TEXT – BOOK OF ADVANCE PHARMACOGNOSY – I

[According to latest syllabus of M. Pharm – I semester (MPG – 102T) of Pharmacy Council of India]

Dr. Deepa Shrivastava

Associate Professor

Radha Raman college of Pharmacy,

Bhopal (Madhya Pradesh)

Mrs. Swati Kumari

Assistant Professor

Muzaffarpur Institute of Technology

Muzaffarpur (Bihar)

Mr. Pallab Dasgupta

Assistant Professor

BCDA College of Pharmacy &

Technology,

Hridaypur, Barasat, Kolkata

Prof. (Dr.) M. K. Senthil Kumar

Professor

Caritas College of Pharmacy,

Caritas Educity,

Ettumanoor, Kottayam

Ms. Surabhi Saksena

Assistant Professor

Radha Raman Institute of

Pharmaceutical Sciences,

Bhopal (Madhya Pradesh)

TEXT – BOOK OF ADVANCE PHARMACOGNOSY – I
NOTION PRESS
PREFACE

The authors feel great pleasure in presenting the first edition of the book **"Text – Book of Advance Pharmacognosy – I"** for graduate and post graduate students. The present book on **Text – Book of Advance Pharmacognosy – I** has been written according to the syllabus of M. Pharm – I semester (MPG – 102T) of Pharmacy Council of India and covers full course of the subject.

THE SALIENT FEATURES OF THE BOOK ARE: -

- *Easy to understand style of writing* which makes the book a self-study material.

- *Each new concept has been introduced through day-today problem of interest* to the students which makes the subject matter interesting.

- *The language of the book, on the whole, is lucid and easy to understand.*

- Wherever needed *neatly labeled figures have been drawn.*

The authors hope that the students, teachers and other readers will find the book interesting and to the point covering the course. We hope that the students will receive the book warmly.

I express a sincere thank you to the Management of Radha Raman college of Pharmacy, Muzaffarpur Institute of Technology, BCDA College of Pharmacy & Technology, Caritas College of Pharmacy and Radharaman group of Institute for their support during the writing of this book.

Every effort is made to keep the book error free. The author will gratefully acknowledge the suggestions to improve the book to make it more useful.

Wishing our readers success in examination and life ahead. The authors feel that their efforts will be fully rewarded if the book serves the purpose for which it is written.

TEXT – BOOK OF ADVANCE PHARMACOGNOSY – I
CONTENTS

1. Plant drug cultivation **6**

   a. General introduction to the importance of Pharmacognosy in herbal drug industry

   b. Indian Council of Agricultural Research

   c. Current Good Agricultural Practices

   d. Current Good Cultivation Practices

   e. Current Good Collection Practices,

   f. Conservation of medicinal plants- Ex-situ and In-situ

   g. Conservation of medicinal plants.

2. Marine natural products **61**

   a. General methods of isolation and purification of Marine natural products,

   b. Study of Marine toxins

   c. Recent advances in research in marine drugs

   d. Problems faced in research on marine drugs such as taxonomical identification, chemical screening and their solution.

3. Nutraceuticals **107**

   a. Current trends and future scope of Nutraceuticals

   b. Inorganic mineral supplements

   c. Vitamin supplements

   d. Digestive enzymes

   e. Dietary fibres

   f. Cereals and grains

   g. Health drinks of natural origin

   h. Antioxidants

   i. Polyunsaturated fatty acids

j. Herbs as functional foods

k. Formulation and standardization of Nutraceuticals

l. Regulatory aspects

m. FSSAI guidelines.

4. Nutraceuticals **158**

a. Spirulina

b. Soya bean

c. Ginseng

d. Garlic

e. Broccoli

f. Green and Herbal Tea

g. Flax seeds

h. Black cohosh

i. Turmeric.

5. Phytopharmaceuticals **207**

a. Carotenoids – i) α and β - Carotene ii) Xanthophyll (Lutein)

b. Limonoids – i) d-Limonene ii) α – Terpineol

c. Saponins – i) Shatavarins

d. Flavonoids – i) Resveratrol ii) Rutin iii) Hesperidin iv) Naringin v) Quercetin

e. Phenolic acids- Ellagic acid

f. Vitamins

g. Tocotrienols and Tocopherols

h. Andrographolide

i. Glycolipids

j. Gugulipids

k. Withanolides

l. Vascine

m. Taxol

6. Pharmacovigilance of drugs of natural origin **257**

    a. WHO guidelines for safety monitoring of natural medicine

    b. AYUSH guidelines for safety monitoring of natural medicine,

    c. Spontaneous reporting schemes for bio drug adverse reactions,

    d. Bio drug-drug interactions with suitable examples

    e. Bio drug-food interactions with suitable examples

CHAPTER – 1

PLANT DRUG CULTIVATION

INTRODUCTION:

Plant drug cultivation refers to the systematic and controlled process of growing plants specifically for the production of pharmaceutical compounds. These plants, often referred to as medicinal plants, have been utilized for centuries in traditional and modern medicine. The cultivation of these plants involves various techniques and practices to ensure the consistent and high-quality production of the desired compounds.

Importance of Plant Drug Cultivation:

Plant drug cultivation plays a crucial role in the pharmaceutical and herbal medicine industries, providing valuable medicinal compounds derived from plants. This cultivation is significant for several reasons:

1. Source of Medicinal Compounds

    a. **Natural Products**: Many pharmaceutical drugs and herbal medicines are derived from plant extracts. These compounds serve as active ingredients in treatments for various diseases and health conditions.

    b. **Diversity of Compounds**: Plants produce a wide range of bioactive compounds such as alkaloids, flavonoids, terpenoids, and phenolic compounds, each with potential therapeutic properties.

2. Traditional and Modern Medicine

    a. **Traditional Medicine**: Plants have been used in traditional medicine systems worldwide for centuries. Cultivating medicinal plants supports the preservation and continuation of traditional healing practices.

    b. **Integration with Modern Medicine**: Plant-derived compounds are extensively studied and integrated into modern medicine, providing effective treatments and contributing to drug discovery and development.

3. Sustainability and Conservation

a. **Preservation of Species**: Cultivation helps reduce pressure on wild plant populations by providing an alternative source of medicinal plants.

b. **Conservation Efforts**: Cultivating medicinal plants can support conservation efforts by promoting sustainable practices and preserving genetic diversity through seed banks and botanical gardens.

4. Economic Importance

a. **Industry and Employment**: Plant drug cultivation supports a significant industry, providing employment opportunities in farming, processing, research, and manufacturing sectors.

b. **Economic Development**: Many regions depend on the cultivation and trade of medicinal plants for economic growth and livelihoods, particularly in rural areas.

5. Research and Innovation

a. **Drug Discovery**: Plants are a valuable source of new drugs and lead compounds. Cultivation supports research into the pharmacological properties and potential uses of medicinal plants.

b. **Biotechnological Advances**: Advances in biotechnology, including tissue culture and genetic modification, enhance the cultivation and production of medicinal plants for pharmaceutical purposes.

6. Quality Control and Standardization

a. **Quality Assurance**: Cultivated plants can be grown under controlled conditions to ensure consistency in the concentration and quality of bioactive compounds.

b. **Standardization**: Establishing cultivation practices and quality standards ensures that medicinal plants meet regulatory requirements for safety, efficacy, and reliability.

7. Public Health Benefits

a. **Access to Healthcare**: Cultivating medicinal plants ensures consistent availability of essential medicines for treating diseases and improving public health outcomes.

b. **Affordability**: Plant-based medicines are often more affordable and accessible than synthetic drugs, especially in low-income regions and developing countries.

Challenges in Plant Drug Cultivation

a. **Environmental Impact**: Agriculture practices can affect soil fertility, water resources, and biodiversity if not managed sustainably.

b. **Climate Change**: Changing climate patterns and extreme weather events can impact plant growth, cultivation practices, and crop yields.

c. **Cultural and Ethical Considerations**: Respecting traditional knowledge and practices, as well as ensuring fair trade and benefit-sharing with local communities, are essential.

Steps in Plant Drug Cultivation:

Plant drug cultivation involves several stages and processes to grow, harvest, process, and utilize medicinal plants for pharmaceutical and herbal medicine purposes. Here's a detailed overview of the steps involved in plant drug cultivation:

1. Selection of Medicinal Plants

a. **Identification**: Choose medicinal plant species based on their therapeutic properties, market demand, and ecological suitability.

b. **Cultivation Suitability**: Assess environmental factors such as soil type, climate, and water availability to ensure the selected plants can thrive in the cultivation area.

2. Site Selection and Preparation

a. **Land Preparation**: Prepare the land by clearing weeds, tilling the soil, and improving soil fertility through organic amendments or fertilizers.

b. **Environmental Factors**: Consider factors like sunlight exposure, drainage, and protection from pests and diseases when selecting cultivation sites.

3. Propagation

a. **Seed Propagation**: Start with seeds obtained from reputable sources or collected from healthy plants. Germinate seeds in nurseries or seedbeds before transplanting to the field.

b. **Vegetative Propagation**: Use cuttings, rhizomes, or tissue culture techniques for plants that do not produce viable seeds or are propagated vegetatively for genetic consistency.

4. Planting

a. **Timing**: Plant medicinal crops during the appropriate season for optimal growth and development.

b. **Spacing**: Follow recommended spacing guidelines to ensure adequate air circulation, sunlight exposure, and nutrient availability for each plant.

5. Crop Management

a. **Watering**: Provide adequate irrigation based on plant requirements and local climate conditions to ensure proper growth and development.

b. **Weed Control**: Implement weed management practices to minimize competition for nutrients and water, using mechanical or organic methods to avoid chemical residues.

c. **Pest and Disease Management**: Monitor plants regularly for pests and diseases, employing integrated pest management (IPM) strategies to minimize chemical inputs.

6. Harvesting

a. **Timing**: Harvest medicinal plants at the optimal stage of growth, usually when active compounds are at their highest concentration.

b. **Techniques**: Use appropriate harvesting techniques to minimize damage to plants and ensure the quality of harvested material.

7. Post-Harvest Processing

a. **Cleaning and Drying**: Clean harvested plants to remove dirt and debris, then dry them using methods that preserve the integrity and potency of medicinal compounds.

b. **Storage**: Store dried plant materials in suitable containers and conditions to protect against moisture, pests, and degradation.

8. Quality Control and Standardization

a. **Testing and Analysis**: Conduct quality control tests to verify the identity, purity, and potency of medicinal plant materials.

b. **Standard Operating Procedures (SOPs)**: Establish SOPs for cultivation, harvesting, and processing to ensure consistency and adherence to regulatory standards.

9. Documentation and Traceability

a. **Record Keeping**: Maintain detailed records of cultivation practices, harvest dates, processing methods, and quality assessments for traceability and regulatory compliance.

b. **Certification**: Obtain organic or other certifications as applicable to demonstrate adherence to quality and sustainability standards.

10. Utilization and Market Access

a. **Product Development**: Process medicinal plants into various forms such as extracts, powders, teas, or capsules for pharmaceutical or herbal medicine applications.

b. **Market Access**: Identify and access markets for medicinal plant products, ensuring compliance with legal and regulatory requirements.

11. Sustainability and Conservation

a. **Environmental Stewardship**: Implement sustainable farming practices to minimize environmental impact and promote biodiversity conservation.

b. **Community Engagement**: Engage with local communities to promote sustainable harvesting practices, fair trade, and benefit-sharing arrangements.

Challenges in Plant Drug Cultivation

a. **Climate Variability**: Changing weather patterns and extreme events can affect crop yields and quality.

b. **Pest and Disease Pressure**: Managing pests and diseases without relying heavily on chemical inputs requires careful planning and monitoring.

c. **Market Demand and Price Fluctuations**: Responding to fluctuations in market demand and ensuring fair prices for growers can be challenging.

Factors Affecting Plant Drug Cultivation:

Factors affecting plant drug cultivation encompass a range of variables that influence the growth, yield, quality, and sustainability of medicinal plants. These factors can be environmental, biological, socio-economic, or related to management practices. Here's a detailed look at the factors affecting plant drug cultivation:

Environmental Factors

1. **Climate and Weather Conditions**

    a. **Temperature**: Optimal temperature ranges vary for different medicinal plants; extremes can affect growth and flowering.

    b. **Rainfall and Irrigation**: Adequate water availability is crucial; insufficient or excessive rainfall can impact plant health and yield.

    c. **Humidity**: High humidity levels can promote fungal diseases, while low humidity can cause water stress.

    d. **Light**: Plants have varying light requirements; insufficient light can affect photosynthesis and growth.

2. **Soil Characteristics**

    a. **Soil Type**: Soil texture (e.g., sandy, clayey) affects water retention and drainage.

b. **Nutrient Content**: Soil fertility, organic matter content, and pH levels influence plant nutrient uptake and growth.

c. **Soil Structure**: Proper soil structure promotes root development and nutrient availability.

3. **Topography**

a. **Slope and Elevation**: Steep slopes may affect water runoff and soil erosion, while elevation can influence temperature and microclimatic conditions.

4. **Microclimate**

a. **Shade and Wind Exposure**: Shelter from wind and appropriate shading can protect plants from physical damage and stress.

Biological Factors

1. **Plant Species and Varieties**

a. **Genetic Diversity**: Different varieties or ecotypes of the same species may have varying tolerance to environmental conditions and pest resistance.

b. **Life Cycle**: Annual, biennial, or perennial growth patterns affect planting and harvesting schedules.

2. **Pests and Diseases**

a. **Pathogens**: Fungal, bacterial, and viral diseases can reduce yield and quality if not managed properly.

b. **Insects and Pests**: Pest infestations can damage plants and reduce yields; integrated pest management (IPM) is essential.

3. **Competition**

a. **Weeds**: Competition from weeds for nutrients, water, and light can reduce crop yields and quality.

Socio-economic Factors

1. **Market Demand and Price Fluctuations**

a. **Market Access**: Access to reliable markets for medicinal plant products influences cultivation decisions.

b. **Price Volatility**: Fluctuations in market prices can affect profitability and economic viability for growers.

2. **Policy and Regulatory Environment**

a. **Government Regulations**: Regulations on cultivation, harvesting, processing, and trade can impact production practices and market access.

b. **Certification Requirements**: Compliance with organic, fair trade, or other certification standards may affect cultivation practices and market opportunities.

3. **Land Tenure and Ownership**

a. **Land Access**: Secure land tenure and access to suitable land for cultivation are critical for long-term planning and investment.

Management Practices

1. **Cultivation Techniques**

a. **Crop Rotation and Intercropping**: Rotating crops and intercropping with compatible species can improve soil fertility and pest management.

b. **Water Management**: Efficient irrigation practices optimize water use efficiency and reduce water stress.

c. **Nutrient Management**: Proper fertilization based on soil testing and plant nutrient requirements enhances plant growth and productivity.

2. **Harvesting and Post-harvest Handling**

a. **Timing**: Harvesting at the right stage of plant growth ensures maximum yield and potency of active compounds.

b. **Processing**: Proper drying, storage, and processing methods maintain product quality and shelf life.

3. **Labor and Skills**

    a. **Labor Availability**: Access to skilled labor for planting, harvesting, and processing affects operational efficiency and quality control.

Challenges in Plant Drug Cultivation:

Plant drug cultivation faces several challenges that impact the growth, yield, quality, and sustainability of medicinal plants. These challenges can vary depending on factors such as environmental conditions, socio-economic factors, biological factors, and management practices. Here's a detailed look at some of the key challenges in plant drug cultivation:

Environmental Challenges

1. **Climate Change**

    a. **Temperature Extremes**: Increased temperatures or fluctuations can affect plant growth cycles, flowering, and overall productivity.

    b. **Altered Precipitation Patterns**: Changes in rainfall patterns, including droughts or floods, can disrupt planting schedules and affect water availability.

    c. **Extreme Weather Events**: Hurricanes, storms, and heatwaves can damage crops and infrastructure, leading to yield losses.

2. **Water Availability**

    a. **Water Scarcity**: Limited access to water for irrigation, exacerbated by climate change and competing demands, can restrict plant growth and development.

    b. **Water Quality**: Poor water quality, contaminated with pollutants or salts, can negatively impact plant health and yield.

3. **Soil Degradation**

    a. **Soil Erosion**: Erosion from wind or water can deplete topsoil and reduce fertility, affecting plant nutrition and growth.

    b. **Soil Compaction**: Heavy machinery or intensive farming practices can compact soil, reducing water infiltration and root growth.

4. **Pests and Diseases**
   a. **Pest Pressure**: Insect pests, fungi, bacteria, and viruses can damage crops, reducing yield and quality.
   b. **Pesticide Resistance**: Overuse of pesticides can lead to resistance in pests and harmful effects on non-target organisms.

Socio-economic Challenges

1. **Market Dynamics**
   a. **Price Volatility**: Fluctuations in market prices for medicinal plants can affect profitability and economic viability for growers.
   b. **Market Access**: Limited access to markets or stringent market requirements can restrict sales opportunities.

2. **Policy and Regulatory Issues**
   a. **Regulatory Compliance**: Meeting regulatory requirements for cultivation practices, product quality, and trade can be complex and costly.
   b. **Land Tenure**: Insecure land tenure can hinder long-term investments in cultivation practices and infrastructure.

3. **Labor and Skills**
   a. **Labor Shortages**: Difficulty in sourcing skilled labor for planting, harvesting, and processing can impact operational efficiency and product quality.
   b. **Training Needs**: Lack of training and knowledge transfer in sustainable cultivation practices and quality control.

Biological Challenges

1. **Genetic Diversity**
   a. **Loss of Biodiversity**: Reduction in genetic diversity within cultivated plant species can limit resilience to pests, diseases, and environmental stresses.

b. **Invasive Species**: Introduction of invasive plants can outcompete native medicinal plants and disrupt ecosystems.

2. **Crop Management**

   a. **Weed Control**: Competition from weeds for nutrients, water, and sunlight requires effective weed management strategies.

   b. **Nutrient Management**: Balancing soil fertility and nutrient requirements to optimize plant growth and minimize environmental impacts.

Management and Operational Challenges

1. **Resource Constraints**

   a. **Limited Inputs**: Access to quality seeds, fertilizers, and pesticides may be limited, especially in remote or economically disadvantaged areas.

   b. **Infrastructure**: Insufficient infrastructure for irrigation, storage, and processing can limit productivity and post-harvest quality.

2. **Quality Control**

   a. **Post-harvest Handling**: Improper drying, storage, and processing can lead to loss of active compounds and degradation of medicinal plant quality.

   b. **Traceability**: Ensuring traceability and documentation throughout the supply chain to maintain product integrity and meet regulatory standards.

Ethical and Cultural Challenges

1. **Traditional Knowledge and Intellectual Property**

   a. **Respect for Indigenous Knowledge**: Safeguarding traditional knowledge and cultural practices related to medicinal plant cultivation and use.

   b. **Intellectual Property Rights**: Ensuring fair compensation and benefit-sharing for communities holding traditional knowledge.

Advances in Plant Drug Cultivation:

Advances in plant drug cultivation have significantly enhanced the efficiency, quality, and sustainability of growing medicinal plants for pharmaceutical and herbal medicine purposes. These advancements span various aspects of cultivation, from biotechnological innovations to sustainable farming practices. Here's a detailed look at some key advances in plant drug cultivation:

Biotechnological Innovations

1. **Tissue Culture and Micropropagation**
   a. **Propagation of Elite Clones**: Tissue culture techniques allow for mass propagation of selected high-yielding or disease-resistant plant varieties.
   b. **Rapid Multiplication**: Micropropagation accelerates the production of uniform plant material under controlled conditions, reducing the dependency on seeds.

2. **Genetic Engineering**
   a. **Improved Traits**: Genetic modification techniques enable the introduction or enhancement of desirable traits such as increased yield, resistance to pests and diseases, and higher content of bioactive compounds.
   b. **Biosynthesis of Medicinal Compounds**: Genetic engineering can be used to enhance the production of specific medicinal compounds within plant tissues.

3. **Marker-Assisted Selection**
   a. **Selection of Traits**: DNA markers are used to identify and select plants with desired traits, such as disease resistance or high medicinal compound content, accelerating breeding programs.

Sustainable Farming Practices

1. **Organic Farming**

a. **Chemical-Free Cultivation**: Organic farming practices eliminate or minimize the use of synthetic pesticides and fertilizers, promoting soil health and reducing environmental impact.

b. **Certification Standards**: Adherence to organic certification standards ensures the production of medicinal plants free from chemical residues, meeting consumer demand for natural products.

2. **Agroforestry and Polyculture**

a. **Diversified Farming Systems**: Integrating medicinal plants with other crops or trees enhances biodiversity, improves soil fertility, and provides ecosystem services.

b. **Companion Planting**: Planting compatible species together can reduce pest infestations and improve nutrient uptake.

3. **Precision Agriculture**

a. **Monitoring and Management**: Use of technology such as sensors, drones, and GIS (Geographic Information System) for precise monitoring of soil conditions, water usage, and plant health.

b. **Optimized Resource Use**: Precision agriculture techniques optimize resource allocation, minimizing inputs while maximizing yield and quality.

Pharmacological and Nutritional Research

1. **Pharmacological Studies**

a. **Identification of Active Compounds**: Advanced analytical techniques help identify and quantify bioactive compounds responsible for medicinal properties.

b. **Pharmacokinetics and Pharmacodynamics**: Understanding how medicinal compounds are absorbed, metabolized, and exert their effects enhances drug development.

2. **Nutritional Enhancement**

a. **Biofortification**: Agronomic practices and genetic modifications can increase the nutritional value of medicinal plants, enhancing their health benefits.

b. **Functional Foods**: Incorporating medicinal plants into functional foods and nutraceuticals expands their use beyond traditional medicine.

Digital and Data-Driven Solutions

1. **Big Data Analytics**

    a. **Decision Support**: Analysis of large datasets helps optimize cultivation practices, predict crop yields, and manage supply chains effectively.

    b. **Crop Modeling**: Using predictive models based on environmental data improves crop management decisions and resilience to climate variability.

2. **Blockchain Technology**

    a. **Traceability and Transparency**: Blockchain platforms enable secure and transparent tracking of medicinal plant supply chains, ensuring product authenticity and compliance with regulatory standards.

    b. **Supply Chain Efficiency**: Streamlining transactions and reducing fraud through blockchain enhances market access and consumer trust.

Integration of Traditional Knowledge with Modern Science

1. **Ethnobotanical Studies**

    a. **Documentation and Conservation**: Recording and preserving traditional knowledge of medicinal plant use by indigenous communities.

b. **Validation and Integration**: Scientific validation of traditional medicinal practices facilitates the integration of traditional remedies into mainstream healthcare systems.

GENERAL INTRODUCTION TO THE IMPORTANCE OF PHARMACOGNOSY IN HERBAL DRUG INDUSTRY

Introduction to Pharmacognosy

Pharmacognosy plays a pivotal role in the cultivation and utilization of medicinal plants for pharmaceutical and herbal medicine purposes. It encompasses the study of natural products derived from plants and other organisms, focusing on their bioactive compounds, medicinal properties, and therapeutic applications. Here's a detailed introduction to pharmacognosy in the context of plant drug cultivation:

Definition and Scope

1. **Natural Products**: Pharmacognosy primarily deals with the study of natural products obtained from plants, fungi, marine organisms, and other biological sources.

2. **Bioactive Compounds**: It involves identifying, isolating, and characterizing bioactive compounds such as alkaloids, flavonoids, terpenoids, and phenolic compounds that contribute to medicinal properties.

3. **Therapeutic Applications**: Pharmacognosy explores the traditional and modern uses of natural products in treating diseases and promoting health.

Importance in Plant Drug Cultivation

1. **Drug Discovery and Development**

   a. **Source of Medicinal Compounds**: Medicinal plants are valuable sources of bioactive compounds used in drug discovery and development.

   b. **Lead Compounds**: Pharmacognosy identifies potential lead compounds for pharmaceutical research, providing starting points for drug synthesis or modification.

2. **Traditional Medicine Systems**

   a. **Ethnopharmacology**: Studies traditional medicinal practices and indigenous knowledge related to medicinal plants, guiding cultivation and utilization.

   b. **Cultural Significance**: Many cultures rely on pharmacognosy to preserve and utilize traditional herbal remedies, fostering cultural continuity and healthcare practices.

3. **Quality Control and Standardization**

   a. **Standardized Extracts**: Pharmacognosy establishes methods for standardizing plant extracts, ensuring consistent levels of bioactive compounds for efficacy and safety.

   b. **Quality Assurance**: Techniques such as chromatography, spectroscopy, and bioassays verify the identity, purity, and potency of medicinal plant materials.

Techniques and Methods

1. **Extraction and Isolation**

   a. **Solvent Extraction**: Techniques like maceration, percolation, and Soxhlet extraction isolate bioactive compounds from plant materials.

   b. **Purification**: Column chromatography, thin-layer chromatography (TLC), and preparative HPLC purify compounds for pharmacological testing.

2. **Identification and Characterization**

   a. **Spectroscopic Techniques**: UV-Vis spectroscopy, IR spectroscopy, NMR spectroscopy, and mass spectrometry identify and characterize chemical structures.

   b. **Bioassays**: Pharmacological testing evaluates the biological activity and therapeutic potential of isolated compounds.

3. **Biotechnological Approaches**
    a. **Plant Cell Culture**: Tissue culture techniques propagate plant cells and tissues under controlled conditions, producing bioactive compounds in vitro.
    b. **Genetic Engineering**: Modifies plant genomes to enhance the production of specific medicinal compounds or improve plant traits.

Conservation and Sustainability

1. **Ethical Harvesting Practices**
    a. **Wild Harvesting**: Sustainable collection methods promote conservation of wild plant populations and biodiversity.
    b. **Cultivation Initiatives**: Pharmacognosy supports efforts to cultivate medicinal plants under sustainable agricultural practices, reducing pressure on wild populations.

2. **Biodiversity Conservation**
    a. **In-situ and Ex-situ Conservation**: Pharmacognosy contributes to preserving plant species diversity through botanical gardens, seed banks, and conservation programs.
    b. **Ethnobotanical Studies**: Documenting traditional knowledge and practices aids in sustainable plant use and conservation efforts.

Challenges and Future Directions

1. **Environmental Impact**: Balancing plant cultivation with environmental sustainability and climate resilience.
2. **Regulatory Compliance**: Meeting legal requirements for cultivation, harvesting, and trade of medicinal plants.
3. **Integration with Modern Medicine**: Enhancing collaboration between pharmacognosy and modern pharmacology for drug discovery and development.

Importance of Pharmacognosy in the Herbal Drug Industry:

1. **Identification and Characterization**

a. **Plant Identification**: Pharmacognosy helps in accurately identifying medicinal plants through macroscopic and microscopic examination. This ensures that the correct species are used, avoiding substitution or adulteration.

b. **Compound Characterization**: It involves isolating, identifying, and characterizing bioactive compounds. Techniques such as chromatography, spectroscopy, and molecular biology are used to understand the structure and activity of these compounds.

2. **Quality Control**

a. **Standardization**: Pharmacognosy establishes standards for the purity, potency, and quality of herbal products. This is crucial for ensuring consistency and efficacy in herbal medicine.

b. **Phytochemical Screening**: It includes the qualitative and quantitative analysis of active constituents to ensure that the medicinal properties of the plants are retained.

3. **Safety and Efficacy**

a. **Toxicological Studies**: Pharmacognosy assesses the safety of herbal drugs through toxicological studies. It helps in identifying potential toxic compounds and understanding their effects on human health.

b. **Pharmacological Evaluation**: It involves studying the pharmacological effects of herbal extracts and their mechanisms of action. This helps in validating the traditional uses of medicinal plants and discovering new therapeutic applications.

4. **Sustainable Use of Medicinal Plants**

a. **Conservation**: Pharmacognosy promotes the conservation of medicinal plants by encouraging sustainable harvesting practices and cultivation. It helps in identifying endangered species and developing strategies for their preservation.

b. **Ethnobotanical Studies**: Understanding traditional knowledge and practices related to medicinal plants aids in the conservation of biodiversity and cultural heritage.

5. **Drug Development**

    a. **New Drug Discovery**: Pharmacognosy plays a pivotal role in the discovery of new drugs from natural sources. Many modern drugs have been developed based on compounds originally derived from plants.

    b. **Herbal Formulations**: It helps in the development of standardized herbal formulations with proven efficacy and safety.

Role of Pharmacognosy in Plant Drug Cultivation;

1. **Selection of Plant Species**

    a. **Ethnobotanical Knowledge**: Pharmacognosy utilizes ethnobotanical information to select plants with medicinal properties. This traditional knowledge guides researchers in identifying promising plant species.

    b. **Biodiversity Studies**: It involves the study of plant biodiversity to discover new medicinal plants and ensure a diverse genetic pool for cultivation.

2. **Cultivation Practices**

    a. **Optimal Growing Conditions**: Pharmacognosy helps in determining the optimal soil, climate, and cultivation practices for different medicinal plants. This ensures the highest yield and quality of bioactive compounds.

    b. **Propagation Techniques**: It includes developing efficient propagation techniques, such as tissue culture, to produce high-quality planting material and preserve genetic traits.

3. **Phytochemical Variation**

    a. **Environmental Impact**: Understanding how environmental factors (e.g., soil, climate, altitude) affect the phytochemical composition of plants is crucial. Pharmacognosy studies these variations to optimize cultivation practices.

    b. **Chemotype Identification**: It involves identifying different chemotypes (plants with the same species but different chemical compositions) to select those with the highest medicinal value.

4. **Harvesting and Post-Harvest Processing**

    a. **Optimal Harvest Time**: Pharmacognosy determines the best time to harvest medicinal plants to ensure maximum potency of active compounds.

    b. **Post-Harvest Handling**: It includes methods for drying, storing, and processing plant materials to preserve their medicinal properties and prevent degradation.

5. **Quality Assurance**

    a. **Analytical Techniques**: Pharmacognosy employs advanced analytical techniques to monitor the quality of medicinal plants throughout the cultivation process.

    b. **Standardization Protocols**: Developing standard operating procedures for cultivation, harvesting, and processing ensures consistent quality and efficacy of herbal drugs.

INDIAN COUNCIL OF AGRICULTURAL RESEARCH

Introduction to ICAR:

The Indian Council of Agricultural Research (ICAR) is an autonomous organization under the Department of Agricultural Research and Education (DARE), Ministry of Agriculture and Farmers Welfare, Government of India. It was established in 1929 and has since played a pivotal role in coordinating, guiding, and managing research and education in agriculture and related fields in India. ICAR's extensive network includes research institutions, agricultural universities, and other organizations focused on advancing agricultural science and technology.

Role of ICAR in Plant Drug Cultivation:

ICAR is significantly involved in the cultivation of medicinal plants and the development of plant-based drugs through various initiatives, research programs, and institutions. Its role encompasses several key areas:

1. **Research and Development**
   a. **Dedicated Research Institutes**: ICAR oversees specialized institutes such as the National Research Centre for Medicinal and Aromatic Plants (NRCMAP), which focuses on research and development in medicinal plant cultivation.
   b. **Collaborative Projects**: ICAR collaborates with national and international organizations to conduct research on medicinal plants, aiming to improve cultivation practices, enhance yield, and discover new bioactive compounds.
2. **Germplasm Conservation and Improvement**
   a. **Germplasm Banks**: ICAR maintains germplasm banks to preserve the genetic diversity of medicinal plants. These banks store seeds and plant material to ensure the availability of diverse genetic resources for future research and cultivation.
   b. **Breeding Programs**: ICAR conducts breeding programs to develop high-yielding, disease-resistant, and high-quality varieties of medicinal plants. These programs aim to enhance the medicinal properties and adaptability of these plants to various environmental conditions.
3. **Cultivation Practices**
   a. **Standardization of Cultivation Techniques**: ICAR develops and disseminates standardized cultivation techniques for different medicinal plants. These guidelines help farmers achieve optimal growth conditions and maximize the production of bioactive compounds.

b. **Integrated Pest Management (IPM)**: ICAR promotes IPM practices to manage pests and diseases in medicinal plant cultivation. These practices include the use of biological control agents, organic pesticides, and cultural practices to minimize chemical inputs.

4. **Extension and Outreach**

   a. **Training and Capacity Building**: ICAR conducts training programs and workshops for farmers, researchers, and extension workers on the cultivation of medicinal plants. These programs cover topics such as propagation techniques, soil management, pest control, and post-harvest processing.

   b. **Information Dissemination**: ICAR publishes research findings, technical bulletins, and cultivation manuals to disseminate knowledge on medicinal plant cultivation to a wider audience.

5. **Sustainable Practices**

   a. **Organic Farming**: ICAR promotes organic farming practices in medicinal plant cultivation to ensure the sustainability and environmental friendliness of production systems. Organic farming reduces the use of synthetic chemicals and enhances soil health.

   b. **Water and Soil Conservation**: ICAR advocates for efficient water and soil management practices, such as drip irrigation and mulching, to conserve natural resources and improve the sustainability of medicinal plant cultivation.

6. **Quality Control and Standardization**

   a. **Phytochemical Analysis**: ICAR conducts phytochemical analyses to identify and quantify the active compounds in medicinal plants. This helps in ensuring the quality and efficacy of the plant materials used in drug production.

   b. **Good Agricultural Practices (GAP)**: ICAR promotes GAP for medicinal plant cultivation. GAP guidelines encompass all aspects of cultivation, from seed selection to post-harvest handling, to ensure the production of high-quality medicinal plants.

7. **Policy Advocacy and Support**

   a. **Policy Development**: ICAR provides scientific inputs for the development of policies related to the cultivation and use of medicinal plants. These policies aim to support the sustainable growth of the medicinal plant sector and benefit farmers and the herbal drug industry.

   b. **Financial and Technical Support**: ICAR offers financial and technical support to research projects and initiatives aimed at improving medicinal plant cultivation. This includes funding for research, infrastructure development, and capacity-building activities.

Key ICAR Institutes Involved in Medicinal Plant Research

1. **National Research Centre for Medicinal and Aromatic Plants (NRCMAP)**

   a. Located in Anand, Gujarat, NRCMAP is a premier institute under ICAR dedicated to research on medicinal and aromatic plants. It focuses on germplasm collection, genetic improvement, and the development of cultivation technologies.

2. **Central Institute of Medicinal and Aromatic Plants (CIMAP)**

   a. Although CIMAP is primarily under the Council of Scientific and Industrial Research (CSIR), it collaborates with ICAR on various projects related to medicinal plant research and cultivation. It is headquartered in Lucknow, Uttar Pradesh.

3. **Directorate of Medicinal and Aromatic Plants Research (DMAPR)**

   a. Also located in Anand, Gujarat, DMAPR is another key ICAR institute that conducts research on the cultivation, improvement, and utilization of medicinal and aromatic plants.

CURRENT GOOD AGRICULTURAL PRACTICES

Good Agricultural Practices (GAP) are a set of guidelines aimed at ensuring the sustainable production of high-quality agricultural products, including medicinal plants. GAP focuses on optimizing farming practices to improve yield, quality, and safety while minimizing environmental impact and ensuring the welfare of workers.

Key Components of GAP in Plant Drug Cultivation:

1. **Site Selection and Land Preparation**
    a. **Appropriate Location**: Select a site with suitable soil, climate, and water availability for the specific medicinal plant species.
    b. **Soil Testing**: Conduct soil tests to determine pH, nutrient levels, and the presence of contaminants. Amend the soil as needed to meet the requirements of the crop.
    c. **Land Preparation**: Prepare the land by removing weeds, rocks, and debris. Use proper tillage techniques to create a suitable seedbed.

2. **Planting Material**
    a. **Quality Seeds and Propagules**: Use certified seeds or planting material from reputable sources to ensure genetic purity and disease-free propagation.
    b. **Varietal Selection**: Choose plant varieties that are well-adapted to local growing conditions and have high medicinal value.

3. **Cultivation Practices**
    a. **Crop Rotation and Intercropping**: Practice crop rotation and intercropping to maintain soil fertility, reduce pest and disease incidence, and improve biodiversity.
    b. **Soil Management**: Implement soil conservation measures such as contour plowing, terracing, and cover cropping to prevent erosion and improve soil health.

c. **Water Management**: Use efficient irrigation systems like drip or sprinkler irrigation to optimize water use. Ensure proper drainage to avoid waterlogging and salinity.

4. **Nutrient Management**

   a. **Balanced Fertilization**: Apply organic and inorganic fertilizers based on soil test results to meet the nutrient requirements of the crop. Avoid over-fertilization to prevent nutrient leaching and pollution.

   b. **Organic Amendments**: Incorporate organic matter such as compost and green manure to improve soil structure, fertility, and microbial activity.

5. **Pest and Disease Management**

   a. **Integrated Pest Management (IPM)**: Employ IPM strategies to manage pests and diseases. This includes biological control, cultural practices, mechanical methods, and the judicious use of chemical pesticides.

   b. **Regular Monitoring**: Conduct regular field inspections to detect and manage pest and disease outbreaks early. Use traps, pheromones, and other monitoring tools.

6. **Harvesting and Post-Harvest Handling**

   a. **Optimal Harvest Time**: Harvest medicinal plants at the right stage of maturity to ensure maximum potency and quality of the active compounds.

   b. **Proper Techniques**: Use appropriate harvesting tools and techniques to minimize damage to the plants and ensure cleanliness.

   c. **Post-Harvest Processing**: Dry, cure, and store plant materials under controlled conditions to preserve their medicinal properties. Avoid contamination and degradation during processing.

7. **Worker Health and Safety**

   a. **Training and Education**: Provide training to workers on GAP, safe handling of chemicals, and the use of personal protective equipment (PPE).

   b. **Health and Hygiene**: Ensure that workers follow good hygiene practices and have access to clean drinking water and sanitary facilities.

8. **Environmental Sustainability**

   a. **Biodiversity Conservation**: Preserve natural habitats and promote the cultivation of a diverse range of plant species to support ecosystem health.

   b. **Resource Management**: Use natural resources such as water, soil, and energy efficiently. Implement practices that reduce waste and promote recycling.

9. **Record Keeping and Documentation**

   a. **Detailed Records**: Maintain detailed records of all farming activities, including soil tests, fertilization, irrigation, pest management, and harvesting. This helps in tracking the production process and ensuring traceability.

   b. **Compliance**: Ensure compliance with national and international standards and regulations related to medicinal plant cultivation and production.

Implementation of GAP in Medicinal Plant Cultivation:

1. **Training and Capacity Building**

   a. Conduct training programs and workshops for farmers, extension workers, and other stakeholders on GAP principles and practices.

   b. Develop and distribute educational materials such as manuals, brochures, and videos.

2. **Certification and Standards**

   a. Encourage farmers to obtain GAP certification from recognized certification bodies. This can enhance market access and consumer trust.

   b. Develop and implement national standards for GAP in medicinal plant cultivation, in line with international guidelines such as those provided by the Food and Agriculture Organization (FAO) and the World Health Organization (WHO).

3. **Research and Development**

   a. Invest in research to develop and refine GAP for different medicinal plant species and growing conditions.

   b. Promote the adoption of innovative technologies and practices that improve efficiency, quality, and sustainability in medicinal plant cultivation.

4. **Monitoring and Evaluation**

   a. Establish monitoring and evaluation systems to assess the adoption and impact of GAP on farm productivity, quality, and sustainability.

   b. Provide feedback and support to farmers to continuously improve their practices.

Benefits of GAP in Plant Drug Cultivation:

1. **Improved Quality and Safety**

   a. Ensures the production of high-quality medicinal plants with consistent potency and purity, meeting the standards required for pharmaceutical use.

   b. Reduces the risk of contamination and ensures the safety of the final product.

2. **Sustainable Production**

a. Promotes environmentally friendly practices that conserve natural resources and reduce the ecological footprint of medicinal plant cultivation.

b. Supports the long-term viability of medicinal plant production systems.

3. **Economic Benefits**

a. Enhances farm productivity and profitability through efficient use of inputs and resources.

b. Opens up new market opportunities by meeting the quality standards and certifications demanded by consumers and the pharmaceutical industry.

4. **Social Benefits**

a. Improves the health, safety, and well-being of farm workers through better training, working conditions, and access to health facilities.

b. Contributes to rural development and livelihoods by providing sustainable income opportunities for farmers and communities.

CURRENT GOOD CULTIVATION PRACTICES

Current Good Cultivation Practices (GCP) are guidelines and practices designed to ensure the consistent production of high-quality medicinal plants. These practices cover every aspect of cultivation, from site selection to post-harvest handling, and emphasize sustainability, safety, and quality control.

Key Components of GCP in Plant Drug Cultivation:

1. **Site Selection and Preparation**

a. **Appropriate Location**: Choose sites with optimal soil, climate, and water conditions for the specific medicinal plant species.

b. **Soil Testing and Preparation**: Conduct soil tests to determine nutrient content, pH levels, and the presence of contaminants. Amend soil as necessary to create optimal growing conditions.

c. **Land Preparation**: Clear the land of weeds, rocks, and other debris. Use proper tillage techniques to prepare a suitable seedbed.

2. **Selection of Plant Varieties**

   a. **Quality Planting Material**: Use high-quality seeds or planting material from reputable sources to ensure genetic purity and disease-free propagation.

   b. **Varietal Selection**: Select plant varieties that are well-suited to local growing conditions and possess desirable medicinal properties.

3. **Propagation Techniques**

   a. **Seed Propagation**: Use certified seeds and follow best practices for germination and planting.

   b. **Vegetative Propagation**: Employ techniques such as cuttings, grafting, and tissue culture for plants that do not reproduce well from seeds.

4. **Soil and Nutrient Management**

   a. **Soil Fertility**: Maintain soil fertility through the application of organic and inorganic fertilizers based on soil test recommendations.

   b. **Organic Amendments**: Use compost, manure, and other organic matter to improve soil structure and nutrient content.

   c. **Crop Rotation and Cover Cropping**: Implement crop rotation and cover cropping to maintain soil health and reduce pest and disease incidence.

5. **Water Management**

   a. **Irrigation Systems**: Use efficient irrigation systems such as drip or sprinkler irrigation to optimize water use and ensure uniform soil moisture.

   b. **Water Quality**: Monitor water quality to prevent contamination of plants with harmful substances.

6. **Pest and Disease Management**

   a. **Integrated Pest Management (IPM)**: Implement IPM strategies, including biological control, cultural practices, mechanical methods, and the judicious use of chemical pesticides.

   b. **Regular Monitoring**: Conduct regular field inspections to detect and manage pests and diseases early. Use traps, pheromones, and other monitoring tools.

7. **Harvesting Practices**

   a. **Optimal Harvest Time**: Harvest plants at the right stage of maturity to ensure maximum potency and quality of active compounds.

   b. **Proper Harvesting Techniques**: Use appropriate tools and techniques to minimize damage and contamination during harvesting.

8. **Post-Harvest Handling**

   a. **Drying and Curing**: Dry and cure plant materials under controlled conditions to preserve their medicinal properties.

   b. **Storage**: Store dried plant materials in a clean, dry, and cool environment to prevent degradation and contamination.

   c. **Packaging**: Use appropriate packaging materials to protect the integrity and quality of the plant materials during storage and transport.

9. **Quality Control**

   a. **Phytochemical Analysis**: Conduct phytochemical analyses to identify and quantify active compounds in plant materials. Ensure the consistency and quality of the final product.

   b. **Standard Operating Procedures (SOPs)**: Develop and implement SOPs for all stages of cultivation, from planting to post-harvest handling, to ensure uniformity and quality control.

10. **Worker Health and Safety**

   a. **Training and Education**: Provide training to workers on GCP, safe handling of chemicals, and the use of personal protective equipment (PPE).

   b. **Health and Hygiene**: Ensure that workers follow good hygiene practices and have access to clean drinking water and sanitary facilities.

11. **Environmental Sustainability**

   a. **Biodiversity Conservation**: Promote the cultivation of a diverse range of plant species to support ecosystem health and resilience.

   b. **Sustainable Practices**: Implement practices that conserve natural resources, reduce waste, and minimize the environmental impact of cultivation activities.

12. **Documentation and Record Keeping**

   a. **Detailed Records**: Maintain detailed records of all cultivation activities, including soil tests, fertilization, irrigation, pest management, harvesting, and post-harvest handling. This helps in tracking the production process and ensuring traceability.

   b. **Compliance**: Ensure compliance with national and international standards and regulations related to medicinal plant cultivation and production.

Implementation of GCP in Medicinal Plant Cultivation:

1. **Training and Capacity Building**

   a. Conduct training programs and workshops for farmers, extension workers, and other stakeholders on GCP principles and practices.

   b. Develop and distribute educational materials such as manuals, brochures, and videos.

2. **Certification and Standards**
   a. Encourage farmers to obtain GCP certification from recognized certification bodies. This can enhance market access and consumer trust.
   b. Develop and implement national standards for GCP in medicinal plant cultivation, in line with international guidelines such as those provided by the Food and Agriculture Organization (FAO) and the World Health Organization (WHO).

3. **Research and Development**
   a. Invest in research to develop and refine GCP for different medicinal plant species and growing conditions.
   b. Promote the adoption of innovative technologies and practices that improve efficiency, quality, and sustainability in medicinal plant cultivation.

4. **Monitoring and Evaluation**
   a. Establish monitoring and evaluation systems to assess the adoption and impact of GCP on farm productivity, quality, and sustainability.
   b. Provide feedback and support to farmers to continuously improve their practices.

Benefits of GCP in Plant Drug Cultivation:

1. **Improved Quality and Safety**
   a. Ensures the production of high-quality medicinal plants with consistent potency and purity, meeting the standards required for pharmaceutical use.
   b. Reduces the risk of contamination and ensures the safety of the final product.

2. **Sustainable Production**

a. Promotes environmentally friendly practices that conserve natural resources and reduce the ecological footprint of medicinal plant cultivation.

b. Supports the long-term viability of medicinal plant production systems.

3. **Economic Benefits**

a. Enhances farm productivity and profitability through efficient use of inputs and resources.

b. Opens up new market opportunities by meeting the quality standards and certifications demanded by consumers and the pharmaceutical industry.

4. **Social Benefits**

a. Improves the health, safety, and well-being of farm workers through better training, working conditions, and access to health facilities.

b. Contributes to rural development and livelihoods by providing sustainable income opportunities for farmers and communities.

CURRENT GOOD COLLECTION PRACTICES

Current Good Collection Practices (GCP) are essential guidelines designed to ensure the sustainable and high-quality collection of wild and cultivated medicinal plants. These practices aim to maintain the potency, purity, and safety of plant materials used in pharmaceuticals, herbal remedies, and other health-related products. Adhering to GCP helps in conserving biodiversity, protecting ecosystems, and ensuring the well-being of local communities involved in plant collection.

Key Components of Good Collection Practices (GCP):

1. **Selection of Collection Sites**

a. **Appropriate Locations**: Choose sites with minimal environmental contamination and avoid areas near industrial activities, roads, or regions exposed to pollutants.

b. **Biodiversity Considerations**: Select collection sites that support biodiversity conservation and avoid overharvesting from sensitive or endangered habitats.

2. **Ethical and Sustainable Collection**

   a. **Permits and Regulations**: Obtain necessary permits and adhere to national and local regulations governing the collection of medicinal plants.

   b. **Sustainable Harvesting Techniques**: Implement techniques that allow for the regeneration of plant populations. Avoid overharvesting and ensure that a significant portion of the plant population is left intact.

3. **Training and Education**

   a. **Collector Training**: Provide training to collectors on sustainable harvesting techniques, plant identification, and the importance of biodiversity conservation.

   b. **Awareness Programs**: Conduct awareness programs for local communities and collectors on the benefits of GCP and the sustainable use of natural resources.

4. **Collection Methods**

   a. **Timing of Collection**: Collect plant materials at the appropriate time of the year or season when the concentration of active compounds is highest.

   b. **Proper Techniques**: Use appropriate tools and methods to minimize damage to the plants and avoid contamination. For example, use clean, sharp tools for cutting and avoid uprooting entire plants unless necessary.

5. **Handling and Transport**

a. **Immediate Processing**: Process collected plant materials as soon as possible to preserve their active compounds. This may include washing, drying, or storing under appropriate conditions.

b. **Clean Containers**: Use clean, dry containers for collecting and transporting plant materials to prevent contamination and spoilage.

c. **Gentle Handling**: Handle plant materials gently to avoid bruising, crushing, or other damage that can degrade their quality.

6. **Post-Collection Processing**

   a. **Drying**: Dry plant materials under controlled conditions to prevent mold growth and preserve their active compounds. Use drying racks, screens, or other appropriate methods to ensure even drying.

   b. **Storage**: Store dried plant materials in a cool, dry, and well-ventilated area. Use airtight containers to protect against moisture, pests, and light.

   c. **Labeling**: Clearly label collected materials with information such as the plant name, collection date, location, and any relevant processing details.

7. **Quality Control**

   a. **Phytochemical Analysis**: Conduct phytochemical analyses to verify the presence and concentration of active compounds in collected plant materials.

   b. **Contamination Checks**: Test for contaminants such as heavy metals, pesticides, and microbial contaminants to ensure the safety and purity of the plant materials.

8. **Documentation and Record Keeping**

   a. **Detailed Records**: Maintain detailed records of collection activities, including site selection, harvesting methods, quantities collected, and processing techniques. This helps in tracking and verifying the quality and sustainability of the collected materials.

b. **Traceability**: Ensure that collected plant materials can be traced back to their source, including information on the collection site, date, and collector.

9. **Environmental and Social Responsibility**

    a. **Ecosystem Protection**: Minimize the environmental impact of collection activities by avoiding damage to non-target species and habitats.

    b. **Community Engagement**: Engage local communities in collection activities, ensuring fair compensation and promoting their involvement in sustainable resource management.

    c. **Cultural Respect**: Respect the traditional knowledge and practices of indigenous and local communities related to plant collection and use.

Implementation of Good Collection Practices (GCP):

1. **Capacity Building**

    a. **Training Programs**: Develop and implement training programs for collectors, farmers, and other stakeholders on GCP principles and practices.

    b. **Technical Assistance**: Provide technical support to collectors and communities to enhance their skills and knowledge in sustainable collection and processing techniques.

2. **Certification and Standards**

    a. **GCP Certification**: Encourage collectors and organizations to obtain GCP certification from recognized certification bodies. This can enhance market access and consumer trust.

    b. **Development of Standards**: Work with national and international organizations to develop and harmonize standards for GCP in medicinal plant collection.

3. **Research and Monitoring**

   a. **Ecological Studies**: Conduct ecological studies to understand the impact of collection on plant populations and ecosystems. Use this information to develop sustainable harvesting guidelines.

   b. **Monitoring Systems**: Establish monitoring systems to assess the compliance and effectiveness of GCP in the field. Regularly review and update practices based on monitoring results.

4. **Policy Advocacy**

   a. **Regulatory Support**: Advocate for the development and enforcement of regulations that support sustainable collection practices and the conservation of medicinal plant resources.

   b. **Incentives**: Promote incentives for sustainable collection practices, such as access to markets, technical support, and financial assistance.

Benefits of Good Collection Practices (GCP):

1. **Quality Assurance**

   a. Ensures the production of high-quality medicinal plant materials with consistent potency and purity, meeting the standards required for pharmaceutical and herbal products.

   b. Reduces the risk of contamination and degradation, ensuring the safety and efficacy of the final products.

2. **Sustainable Resource Management**

   a. Promotes the conservation of plant populations and ecosystems by implementing sustainable collection practices.

   b. Supports the long-term availability of medicinal plant resources for future generations.

3. **Economic and Social Benefits**

   a. Enhances the livelihoods of local communities and collectors through fair compensation and access to sustainable markets.

b. Builds community capacity and promotes the sustainable management of natural resources.

4. **Environmental Protection**

    a. Minimizes the environmental impact of collection activities, protecting biodiversity and ecosystem health.

    b. Supports the sustainable use and conservation of medicinal plant resources.

CONSERVATION OF MEDICINAL PLANTS- EX-SITU AND INSITU

Conserving medicinal plants is crucial for maintaining biodiversity, ensuring the sustainability of natural resources, and preserving the genetic diversity necessary for future research and development. Both ex-situ and in-situ conservation methods are employed to protect these valuable species.

In-situ Conservation:

In-situ conservation refers to the preservation of plants in their natural habitats. This method focuses on maintaining and protecting ecosystems and natural habitats to ensure the survival of species in their original environment.

Key Strategies for In-situ Conservation

1. **Protected Areas**

    a. **National Parks and Reserves**: Establishing national parks, wildlife reserves, and protected areas to safeguard habitats from human activities and environmental degradation.

    b. **Community Reserves**: Involving local communities in the management and protection of natural habitats, promoting sustainable use, and conserving biodiversity.

2. **Sustainable Harvesting Practices**

    a. **Regulated Collection**: Implementing policies and regulations to control the collection of medicinal plants from the wild, ensuring sustainable harvesting levels that do not threaten plant populations.

b. **Education and Awareness**: Educating local communities about the importance of sustainable harvesting and biodiversity conservation.

3. **Habitat Restoration**

    a. **Reforestation and Afforestation**: Planting native trees and plants to restore degraded habitats and improve the ecological balance.

    b. **Erosion Control**: Implementing measures to prevent soil erosion and protect water sources, ensuring a healthy environment for plant growth.

4. **Monitoring and Research**

    a. **Biodiversity Inventories**: Conducting surveys and inventories to identify and monitor the status of medicinal plant species and their habitats.

    b. **Ecological Studies**: Researching the ecological requirements of medicinal plants to inform conservation strategies and habitat management practices.

Ex-situ Conservation:

Ex-situ conservation involves the preservation of plant species outside their natural habitats. This method is employed to safeguard plant genetic resources, especially for species that are threatened or have limited natural populations.

Key Strategies for Ex-situ Conservation

1. **Botanical Gardens and Arboreta**

    a. **Living Collections**: Establishing living collections of medicinal plants in botanical gardens and arboreta, providing a controlled environment for their growth and study.

    b. **Public Education**: Using botanical gardens to educate the public about the importance of plant conservation and the value of medicinal plants.

2. **Seed Banks and Germplasm Storage**

a. **Seed Collection and Storage**: Collecting and storing seeds of medicinal plants in seed banks under controlled conditions to ensure their long-term viability.

b. **Cryopreservation**: Utilizing cryopreservation techniques to store plant tissues, seeds, and cells at ultra-low temperatures for extended periods.

3. **Tissue Culture and Micropropagation**

a. **In-vitro Propagation**: Using tissue culture techniques to propagate medicinal plants in laboratory conditions, producing large numbers of genetically identical plants.

b. **Genetic Conservation**: Maintaining a diverse genetic pool by propagating plants from different genetic backgrounds.

4. **Field Gene Banks**

a. **Cultivation in Controlled Environments**: Establishing field gene banks to cultivate medicinal plants in controlled environments, ensuring their survival and availability for future use.

b. **Genetic Studies**: Conducting genetic studies to understand the diversity and adaptability of medicinal plants, informing breeding and conservation programs.

Integration of In-situ and Ex-situ Conservation:

A comprehensive conservation strategy for medicinal plants often involves integrating both in-situ and ex-situ methods. This approach ensures the preservation of genetic diversity, supports ecosystem health, and provides a safety net for species at risk of extinction.

Key Integration Strategies

1. **Complementary Conservation Plans**

a. **Combined Efforts**: Developing conservation plans that incorporate both in-situ and ex-situ methods, ensuring a holistic approach to preserving medicinal plants.

b. **Resource Allocation**: Allocating resources effectively between in-situ and ex-situ programs based on the specific needs and status of each plant species.

2. **Research and Data Sharing**

   a. **Collaborative Research**: Promoting collaboration between botanical gardens, research institutions, and conservation organizations to share data and research findings.

   b. **Integrated Databases**: Creating integrated databases to document the distribution, genetic diversity, and conservation status of medicinal plants, facilitating informed decision-making.

3. **Community Involvement**

   a. **Local Engagement**: Engaging local communities in conservation efforts, providing them with knowledge, resources, and incentives to participate in both in-situ and ex-situ conservation programs.

   b. **Benefit Sharing**: Ensuring that local communities benefit from the conservation and sustainable use of medicinal plants, promoting long-term commitment to conservation goals.

Benefits of Conserving Medicinal Plants:

1. **Biodiversity Preservation**

   a. **Ecosystem Health**: Conserving medicinal plants contributes to the overall health and stability of ecosystems, supporting a wide range of plant and animal species.

   b. **Genetic Diversity**: Preserving genetic diversity within medicinal plant populations ensures their adaptability to changing environmental conditions and supports future research and development.

2. **Sustainable Resource Management**

   a. **Renewable Resources**: Sustainable conservation practices ensure the continued availability of medicinal plants for future generations.

b. **Economic Benefits**: Promoting the sustainable use of medicinal plants can provide economic opportunities for local communities, fostering a sense of stewardship and conservation.

3. **Cultural and Traditional Value**

    a. **Cultural Heritage**: Many medicinal plants have cultural and traditional significance for indigenous and local communities. Conservation efforts help preserve this cultural heritage.

    b. **Traditional Medicine**: Ensuring the availability of medicinal plants supports traditional medicine practices, which are an important part of healthcare for many communities.

CONSERVATION OF MEDICINAL PLANTS

Conserving medicinal plants is a vital aspect of plant drug cultivation, ensuring the sustainability of these valuable resources for future generations. Conservation efforts focus on preserving genetic diversity, protecting natural habitats, and promoting sustainable use practices. Both in-situ (on-site) and ex-situ (off-site) conservation methods play essential roles in achieving these goals.

Importance of Conservation in Plant Drug Cultivation:

Conserving medicinal plants within the framework of plant drug cultivation is critical for several reasons. These include maintaining biodiversity, ensuring the sustainability of natural resources, preserving genetic diversity, supporting traditional and modern medicine, and promoting environmental health. Here's a detailed look at why conservation is so important in this context:

1. Biodiversity Preservation

    a. **Ecosystem Stability**: Medicinal plants are integral parts of their ecosystems. Conserving them helps maintain ecosystem stability and resilience, supporting a wide range of flora and fauna.

    b. **Species Interdependence**: Many species depend on medicinal plants for their survival, either directly as food or habitat, or indirectly through the ecosystem services they provide.

2. Sustainable Resource Use

a. **Long-term Availability**: Conservation ensures that medicinal plants remain available for future generations, supporting ongoing medical and pharmacological research and use.

b. **Renewable Resources**: By adopting sustainable practices, medicinal plants can be harvested without depleting the resources, ensuring a continuous supply for the pharmaceutical and herbal industries.

3. Genetic Diversity Preservation

a. **Adaptation to Environmental Changes**: Genetic diversity within medicinal plant species allows for greater adaptability to changing environmental conditions, pests, and diseases.

b. **Research and Development**: A diverse genetic pool is crucial for the development of new drugs. Conserved genetic diversity provides a wider array of phytochemicals for potential therapeutic applications.

4. Support for Traditional and Modern Medicine

a. **Cultural Heritage**: Many medicinal plants are deeply embedded in cultural practices and traditional medicine systems. Conserving these plants helps preserve indigenous knowledge and cultural heritage.

b. **Healthcare Resource**: In many regions, medicinal plants are a primary healthcare resource. Conservation ensures these communities continue to have access to effective and affordable treatments.

5. Environmental Health

a. **Ecosystem Services**: Medicinal plants contribute to ecosystem services such as soil stabilization, water purification, and carbon sequestration. Their conservation helps maintain these critical functions.

b. **Habitat Preservation**: Conserving medicinal plants often involves protecting entire habitats, which benefits other species and contributes to overall environmental health.

6. Economic Benefits

a. **Livelihoods**: Many communities rely on the collection and cultivation of medicinal plants for their livelihoods. Conservation ensures the sustainability of these economic activities.

b. **Market Access**: Sustainable and certified medicinal plant products can access premium markets, providing economic incentives for conservation.

7. Scientific and Educational Value

a. **Research Opportunities**: Conserved medicinal plants provide ongoing opportunities for scientific research, leading to new discoveries in medicine, pharmacology, and botany.

b. **Educational Resources**: Botanical gardens, seed banks, and conservation areas serve as educational resources, promoting awareness and understanding of the importance of medicinal plant conservation.

Strategies for Conservation in Plant Drug Cultivation

To achieve these benefits, a combination of in-situ and ex-situ conservation strategies is often employed.

In-situ Conservation

a. **Protected Areas**: Establishing national parks, reserves, and community conservation areas to protect natural habitats.

b. **Sustainable Harvesting**: Implementing and promoting sustainable harvesting techniques to avoid overexploitation.

c. **Habitat Restoration**: Reforesting and rehabilitating degraded lands to restore natural habitats.

d. **Community Engagement**: Involving local communities in conservation efforts to ensure sustainable use and benefit-sharing.

Ex-situ Conservation

a. **Botanical Gardens**: Maintaining living collections of medicinal plants for research, education, and preservation.

b. **Seed Banks**: Storing seeds under controlled conditions to preserve genetic diversity.

c. **Tissue Culture**: Using tissue culture and micropropagation techniques to propagate and conserve rare or endangered species.

d. **Field Gene Banks**: Establishing field gene banks to grow and maintain medicinal plants in controlled environments.

In-situ Conservation:

In-situ conservation involves protecting and maintaining medicinal plants in their natural habitats. This method focuses on preserving the ecosystems and environments where these plants naturally occur.

Key Strategies for In-situ Conservation

1. **Protected Areas**

    a. **National Parks and Wildlife Reserves**: Establish and manage protected areas to safeguard habitats from human activities and environmental degradation.

    b. **Community Conservation Areas**: Engage local communities in protecting and managing natural habitats, promoting sustainable use and conservation.

2. **Sustainable Harvesting Practices**

    a. **Regulated Collection**: Implement policies to control the collection of medicinal plants from the wild, ensuring sustainable harvesting levels.

    b. **Education and Awareness**: Educate local communities on sustainable harvesting methods and the importance of biodiversity conservation.

3. **Habitat Restoration**

    a. **Reforestation and Afforestation**: Plant native species to restore degraded habitats and enhance plant diversity.

    b. **Erosion Control**: Implement measures to prevent soil erosion and maintain healthy environments for plant growth.

4. **Monitoring and Research**

   a. **Biodiversity Inventories**: Conduct surveys to identify and monitor the status of medicinal plant species and their habitats.

   b. **Ecological Studies**: Research the ecological needs of medicinal plants to inform conservation strategies and habitat management practices.

Ex-situ Conservation:

Ex-situ conservation involves preserving plant species outside their natural habitats. This method is crucial for safeguarding plant genetic resources, especially for species that are endangered or have limited populations.

Key Strategies for Ex-situ Conservation

1. **Botanical Gardens and Arboreta**

   a. **Living Collections**: Maintain living collections of medicinal plants, providing controlled environments for their growth and study.

   b. **Public Education**: Use botanical gardens to educate the public on the importance of plant conservation and the value of medicinal plants.

2. **Seed Banks and Germplasm Storage**

   a. **Seed Collection and Storage**: Collect and store seeds of medicinal plants in seed banks under controlled conditions for long-term viability.

   b. **Cryopreservation**: Use cryopreservation to store plant tissues, seeds, and cells at ultra-low temperatures for extended periods.

3. **Tissue Culture and Micropropagation**

   a. **In-vitro Propagation**: Use tissue culture to propagate medicinal plants in laboratory conditions, producing large numbers of genetically identical plants.

   b. **Genetic Conservation**: Maintain diverse genetic pools by propagating plants from different genetic backgrounds.

4. **Field Gene Banks**

a. **Cultivation in Controlled Environments**: Establish field gene banks to cultivate medicinal plants in controlled environments, ensuring their survival and availability.

b. **Genetic Studies**: Conduct genetic studies to understand the diversity and adaptability of medicinal plants.

Integration of In-situ and Ex-situ Conservation:

A comprehensive conservation strategy often integrates both in-situ and ex-situ methods to ensure the preservation of genetic diversity and support ecosystem health.

Key Integration Strategies

1. **Complementary Conservation Plans**

    a. **Combined Efforts**: Develop plans that incorporate both in-situ and ex-situ methods for a holistic conservation approach.

    b. **Resource Allocation**: Allocate resources effectively between in-situ and ex-situ programs based on specific needs and species status.

2. **Research and Data Sharing**

    a. **Collaborative Research**: Promote collaboration between botanical gardens, research institutions, and conservation organizations to share data and findings.

    b. **Integrated Databases**: Create databases to document the distribution, genetic diversity, and conservation status of medicinal plants.

3. **Community Involvement**

    a. **Local Engagement**: Involve local communities in conservation efforts, providing knowledge, resources, and incentives to participate in sustainable practices.

    b. **Benefit Sharing**: Ensure that local communities benefit from the conservation and sustainable use of medicinal plants.

Benefits of Conserving Medicinal Plants

1. **Quality Assurance**

a. **Ensuring Consistency**: Conservation helps maintain the quality and consistency of medicinal plants, ensuring their efficacy for pharmaceutical use.

b. **Safety**: Reduces the risk of contamination and ensures the safety of medicinal plant products.

2. **Sustainable Resource Management**

   a. **Long-term Availability**: Promotes sustainable practices that ensure the continued availability of medicinal plants.

   b. **Economic Benefits**: Provides economic opportunities for local communities, fostering stewardship and conservation.

3. **Environmental Protection**

   a. **Ecosystem Health**: Supports the health and stability of ecosystems, promoting biodiversity and ecological balance.

   b. **Minimized Impact**: Reduces the environmental impact of plant collection and cultivation activities.

4. **Cultural and Traditional Value**

   a. **Cultural Preservation**: Helps preserve traditional knowledge and practices related to medicinal plants.

   b. **Healthcare Support**: Ensures the availability of medicinal plants for traditional medicine, which is vital for many communities.

Multiple Choice Questions (MCQs)

1. What is plant drug cultivation?

   A) Growing plants for decorative purposes

   B) Growing plants specifically for pharmaceutical compounds

   C) Growing plants for food production

   D) Growing plants for industrial raw materials

2. Which of the following is a primary source of medicinal compounds in plants?

   A) Alkaloids

   B) Plastics

   C) Metals

   D) Fossil fuels

3. How does plant drug cultivation support traditional medicine?

   A) By replacing traditional medicine with modern pharmaceuticals

   B) By preserving and continuing traditional healing practices

   C) By eliminating the need for medicinal plants

   D) By converting traditional knowledge into digital formats

4. What is one of the economic benefits of plant drug cultivation?

   A) Decreased employment opportunities

   B) Reduction in pharmaceutical prices

   C) Providing employment in farming, processing, and research

   D) Increasing the cost of traditional medicines

5. Which of the following is a challenge in plant drug cultivation?

   A) Abundance of water resources

   B) Climate change and extreme weather events

   C) High soil fertility

   D) Easy market access

6. What is the purpose of site selection and preparation in plant drug cultivation?

   A) To improve plant aesthetics

   B) To ensure optimal growth conditions

   C) To increase pesticide use

   D) To decrease soil fertility

7. Which propagation technique is used for plants that do not produce viable seeds?

A) Seed propagation

B) Vegetative propagation

C) Chemical propagation

D) Water propagation

8. What is one of the benefits of in-situ conservation?

A) Preserving plants in their natural habitat

B) Storing plants in botanical gardens

C) Freezing plant tissues at ultra-low temperatures

D) Using plants for decorative purposes

9. What is the role of seed banks in ex-situ conservation?

A) To store seeds under controlled conditions for long-term viability

B) To plant seeds in their natural habitat

C) To destroy seeds of endangered species

D) To convert seeds into fossil fuels

10. Which organization is responsible for coordinating agricultural research in India?

A) WHO

B) ICAR

C) FAO

D) UNESCO

11. What is the purpose of phytochemical analysis in plant drug cultivation?

A) To enhance plant aesthetics

B) To identify and quantify active compounds

C) To increase soil erosion

D) To reduce plant growth

12. Which technique is used to propagate medicinal plants in laboratory conditions?

A) Traditional farming

B) Tissue culture

C) Pesticide application

D) Watering

13. What is the main focus of Good Agricultural Practices (GAP)?

A) Maximizing pesticide use

B) Ensuring the sustainable production of high-quality agricultural products

C) Decreasing soil fertility

D) Increasing water pollution

14. Which method involves the preservation of plants in their natural habitats?

A) Ex-situ conservation

B) In-situ conservation

C) Chemical preservation

D) Genetic engineering

15. What is one of the key components of Good Collection Practices (GCP)?

A) Harvesting plants during inappropriate seasons

B) Using inappropriate tools for collection

C) Ensuring sustainable harvesting levels

D) Avoiding the use of clean containers

16. Which strategy involves planting native species to restore degraded habitats?

A) Soil compaction

B) Erosion control

C) Reforestation and afforestation

D) Waterlogging

17. What is the benefit of community engagement in plant conservation efforts?

A) Promoting overharvesting

B) Ensuring fair compensation and sustainable practices

C) Reducing biodiversity

D) Decreasing environmental awareness

18. Which organization maintains germplasm banks to preserve genetic diversity of medicinal plants in India?

    A) WHO

    B) FAO

    C) ICAR

    D) UNESCO

19. What is one of the primary goals of ex-situ conservation?

    A) To eliminate the need for genetic diversity

    B) To safeguard plant genetic resources outside their natural habitats

    C) To decrease plant populations

    D) To promote soil erosion

20. What is the significance of maintaining detailed records in plant drug cultivation?

    A) To increase soil erosion

    B) To ensure traceability and regulatory compliance

    C) To decrease plant quality

    D) To eliminate the need for quality control

Short Answer Type Questions

1. What is plant drug cultivation?

2. Why is plant drug cultivation important for the pharmaceutical and herbal medicine industries?

3. Name two bioactive compounds commonly found in medicinal plants.

4. How does plant drug cultivation support traditional medicine?

5. What role does biotechnology play in plant drug cultivation?

6. Explain the significance of quality control and standardization in plant drug cultivation.

7. What are the key steps involved in plant drug cultivation?

8. Why is site selection and preparation crucial in plant drug cultivation?

9. Describe the process of vegetative propagation.

10. What are the main components of integrated pest management (IPM) in plant drug cultivation?

11. What is the importance of post-harvest processing in plant drug cultivation?

12. Define in-situ conservation of medicinal plants.

13. How does ex-situ conservation differ from in-situ conservation?

14. What are the key strategies for sustainable harvesting of medicinal plants?

15. Explain the role of the Indian Council of Agricultural Research (ICAR) in plant drug cultivation.

16. What are Good Agricultural Practices (GAP) and why are they important?

17. What is the significance of phytochemical analysis in plant drug cultivation?

18. How does community engagement contribute to the conservation of medicinal plants?

19. Describe one challenge faced in plant drug cultivation and its impact.

20. What are the benefits of conserving medicinal plants?

Long Answer Type Questions

1. Discuss the importance of plant drug cultivation in modern and traditional medicine, highlighting its economic, ecological, and healthcare impacts.

2. Explain the various steps involved in plant drug cultivation, from the selection of medicinal plants to market access.

3. Analyze the environmental, biological, socio-economic, and management factors that affect plant drug cultivation.

4. What are the main challenges in plant drug cultivation? Discuss potential solutions to these challenges.

5. Describe the advances in biotechnological innovations and sustainable farming practices that have enhanced plant drug cultivation.

6. Explain the role of Pharmacognosy in the herbal drug industry, focusing on the identification, characterization, and standardization of medicinal plants.

7. How does ICAR contribute to the cultivation of medicinal plants and the development of plant-based drugs in India?

8. Discuss the key components of Good Agricultural Practices (GAP) and Current Good Cultivation Practices (GCP) in plant drug cultivation.

9. Compare and contrast in-situ and ex-situ conservation methods, providing examples of strategies used in each approach.

10. Explain the integration of traditional knowledge with modern science in the conservation and cultivation of medicinal plants. Discuss the benefits and challenges of this integration.

Answer Key

1. B) Growing plants specifically for pharmaceutical compounds
2. A) Alkaloids
3. B) By preserving and continuing traditional healing practices
4. C) Providing employment in farming, processing, and research
5. B) Climate change and extreme weather events
6. B) To ensure optimal growth conditions
7. B) Vegetative propagation
8. A) Preserving plants in their natural habitat
9. A) To store seeds under controlled conditions for long-term viability
10. B) ICAR
11. B) To identify and quantify active compounds
12. B) Tissue culture
13. B) Ensuring the sustainable production of high-quality agricultural products
14. B) In-situ conservation
15. C) Ensuring sustainable harvesting levels
16. C) Reforestation and afforestation
17. B) Ensuring fair compensation and sustainable practices
18. C) ICAR

19.B) To safeguard plant genetic resources outside their natural habitats

20.B) To ensure traceability and regulatory compliance

CHAPTER – 2

MARINE NATURAL PRODUCTS

INTRODUCTION:

Marine natural products refer to chemical compounds derived from marine organisms such as sponges, algae, bacteria, fungi, and marine invertebrates. These compounds have garnered significant interest due to their diverse structures and potent biological activities, making them valuable for pharmaceutical, agricultural, and industrial applications.

Types of Marine Natural Products:

Marine natural products encompass a diverse array of chemical compounds derived from marine organisms, including microorganisms, algae, invertebrates, and vertebrates. These compounds have shown remarkable biological activities and have the potential for various applications, including pharmaceuticals, cosmetics, and biotechnology. Here's an overview of the main types of marine natural products:

1. Peptides and Proteins:

    a. **Examples:** Cyanopeptolins, Didemnins, Conotoxins.

    b. **Source:** Often produced by marine organisms like sponges, tunicates, and cone snails.

    c. **Biological Activities:** Antibacterial, antifungal, antiviral, and anticancer activities.

    d. **Applications:** Potential therapeutic agents due to their specific biological activities and structural diversity.

2. Terpenes and Terpenoids:

    a. **Examples:** Diterpenes (e.g., Sarcophytol A), Sesquiterpenes, Steroids.

    b. **Source:** Found in marine algae (e.g., seaweeds) and some marine invertebrates.

c. **Biological Activities:** Antimicrobial, antifouling (preventing attachment of marine organisms), and anticancer properties.

d. **Applications:** Used in pharmaceuticals, cosmetics, and as antifouling agents in marine coatings.

3. Polyketides:

a. **Examples:** Discodermolide, Bryostatins, Halichondrins.

b. **Source:** Produced by marine sponges, bacteria, and fungi.

c. **Biological Activities:** Anticancer, antibacterial, and antifungal activities.

d. **Applications:** Potential drug leads due to their complex structures and potent bioactivities.

4. Alkaloids:

a. **Examples:** Bromotyrosines (e.g., Aplysinopsins), Indole alkaloids.

b. **Source:** Found in marine sponges, tunicates, and some marine plants.

c. **Biological Activities:** Neurotoxic, antimicrobial, and antiviral activities.

d. **Applications:** Pharmaceuticals and biomedical research due to their diverse pharmacological properties.

5. Pigments:

a. **Examples:** Astaxanthin, Phycobilins (from red algae), Chlorophylls.

b. **Source:** Commonly found in marine algae and some marine bacteria.

c. **Biological Activities:** Antioxidant, photoprotective (UV protection), and potential health benefits.

d. **Applications:** Used in cosmetics, nutraceuticals, and food coloring agents.

6. Glycosides:

a. **Examples:** Saponins, Glycosylated fatty acids.

b. **Source:** Found in marine organisms such as sea cucumbers, marine plants, and some marine microbes.

c. **Biological Activities:** Anti-inflammatory, antitumor, and immune-modulating properties.

d. **Applications:** Pharmaceutical development and as bioactive compounds in functional foods.

7. Lipids and Fatty Acids:

a. **Examples:** Omega-3 fatty acids (e.g., EPA, DHA), Wax esters.

b. **Source:** Derived from marine algae, fish, and some marine invertebrates.

c. **Biological Activities:** Cardiovascular health benefits, anti-inflammatory effects, and skin barrier enhancement.

d. **Applications:** Nutraceuticals, dietary supplements, and pharmaceutical formulations.

8. Marine Polysaccharides:

a. **Examples:** Alginate, Carrageenans, Fucoidan.

b. **Source:** Found in marine algae (e.g., brown algae, red algae) and some marine bacteria.

c. **Biological Activities:** Antioxidant, anticoagulant, and immunomodulatory properties.

d. **Applications:** Used in pharmaceuticals, cosmetics, and as functional food ingredients.

Importance and Future Directions

Marine natural products offer immense potential for drug discovery and other biotechnological applications due to their unique chemical structures and diverse biological activities. Continued exploration of marine biodiversity, coupled with advances in analytical techniques and biotechnology, is essential for harnessing these compounds for sustainable development and innovation in healthcare and other industries. Efforts in biodiversity conservation and sustainable bioprospecting practices are critical to ensuring the long-term availability and ethical use of marine natural products.

Biological Activities and Applications:

Marine natural products exhibit a wide range of biological activities that make them valuable for various applications in pharmaceuticals, biotechnology, cosmetics, and other industries. Here's a detailed exploration of their biological activities and applications:

Biological Activities

1. **Anticancer Activity**
    a. **Examples:** Marine natural products like Bryostatins, Discodermolide, and Halichondrins have shown potent anticancer properties.
    b. **Mechanisms:** Inhibit tumor cell proliferation, induce apoptosis (programmed cell death), and disrupt cancer cell signaling pathways.
    c. **Applications:** Potential as chemotherapeutic agents for treating various types of cancer.

2. **Antimicrobial and Antifungal Activity**
    a. **Examples:** Marine peptides (e.g., Cyanopeptolins, Didemnins) and polyketides (e.g., Pseudopterosins) exhibit antimicrobial and antifungal activities.
    b. **Mechanisms:** Disrupt bacterial cell membranes, inhibit bacterial and fungal enzymes, and interfere with microbial DNA replication.
    c. **Applications:** Development of antibiotics, antifungal agents, and antiseptics to combat drug-resistant pathogens.

3. **Antiviral Activity**
    a. **Examples:** Marine-derived compounds such as Manzamine alkaloids and Spongouridine show antiviral activity against viruses.
    b. **Mechanisms:** Inhibit viral replication, block viral entry into host cells, or modulate host immune responses against viral infections.
    c. **Applications:** Potential for developing antiviral drugs and treatments for viral infections.

4. **Anti-inflammatory and Immunomodulatory Properties**

    a. **Examples:** Marine glycosides (e.g., Saponins), fatty acids (e.g., Omega-3 fatty acids), and polysaccharides (e.g., Fucoidans) possess anti-inflammatory and immunomodulatory effects.

    b. **Mechanisms:** Suppress inflammatory cytokines, regulate immune cell function, and modulate immune responses.

    c. **Applications:** Treatment of inflammatory diseases (e.g., arthritis, inflammatory bowel disease) and immune disorders.

5. **Neuroprotective and Neurological Activity**

    a. **Examples:** Marine alkaloids (e.g., Bromotyrosines), peptides (e.g., Conotoxins), and polyketides (e.g., Halichondrins) exhibit neuroprotective effects.

    b. **Mechanisms:** Enhance neuronal survival, modulate neurotransmitter levels, and protect against neurodegenerative processes.

    c. **Applications:** Potential for developing treatments for neurological disorders such as Alzheimer's disease and Parkinson's disease.

6. **Antioxidant and Anti-aging Properties**

    a. **Examples:** Marine pigments (e.g., Astaxanthin), polyphenols (e.g., Phlorotannins), and peptides (e.g., Collagen peptides) possess antioxidant and anti-aging properties.

    b. **Mechanisms:** Scavenge free radicals, prevent oxidative stress-induced damage, and promote collagen synthesis.

    c. **Applications:** Used in cosmetics and skincare products for their anti-aging and skin-protective benefits.

7. **Cardiovascular Health Benefits**

    a. **Examples:** Marine lipids (e.g., Omega-3 fatty acids), peptides (e.g., Bioactive peptides from fish), and polysaccharides (e.g., Carrageenans) contribute to cardiovascular health.

b. **Mechanisms:** Lower cholesterol levels, reduce blood pressure, and enhance vascular function.

c. **Applications:** Used as dietary supplements and functional food ingredients to promote heart health and prevent cardiovascular diseases.

Applications

1. **Pharmaceuticals:** Marine natural products serve as lead compounds or drug candidates for developing novel therapeutics targeting various diseases, including cancer, infectious diseases, and inflammatory disorders.

2. **Biotechnology:** Utilized in biotechnological applications such as enzyme inhibitors, biosurfactants, and biofuels derived from marine microorganisms and algae.

3. **Cosmetics:** Incorporated into skincare products and cosmetics for their antioxidant, anti-aging, and moisturizing properties derived from marine-derived peptides, pigments, and polysaccharides.

4. **Nutraceuticals:** Used as dietary supplements (e.g., Omega-3 fatty acids, marine polysaccharides) for health benefits ranging from cardiovascular support to immune system enhancement.

5. **Environmental and Agricultural Applications:** Marine natural products are explored for their potential as environmentally friendly pesticides, antifouling agents, and soil conditioners.

Future Directions

Continued exploration of marine biodiversity and advances in biotechnological and analytical techniques will unlock further potential for discovering and utilizing marine natural products. Efforts in sustainable bioprospecting, biodiversity conservation, and ethical practices are crucial to ensure responsible utilization of marine resources for human benefit while preserving marine ecosystems. Research collaborations and interdisciplinary approaches will further enhance our understanding of marine natural products and their applications in improving human health and sustainable development.

Challenges and Future Prospects:

Marine natural products offer immense potential for various applications, including pharmaceuticals, biotechnology, cosmetics, and more. However, their exploration and utilization come with several challenges that need to be addressed to fully harness their benefits. Here's an in-depth look at these challenges and future prospects in marine natural products research:

Challenges

1. **Bioprospecting and Access**
    a. **Biodiversity Loss:** Threats to marine biodiversity from climate change, pollution, overfishing, and habitat destruction reduce the availability of novel marine organisms and their natural products.
    b. **Access and Benefit Sharing:** Challenges in navigating international regulations, such as the Nagoya Protocol, for fair and equitable sharing of benefits from genetic resources and traditional knowledge with source countries.

2. **Technological and Analytical Limitations**
    a. **Complexity of Chemical Structures:** Many marine natural products have complex chemical structures, requiring advanced analytical techniques (e.g., NMR spectroscopy, mass spectrometry) for accurate identification and characterization.
    b. **Low Yield and Availability:** Limited availability of certain marine organisms and low yields of bioactive compounds pose challenges in scaling up production for commercial applications.

3. **Regulatory and Commercialization Hurdles**
    a. **Regulatory Approval:** Stringent regulatory requirements for safety, efficacy, and environmental impact assessment delay the development and commercialization of marine-derived drugs and products.

b. **Intellectual Property (IP) Issues:** Challenges in obtaining and protecting IP rights for marine natural products due to prior art, natural occurrence, and complexities in patenting novel discoveries.

4. **Environmental and Ethical Considerations**
   a. **Sustainability:** Balancing bioprospecting activities with sustainable use of marine resources to prevent overexploitation and protect marine ecosystems and biodiversity.
   b. **Ethical Practices:** Respecting indigenous rights, traditional knowledge, and cultural values of communities involved in bioprospecting activities.

5. **Biotechnological Challenges**
   a. **Bioproduction and Synthesis:** Developing sustainable and cost-effective methods for producing marine natural products through biotechnological approaches (e.g., marine microorganism fermentation, genetic engineering).
   b. **Bioactivity Screening:** Enhancing screening methods to identify bioactive compounds efficiently and effectively from diverse marine organisms and habitats.

Future Prospects

1. **Advancements in Technology and Research**
   a. **Omics Technologies:** Integration of genomics, transcriptomics, proteomics, and metabolomics to elucidate biosynthetic pathways of marine natural products and optimize production.
   b. **High-Throughput Screening:** Automation and miniaturization of bioassays for rapid screening of marine natural products for therapeutic and industrial applications.

2. **Collaborative and Interdisciplinary Research**

a. **Global Partnerships:** Strengthening international collaborations among academia, industry, and governments to share resources, expertise, and infrastructure for marine natural product research.

b. **Interdisciplinary Approaches:** Integrating fields such as chemistry, biology, ecology, pharmacology, and biotechnology to comprehensively explore marine biodiversity and natural products.

3. **Sustainable Bioprospecting Practices**

a. **Conservation and Management:** Implementing sustainable harvesting practices, marine protected areas, and ecosystem-based management to conserve marine biodiversity and habitats.

b. **Community Engagement:** Involving local communities in bioprospecting activities through equitable benefit-sharing mechanisms and capacity building.

4. **Innovation in Drug Discovery and Development**

a. **Drug Design and Optimization:** Utilizing marine natural products as leads for drug discovery, optimizing their pharmacokinetic and pharmacodynamic properties through medicinal chemistry and drug design.

b. **Therapeutic Applications:** Expanding the therapeutic potential of marine natural products beyond cancer to include infectious diseases, neurodegenerative disorders, and metabolic diseases.

5. **Education and Public Awareness**

a. **Training and Education:** Investing in training programs and capacity building for scientists, policymakers, and stakeholders involved in marine natural product research and conservation.

b. **Public Outreach:** Increasing awareness among the general public about the value of marine biodiversity, sustainable use of marine resources, and the potential benefits of marine natural products.

GENERAL METHODS OF ISOLATION AND PURIFICATION OF MARINE NATURAL PRODUCTS

Isolating and purifying marine natural products involves several complex steps due to the diversity of marine organisms and the often low concentrations of target compounds. Here are the general methods used in the isolation and purification of marine natural products:

1. **Collection and Identification of Marine Organisms:**
    a. **Collection:** Marine organisms like sponges, algae, and tunicates are collected from their natural habitats, often from diverse marine environments worldwide.
    b. **Identification:** Taxonomic identification ensures correct species identification and facilitates further study of their chemical constituents.

2. **Extraction of Bioactive Compounds:**
    a. **Solvent Extraction:** Typically, organic solvents such as methanol, ethanol, acetone, or dichloromethane are used to extract bioactive compounds from collected organisms.
    b. **Partitioning:** Partitioning between immiscible solvents (e.g., water and organic solvents) helps separate different classes of compounds based on their polarity.

3. **Fractionation and Purification Techniques:**
    a. **Chromatography:** Various chromatographic techniques, such as column chromatography, thin-layer chromatography (TLC), high-performance liquid chromatography (HPLC), and flash chromatography, are used to separate complex mixtures of compounds based on differences in polarity, size, and chemical properties.
    b. **Preparative HPLC:** Enables purification of larger quantities of compounds for further biological testing and structural elucidation.

4. **Structural Elucidation:**
   a. **Spectroscopic Techniques:** Nuclear magnetic resonance (NMR) spectroscopy, mass spectrometry (MS), and infrared (IR) spectroscopy are used to determine the chemical structure and confirm the purity of isolated compounds.
   b. **X-ray Crystallography:** Provides detailed three-dimensional structural information for solid compounds.
5. **Bioassay-Guided Fractionation:**
   a. **Bioactivity Testing:** Bioassays are used to identify fractions or compounds with specific biological activities (e.g., anticancer, antibacterial). This approach guides the isolation of bioactive compounds.
6. **Scale-Up and Yield Optimization:**
   a. **Fermentation:** For microorganisms, fermentation techniques can be scaled up to produce larger quantities of compounds.
   b. **Synthetic Biology:** Genetic engineering of marine microorganisms to increase production of desired natural products.
7. **Storage and Stability Testing:**
   a. **Storage:** Proper storage conditions (e.g., temperature, light exposure) are crucial to maintain the stability and biological activity of purified compounds.
8. **Ethical and Regulatory Considerations:**
   a. **Conservation:** Sustainable harvesting practices to minimize environmental impact and protect marine biodiversity.
   b. **Regulation:** Compliance with international regulations and conventions governing access to and utilization of marine genetic resources.

STUDY OF MARINE TOXINS

Marine toxins are a fascinating and diverse group of natural compounds produced by various marine organisms, often as a defense mechanism or for predation. These toxins can have potent biological activities and pose risks to human health if consumed or encountered. Here's an overview of the study of marine toxins:

Types of Marine Toxins:

Marine toxins are potent natural compounds produced by various marine organisms, primarily for defense against predators or competition for resources. These toxins can have significant biological effects, ranging from neurotoxicity to cytotoxicity, and their study is crucial for understanding marine ecology, human health impacts, and potential biomedical applications. Here's an overview of some major types of marine toxins:

1. Ciguatoxins:

a. **Source:** Produced by marine dinoflagellates (Gambierdiscus spp.) and bioaccumulate in reef fish (e.g., barracuda, grouper).

b. **Mechanism:** Act as sodium channel activators, leading to disruption of nerve cell function and causing ciguatera fish poisoning (CFP) in humans.

c. **Symptoms:** Neurological symptoms (e.g., numbness, tingling), gastrointestinal disturbances, and cardiovascular effects.

d. **Impacts:** CFP is a common seafood poisoning in tropical and subtropical regions, affecting fish consumers and causing economic losses in fisheries.

2. Saxitoxins:

a. **Source:** Produced by marine dinoflagellates (e.g., Alexandrium spp.) and some cyanobacteria.

b. **Mechanism:** Block voltage-gated sodium channels, leading to inhibition of nerve impulse transmission and causing paralytic shellfish poisoning (PSP).

c. **Symptoms:** Neurological symptoms (e.g., numbness, tingling, paralysis), respiratory distress, and potentially fatal respiratory failure.

d. **Impacts:** PSP affects shellfish consumers, posing risks to public health and leading to regulatory monitoring of shellfish harvesting.

3. Tetrodotoxin (TTX):

a. **Source:** Found in certain marine pufferfish (e.g., Fugu spp.), blue-ringed octopuses, and some marine invertebrates.

b. **Mechanism:** Blocks voltage-gated sodium channels, causing neuromuscular paralysis and potentially lethal respiratory and cardiovascular failure.

c. **Symptoms:** Neurological symptoms (e.g., numbness, paralysis), nausea, and potentially fatal respiratory arrest.

d. **Impacts:** TTX poisoning is a serious concern in regions where pufferfish consumption is culturally practiced, necessitating strict regulation of its sale and preparation.

4. Brevetoxins:

a. **Source:** Produced by marine dinoflagellates (Karenia brevis) during harmful algal blooms (red tides).

b. **Mechanism:** Bind to voltage-gated sodium channels, disrupting nerve cell function and causing neurotoxic shellfish poisoning (NSP).

c. **Symptoms:** Neurological symptoms (e.g., dizziness, nausea, respiratory distress), particularly affecting shellfish consumers.

d. **Impacts:** NSP outbreaks are monitored closely in shellfish harvesting areas, impacting local economies and public health.

5. Okadaic Acid and Dinophysistoxins:

a. **Source:** Produced by marine dinoflagellates (e.g., Dinophysis spp.) and accumulate in shellfish.

b. **Mechanism:** Inhibit protein phosphatases, leading to disruption of cellular processes and causing diarrhetic shellfish poisoning (DSP).

c. **Symptoms:** Gastrointestinal symptoms (e.g., diarrhea, nausea, vomiting), affecting shellfish consumers.

d. **Impacts:** DSP outbreaks necessitate monitoring of shellfish toxicity levels and closures of affected harvesting areas to prevent human illness.

6. Palytoxins:

a. **Source:** Produced by marine dinoflagellates (Ostreopsis spp.) and certain coral species (e.g., Palythoa spp.).

b. **Mechanism:** Act as sodium channel activators and disrupt cellular function, causing severe toxicity in marine organisms and humans.

c. **Symptoms:** Severe skin and mucosal irritation, respiratory distress, and potentially fatal cardiovascular effects.

d. **Impacts:** Palytoxin exposure can occur through inhalation of aerosols during algal blooms, affecting coastal residents and divers.

Importance and Research Focus

Studying marine toxins is critical for understanding their ecological roles, impacts on marine ecosystems, and risks to human health. Ongoing research focuses on toxin detection methods, mechanisms of toxicity, ecological factors influencing toxin production, and development of mitigation strategies to reduce human exposure. Regulatory agencies monitor toxin levels in seafood and recreational waters to protect public health and ensure sustainable use of marine resources amidst environmental changes and anthropogenic pressures.

Methods of Study and Detection:

The study and detection of marine toxins are essential for understanding their ecological impact, monitoring seafood safety, and protecting human health.

Various methods are employed to identify, quantify, and analyze marine toxins in both marine organisms and environmental samples. Here's a detailed exploration of the methods used in the study of marine toxins:

1. Biological Assays

a. **Bioassays:** Utilize living organisms or tissues to detect biological activity and toxicity of marine toxins.

  i. **Examples:** Mouse bioassay (for detection of paralytic shellfish toxins), brine shrimp lethality assay (for general toxicity screening), and cell-based assays (e.g., cytotoxicity assays).

  ii. **Advantages:** Direct measurement of biological effects, sensitive to complex toxin mixtures.

  iii. **Limitations:** Lack of specificity for individual toxins, ethical considerations (e.g., animal use).

2. Chemical Analysis

a. **Chromatography Techniques:** Separation and quantification of toxins based on their chemical properties.

  i. **High-Performance Liquid Chromatography (HPLC):** Separates toxins based on their polarity and interaction with a stationary phase.

  ii. **Gas Chromatography (GC):** Separates volatile toxins based on their vapor pressure and interaction with a stationary phase.

  iii. **Advantages:** High specificity and sensitivity for toxin detection, quantitative analysis.

  iv. **Limitations:** Requires standards for accurate identification, may not distinguish between structural analogs without additional techniques.

3. Mass Spectrometry (MS)

a. **Liquid Chromatography-Mass Spectrometry (LC-MS) and Gas Chromatography-Mass Spectrometry (GC-MS):** Combine chromatography with mass spectrometric detection for identification and quantification of toxins.

    i. **Advantages:** Provides structural information, high sensitivity for trace analysis, can distinguish between structural isomers and analogs.

    ii. **Limitations:** Requires expertise in mass spectrometry, expensive equipment, and standards for accurate quantification.

4. Immunoassays

a. **Enzyme-Linked Immunosorbent Assay (ELISA):** Uses antibodies specific to toxins to detect and quantify their presence.

    i. **Advantages:** Rapid, sensitive, and cost-effective screening method.

    ii. **Limitations:** Cross-reactivity with structurally similar compounds, requires validation against chemical analysis methods.

5. Molecular Techniques

a. **Polymerase Chain Reaction (PCR):** Detects and quantifies toxin-producing organisms (e.g., dinoflagellates) based on their DNA or RNA.

    i. **Advantages:** Specific detection of toxin-producing species, rapid results.

    ii. **Limitations:** Limited to known toxin-producing species, requires reference sequences for identification.

6. Electrophysiological Assays

a. **Electrophysiological Techniques:** Measure changes in ion channel activity or membrane potential caused by toxins.

    i. **Examples:** Patch clamp electrophysiology to study sodium channel activity affected by toxins like saxitoxin.

    ii. **Advantages:** Direct measurement of toxin effects on cellular function.

iii. **Limitations:** Requires specialized equipment and expertise, may not be suitable for high-throughput screening.

7. Remote Sensing and Monitoring

a. **Remote Sensing:** Use satellite imagery and environmental sensors to detect harmful algal blooms (HABs) associated with toxin-producing organisms.

   i. **Advantages:** Early warning systems for HABs, monitoring of bloom dynamics.

   ii. **Limitations:** Cannot directly detect toxins, requires ground validation and integration with chemical analysis.

Importance and Future Directions

Advancements in analytical techniques, including multi-method approaches combining chromatography, mass spectrometry, and immunoassays, enhance our ability to detect and monitor marine toxins with greater accuracy and efficiency. Future research focuses on developing rapid, field-deployable methods for on-site toxin detection, improving toxin standardization for method validation, and understanding the ecological factors influencing toxin production in marine environments. These efforts are crucial for mitigating risks to human health, ensuring seafood safety, and conserving marine ecosystems impacted by toxin-producing organisms.

Health and Environmental Implications:

The study of marine toxins is pivotal due to their significant health and environmental implications. These toxins, produced by various marine organisms, can adversely affect both marine ecosystems and human populations through seafood contamination and ecosystem disruption. Here's a detailed exploration of the health and environmental implications associated with marine toxins:

Health Implications:

1. **Seafood Poisoning**

    a. **Paralytic Shellfish Poisoning (PSP):** Caused by saxitoxins and related compounds produced by dinoflagellates during harmful algal blooms (HABs). Symptoms include numbness, tingling, respiratory distress, and potentially fatal paralysis.

    b. **Neurotoxic Shellfish Poisoning (NSP):** Resulting from brevetoxins produced by Karenia brevis during red tides. Symptoms include gastrointestinal distress, neurological symptoms (e.g., dizziness, coordination problems), and respiratory issues.

    c. **Ciguatera Fish Poisoning (CFP):** Caused by ciguatoxins produced by Gambierdiscus spp. in reef fish. Symptoms include gastrointestinal symptoms (e.g., nausea, vomiting), neurological effects (e.g., numbness, tingling), and potentially severe cardiovascular complications.

    d. **Diarrhetic Shellfish Poisoning (DSP):** Due to okadaic acid and dinophysistoxins produced by dinoflagellates. Symptoms include diarrhea, nausea, vomiting, and gastrointestinal distress.

    e. **Amnesic Shellfish Poisoning (ASP):** Caused by domoic acid produced by diatoms. Symptoms include gastrointestinal symptoms, neurological effects (e.g., seizures, memory loss), and potential long-term neurological damage.

2. **Human Exposure and Health Risks**

    a. **Acute Toxicity:** Immediate symptoms upon ingestion of contaminated seafood, ranging from mild gastrointestinal upset to severe neurological and respiratory effects.

    b. **Chronic Effects:** Prolonged exposure to low levels of marine toxins may lead to cumulative health effects, including neurological disorders and increased cancer risks.

3. **Public Health Concerns**
   a. **Regulatory Monitoring:** Regular monitoring of seafood harvesting areas for toxin levels to prevent outbreaks of seafood poisoning and ensure food safety regulations are met.
   b. **Risk Communication:** Educating seafood consumers, healthcare providers, and coastal communities about the risks of marine toxins and appropriate precautions.

Environmental Implications:

1. **Impact on Marine Ecosystems**
   a. **Harmful Algal Blooms (HABs):** Rapid growth of toxin-producing algae (dinoflagellates, diatoms) due to nutrient pollution, climate change, and other factors.
   b. **Ecosystem Disruption:** HABs can lead to oxygen depletion, fish kills, and harmful effects on marine flora and fauna, disrupting ecosystem balance and biodiversity.

2. **Bioaccumulation and Biomagnification**
   a. **Bioaccumulation:** Toxins accumulate in the tissues of filter-feeding organisms (e.g., shellfish, bivalves) that ingest toxin-producing algae.
   b. **Biomagnification:** Toxins become more concentrated as they move up the food chain, posing higher risks to predators and humans consuming contaminated seafood.

3. **Economic and Societal Impact**
   a. **Fisheries and Aquaculture:** Closures of fishing grounds and shellfish harvesting areas during HAB events impact local economies and seafood industries.
   b. **Tourism:** Algal blooms and associated toxin outbreaks can deter tourists from visiting affected coastal areas, affecting tourism-dependent economies.

Mitigation and Management Strategies:

1. **Monitoring and Early Warning Systems**
   a. **Remote Sensing:** Use of satellite imagery and environmental sensors to detect HABs and predict their movement and intensity.
   b. **Biomonitoring:** Monitoring toxin levels in sentinel species (e.g., mussels, clams) to assess environmental contamination and human health risks.
2. **Regulatory Measures**
   a. **Shellfish Monitoring Programs:** Regular testing of shellfish for toxin levels and closure of harvesting areas when toxin levels exceed safe limits.
   b. **Water Quality Regulations:** Implementation of nutrient management strategies and pollution controls to mitigate factors contributing to HABs.
3. **Public Awareness and Education**
   a. **Health Advisories:** Issuing advisories to seafood consumers during toxin outbreaks to prevent illness and reduce human exposure.
   b. **Community Engagement:** Educating coastal communities, fishermen, and aquaculture operators about the risks of marine toxins and measures to protect public health and marine ecosystems.

Regulation and Management:

Regulation and management of marine toxins are crucial aspects of ensuring public health safety, protecting marine ecosystems, and maintaining sustainable fisheries. The study of marine toxins involves regulatory frameworks, monitoring programs, and management strategies aimed at preventing toxin-related illnesses and minimizing environmental impacts. Here's a detailed exploration of regulation and management in the study of marine toxins:

Regulatory Frameworks

1. **International Regulations**

a. **Codex Alimentarius Commission:** Sets international food standards and guidelines, including maximum levels for marine toxins in seafood to ensure food safety.

b. **International Maritime Organization (IMO):** Implements regulations to prevent ship-induced pollution and environmental impacts, including measures related to harmful algal blooms (HABs).

c. **United Nations Environment Programme (UNEP):** Promotes international cooperation and treaties addressing marine pollution and ecosystem management, indirectly influencing toxin-related regulations.

2. **Regional and National Regulations**

a. **European Union (EU):** Implements regulations (e.g., EU Directive 91/492/EEC) for monitoring and controlling marine biotoxins in seafood, ensuring compliance with food safety standards.

b. **United States:** The Food and Drug Administration (FDA) and National Oceanic and Atmospheric Administration (NOAA) regulate marine toxins in seafood through monitoring programs, closure of affected harvesting areas, and issuing public health advisories.

c. **Australia:** The Australian Government Department of Agriculture, Water and the Environment monitors marine biotoxins under the National Shellfish Program, ensuring seafood safety through testing and regulatory enforcement.

Monitoring Programs

1. **Shellfish Monitoring Programs**

a. **Sampling and Analysis:** Regular testing of shellfish (e.g., mussels, clams) for marine toxins (e.g., saxitoxins, domoic acid) to detect contamination levels and ensure compliance with regulatory standards.

b. **Closure and Reopening:** Temporary closure of shellfish harvesting areas when toxin levels exceed safe thresholds, followed by reopening after toxin levels decrease to safe levels.

2. **Environmental Monitoring**

    a. **Harmful Algal Bloom (HAB) Monitoring:** Use of satellite imagery, environmental sensors, and water quality monitoring to detect and track HABs, which can lead to toxin-producing algal blooms.

    b. **Early Warning Systems:** Implementation of systems to provide timely alerts to stakeholders (e.g., fishermen, seafood processors) about potential toxin outbreaks and associated risks.

Management Strategies

1. **Risk Assessment and Communication**

    a. **Health Advisories:** Issuance of advisories to the public, seafood industry, and healthcare providers during toxin outbreaks, providing guidance on safe consumption practices and symptoms of toxin-related illnesses.

    b. **Public Outreach:** Educational campaigns to raise awareness about marine toxins, their health risks, and measures to minimize exposure through responsible seafood consumption.

2. **Research and Development**

    a. **Toxin Detection Methods:** Advancements in analytical techniques (e.g., chromatography, mass spectrometry) for accurate detection and quantification of marine toxins in seafood and environmental samples.

    b. **Toxin Standards and Reference Materials:** Development and validation of certified reference materials and standards for use in toxin analysis, ensuring reliability and comparability of results across laboratories.

Challenges and Future Directions

1. **Emerging Toxins and Climate Change**

a. **New Toxin Variants:** Monitoring and managing emerging toxins and toxin-producing species influenced by changing environmental conditions and ocean warming.

b. **Adaptation Strategies:** Developing adaptive management strategies to address unpredictable HAB events and mitigate their impacts on human health and marine ecosystems.

2. **International Cooperation and Collaboration**

a. **Data Sharing:** Enhancing global cooperation and data sharing among countries and international organizations to improve understanding of marine toxins and harmonize regulatory approaches.

b. **Capacity Building:** Supporting capacity building in developing countries to strengthen their ability to monitor, detect, and manage marine toxins and protect vulnerable coastal communities.

RECENT ADVANCES IN RESEARCH IN MARINE DRUGS

Recent advances in marine drug research have significantly expanded our understanding of the potential therapeutic applications of marine natural products. Here are some key advancements:

1. **Genomic and Metagenomic Approaches:**

a. **Metagenomics:** Studying genetic material recovered directly from environmental samples (e.g., seawater, sediments) has enabled the discovery of novel biosynthetic gene clusters responsible for producing bioactive compounds.

b. **Genome Mining:** Computational tools identify potential biosynthetic pathways in marine microorganisms, facilitating targeted discovery of new drug leads.

2. **Biotechnological Innovations:**

a. **Synthetic Biology:** Engineering marine microorganisms to optimize production of desired natural products or to create novel derivatives with improved pharmacological properties.

b. **Heterologous Expression:** Transferring biosynthetic gene clusters into host organisms to produce complex natural products that are difficult to obtain from their native sources.

3. **Advanced Analytical Techniques:**

    a. **High-Resolution Mass Spectrometry (HR-MS):** Enables precise identification and structural characterization of complex marine natural products, even in minute quantities.

    b. **Cryogenic NMR Techniques:** Enhances resolution and sensitivity in structural elucidation of marine compounds, particularly those with complex structures.

4. **Bioinformatics and Computational Modeling:**

    a. **Virtual Screening:** Computational methods predict the binding affinity of marine natural products to target proteins, accelerating drug discovery.

    b. **Structure-Based Drug Design:** Utilizes 3D structural information of target proteins and marine compounds to design novel drugs with enhanced specificity and efficacy.

5. **Ecological and Pharmacological Studies:**

    a. **Chemical Ecology:** Investigating ecological interactions between marine organisms and their chemical defenses, guiding the search for bioactive compounds.

    b. **Pharmacokinetics and Pharmacodynamics:** Studying absorption, distribution, metabolism, and excretion (ADME) profiles of marine drugs to optimize their therapeutic use.

6. **Clinical Trials and Drug Development:**

    a. **Anticancer Agents:** Marine-derived compounds like trabectedin (from sea squirt) and eribulin (from marine sponge) have been approved for cancer treatment, demonstrating efficacy in clinical trials.

b. **Neurological Disorders:** Compounds targeting neurodegenerative diseases (e.g., Alzheimer's, Parkinson's) show promise in preclinical studies, advancing toward clinical evaluation.

c. **Antimicrobial Resistance:** Marine peptides and polyketides exhibit potent activity against drug-resistant bacteria, offering new options for combating antimicrobial resistance.

7. **Commercialization and Market Expansion:**

a. **Bioprospecting and Biodiversity Conservation:** Sustainable sourcing of marine natural products while preserving marine ecosystems.

b. **Collaborations:** Industry-academic partnerships accelerate drug development and commercialization, bridging gaps between discovery research and market availability.

PROBLEMS FACED IN RESEARCH ON MARINE DRUGS SUCH AS TAXONOMICAL IDENTIFICATION, CHEMICAL SCREENING AND THEIR SOLUTION

Research on marine drugs faces several challenges that stem from the unique characteristics of marine organisms and their environments. Here are the key problems encountered in this field and potential solutions:

Taxonomical Identification:

Taxonomical identification in marine drug research poses significant challenges due to the vast diversity of marine organisms, taxonomic complexities, and the critical need for accurate species attribution. Here's a detailed exploration of the issues, solutions, and methodologies involved:

Problems with Taxonomical Identification

1. **Taxonomic Complexity:**

a. **Morphological Variability:** Many marine organisms exhibit phenotypic plasticity, making traditional morphological identification challenging.

b. **Cryptic Species:** Species that appear identical morphologically but are genetically distinct pose identification difficulties.

c. **Incomplete Taxonomic Knowledge:** Limited taxonomic expertise and databases for some marine taxa further complicate accurate identification.

2. **Misidentification and Misattribution:**

a. Incorrect species identification can lead to misattribution of bioactive compounds to the wrong taxa, impacting subsequent research and development efforts.

b. Lack of standardized protocols and criteria for taxonomic identification across different research groups can lead to inconsistencies.

Solutions and Methodologies

1. DNA Barcoding and Molecular Techniques

a. **DNA Barcoding:** Utilizing short, standardized gene sequences (e.g., mitochondrial COI gene) to identify species accurately, even when morphological identification is challenging.

   i. **Advantages:** Provides rapid and reliable species identification, facilitates large-scale biodiversity assessments, and supports taxonomic revisions.

   ii. **Applications:** Applied widely in marine biodiversity studies and ecological assessments to link genetic data with species identities.

2. Integrative Taxonomy

a. **Combining Multiple Data Sources:** Integrating morphological, molecular, ecological, and biogeographical data for comprehensive species characterization.

   i. **Holistic Approach:** Helps resolve taxonomic uncertainties and validate species identities by cross-referencing multiple lines of evidence.

ii. **Collaborative Efforts:** Collaboration among taxonomists, molecular biologists, and ecologists enhances accuracy and reliability in species identification.

3. Next-Generation Sequencing (NGS) and Metagenomics

a. **NGS Techniques:** High-throughput sequencing of environmental DNA (eDNA) and metagenomic samples to detect and characterize species diversity in marine environments.

    i. **Environmental DNA (eDNA):** Allows detection of species presence without direct sampling, enhancing biodiversity assessments and identifying cryptic species.

    ii. **Metagenomics:** Identifying biosynthetic gene clusters responsible for producing bioactive compounds in marine microorganisms, guiding bioprospecting efforts.

4. Collaborative Networks and Databases

a. **Global Taxonomic Initiatives:** Participation in international taxonomic networks (e.g., Barcode of Life, Global Biodiversity Information Facility) fosters data-sharing, standardization of methods, and global collaboration in marine taxonomy.

b. **Digital Repositories:** Curating and maintaining comprehensive databases of genetic sequences, morphological data, and ecological information for marine organisms.

    i. **Facilitates:** Access to reference sequences for accurate species identification and supports biodiversity conservation efforts.

5. Advanced Imaging and Bioinformatics

a. **Advanced Imaging Techniques:** Utilizing high-resolution imaging (e.g., scanning electron microscopy, confocal microscopy) to capture detailed morphological features for taxonomic studies.

b. **Bioinformatics Tools:** Developing computational algorithms for species delimitation, phylogenetic analysis, and taxonomic classification based on genetic and morphological data integration.

Importance in Marine Drug Research

Accurate taxonomic identification is foundational in marine drug research for several reasons:

a. **Bioprospecting:** Ensures that bioactive compounds are correctly attributed to their source organisms, supporting targeted bioprospecting efforts.

b. **Ecological Context:** Facilitates understanding of ecological interactions and evolutionary relationships among marine organisms producing bioactive compounds.

c. **Conservation:** Supports biodiversity conservation efforts by accurately documenting species distributions and identifying species of conservation concern.

Chemical Screening and Isolation:

Chemical screening and isolation are critical steps in marine drug research but are fraught with challenges due to the complex nature of marine natural product mixtures and the need for efficient identification and isolation of bioactive compounds. Here's a detailed exploration of the issues, solutions, and methodologies involved in chemical screening and isolation:

Problems with Chemical Screening and Isolation

1. **Complex Mixtures of Natural Products:**

    a. Marine organisms produce a diverse array of secondary metabolites, often in complex mixtures with varying chemical properties.

    b. Identifying and isolating specific bioactive compounds from these mixtures can be time-consuming and resource-intensive.

2. **Low Concentrations of Target Compounds:**
   a. Bioactive compounds in marine organisms are often present in trace amounts, requiring sensitive detection methods and efficient extraction techniques.

3. **Structural Elucidation:**
   a. Determining the chemical structure of isolated compounds, particularly those with novel scaffolds or complex structures, can be challenging and may require advanced spectroscopic techniques.

4. **Isolation Techniques:**
   a. Traditional isolation methods (e.g., solvent extraction, chromatography) may not always yield pure compounds or may result in degradation or loss of bioactivity during purification.

Solutions and Methodologies

1. Bioassay-Guided Fractionation

   i. **Principle:** Utilizing biological assays to guide the sequential fractionation and isolation of bioactive compounds from crude extracts.

   ii. **Process:**
   a. Initial screening of crude extracts using bioassays (e.g., cytotoxicity assays, antimicrobial assays) to identify fractions with desired biological activities.
   b. Fractionation of active fractions using chromatographic techniques (e.g., column chromatography, HPLC) to separate and purify individual compounds.
   c. Repeated bioassays to assess bioactivity of isolated compounds and guide further purification steps if necessary.

2. High-Throughput Screening (HTS) and Virtual Screening

   i. **HTS:** Screening large compound libraries or natural product extracts against biological targets using automated assays to identify bioactive compounds.

a. Advances in robotics and miniaturization enable rapid screening of marine natural product libraries for drug discovery.

ii. **Virtual Screening:** Computational methods to predict the binding affinity of marine natural products to target proteins, facilitating prioritization of compounds for experimental validation.

3. Advanced Chromatographic Techniques

i. **Preparative Chromatography:** High-resolution techniques such as preparative HPLC and flash chromatography for efficient isolation of pure compounds from complex mixtures.

a. Utilizes automated fraction collectors and optimized separation conditions to improve yield and purity.

ii. **Solid-Phase Extraction (SPE):** Extraction method that uses solid matrices to selectively retain and elute target compounds from crude extracts, minimizing solvent use and improving efficiency.

4. Structural Elucidation Techniques

i. **Nuclear Magnetic Resonance (NMR) Spectroscopy:** Provides detailed information about the molecular structure, connectivity, and stereochemistry of isolated compounds.

a. Advances in cryogenic NMR techniques enhance sensitivity and resolution for complex marine natural products.

ii. **Mass Spectrometry (MS):** Determines molecular weights and fragment patterns of compounds, complementing NMR data for structural confirmation.

5. Metabolomics and Dereplication Strategies

i. **Metabolomics:** Comprehensive analysis of metabolites produced by marine organisms to profile chemical diversity and identify novel bioactive compounds.

ii. **Dereplication:** Combining analytical techniques (e.g., LC-MS, NMR) with databases and bioinformatics tools to rapidly identify known compounds in natural product extracts, facilitating prioritization of novel compounds.

Importance in Marine Drug Research

i. **Efficient Drug Discovery:** Effective chemical screening and isolation methodologies accelerate the discovery of bioactive marine natural products with potential pharmaceutical applications.

ii. **Structural Diversity:** Enables exploration of diverse chemical scaffolds and novel mechanisms of action for drug development.

iii. **Bioprospecting Efficiency:** Optimizes utilization of marine biodiversity while minimizing environmental impact through targeted extraction and isolation techniques.

Ecological and Environmental Considerations:

Ecological and environmental considerations are crucial aspects of marine drug research, influencing various stages from taxonomical identification to chemical screening and beyond. Here's a detailed exploration of the challenges, solutions, and methodologies related to ecological and environmental considerations in this field:

Challenges in Ecological and Environmental Considerations

1. **Sustainability of Marine Resources:**
   a. **Overexploitation:** Unsustainable harvesting practices can deplete marine populations of bioactive organisms, impacting biodiversity and ecosystem health.
   b. **Habitat Destruction:** Collection methods may damage sensitive marine habitats (e.g., coral reefs, seagrass beds), affecting associated species and ecosystem services.

2. **Biodiversity Conservation:**
   a. **Impact on Non-Target Species:** Extraction activities may unintentionally harm non-target species, including ecologically important organisms and vulnerable species.

b. **Species Interactions:** Disruption of ecological interactions (e.g., predator-prey dynamics, symbiotic relationships) can have cascading effects on marine ecosystems.

3. **Environmental Monitoring and Regulation:**

   a. **Pollution and Contamination:** Chemical pollutants (e.g., heavy metals, persistent organic pollutants) in marine environments can accumulate in marine organisms, affecting their suitability for drug discovery.

   b. **Climate Change:** Altered ocean conditions (e.g., temperature, pH) due to climate change can impact the distribution and productivity of marine organisms producing bioactive compounds.

Solutions and Methodologies

1. Sustainable Harvesting Practices

   a. **Ecosystem-Based Management:** Adopting practices that consider ecological interactions and ecosystem health when harvesting marine organisms.

   b. **Quotas and Regulations:** Implementing quotas, seasonal closures, and protected areas to manage and conserve target species and habitats.

   c. **Alternative Sourcing:** Exploring sustainable alternatives such as aquaculture and mariculture for cultivating marine organisms under controlled conditions.

2. Biodiversity Monitoring and Impact Assessment

   a. **Environmental Impact Assessments (EIAs):** Conducting assessments prior to research activities to evaluate potential impacts on marine biodiversity and ecosystems.

   b. **Long-Term Monitoring:** Establishing monitoring programs to track changes in biodiversity, population dynamics, and habitat integrity over time.

3. Bioprospecting and Benefit Sharing

    a. **Access and Benefit-Sharing (ABS) Agreements:** Engaging in fair and equitable partnerships with local communities and countries of origin to share benefits derived from marine biodiversity.

    b. **Ethical Guidelines:** Adhering to international conventions (e.g., Nagoya Protocol) and ethical principles to ensure respect for indigenous knowledge and rights.

4. Green Chemistry and Sustainable Technologies

    a. **Green Extraction Methods:** Developing and adopting environmentally friendly extraction techniques (e.g., supercritical fluid extraction, microwave-assisted extraction) to reduce solvent use and minimize environmental impact.

    b. **Biodegradable Products:** Promoting the development of biodegradable and eco-friendly products derived from marine natural products to minimize waste and pollution.

5. Public Awareness and Education

    a. **Stakeholder Engagement:** Involving local communities, stakeholders, and policymakers in decision-making processes to promote sustainable practices and conservation efforts.

    b. **Educational Outreach:** Raising awareness about the importance of marine biodiversity, sustainable resource use, and the potential benefits of marine natural products for drug discovery.

Importance in Marine Drug Research

    a. **Long-Term Viability:** Ensuring the continued availability of marine resources for future generations of researchers and industries engaged in marine drug discovery.

    b. **Ethical Responsibility:** Upholding ethical standards and principles in accessing and utilizing marine biodiversity, respecting the rights and knowledge of local communities.

c. **Environmental Stewardship:** Contributing to marine conservation and sustainable development goals through responsible research practices and resource management.

Technological and Analytical Limitations:

Technological and analytical limitations pose significant challenges in marine drug research, affecting various aspects from taxonomical identification to chemical screening and beyond. Here's an in-depth exploration of these challenges, along with potential solutions and methodologies:

Technological and Analytical Limitations

1. **Analytical Sensitivity and Specificity:**
   a. **Detection Limits:** Difficulty in detecting and quantifying trace amounts of bioactive compounds in complex marine matrices.
   b. **Specificity:** Discriminating between structurally similar compounds or contaminants in natural product extracts.

2. **Structural Elucidation:**
   a. **Complexity of Structures:** Marine natural products often have complex chemical structures, requiring advanced spectroscopic techniques for accurate characterization.
   b. **Resolution and Sensitivity:** Achieving high resolution and sensitivity in structural elucidation, particularly for compounds with low abundance.

3. **Data Integration and Interpretation:**
   a. **Multidimensional Data:** Integrating diverse datasets (e.g., genomic, metabolomic, ecological) to correlate chemical profiles with biological activities and ecological contexts.
   b. **Bioinformatics Challenges:** Developing computational tools and algorithms for data mining, dereplication, and predictive modeling in marine natural product research.

4. **Access to Advanced Technologies:**
   a. **Instrumentation:** Availability and affordability of high-end analytical instruments (e.g., high-resolution mass spectrometers, cryogenic NMR spectrometers) for comprehensive compound analysis.
   b. **Technological Expertise:** Training and expertise in operating and interpreting data from advanced analytical technologies in marine drug discovery.

Solutions and Methodologies

1. Advanced Analytical Techniques

   i. **High-Resolution Mass Spectrometry (HR-MS):**
      a. **Advantages:** Provides accurate mass measurement and fragmentation patterns for rapid identification of unknown compounds in marine extracts.
      b. **Applications:** Enables dereplication, structural elucidation, and metabolomics studies to identify novel bioactive compounds.

   ii. **Nuclear Magnetic Resonance (NMR) Spectroscopy:**
      a. **Capabilities:** Offers detailed structural information, including molecular connectivity and stereochemistry, essential for characterizing complex natural products.
      b. **Enhancements:** Advances in cryogenic probes and 2D NMR techniques improve sensitivity and resolution for challenging marine compounds.

2. Computational and Bioinformatics Tools

   i. **Virtual Screening and Molecular Docking:**
      a. **Prediction:** Computational methods predict binding affinities and interactions between marine natural products and target proteins, guiding prioritization for experimental validation.

b. **Structure-Based Drug Design:** Utilizes 3D structural information from computational models to design and optimize drug candidates.

ii. **Metabolomics and Bioinformatics:**

a. **Metabolomic Profiling:** Comprehensive analysis of metabolic profiles in marine organisms to discover and prioritize bioactive compounds.

b. **Data Integration:** Integrating omics data with ecological and taxonomic information for holistic understanding of marine natural product biosynthesis and function.

3. Technological Innovation and Collaboration

i. **Collaborative Networks:** Forming interdisciplinary collaborations among chemists, biologists, bioinformaticians, and environmental scientists to leverage expertise and resources.

ii. **Technological Advancements:** Investing in research and development of new analytical technologies tailored for marine natural product research, enhancing sensitivity, specificity, and throughput.

4. Open Data Sharing and Standards

i. **Data Repositories:** Establishing centralized repositories for marine natural product data, promoting transparency, reproducibility, and collaborative research efforts.

ii. **Standardization:** Developing standardized protocols and criteria for data collection, analysis, and reporting in marine drug discovery to facilitate comparison and meta-analysis.

Importance in Marine Drug Research

i. **Innovation and Discovery:** Overcoming technological limitations fosters innovation in identifying novel marine natural products and drug leads with therapeutic potential.

ii. **Efficiency and Cost-Effectiveness:** Enhancing analytical capabilities reduces time and resources required for compound discovery and development.

iii. **Sustainability and Conservation:** Facilitating sustainable bioprospecting practices through accurate compound identification and ecological understanding.

Commercialization and Regulatory Hurdles:

Commercialization and regulatory hurdles present significant challenges in marine drug research, influencing various stages from initial discovery to market approval. Here's a detailed exploration of these challenges, along with potential solutions and methodologies:

Commercialization and Regulatory Hurdles

1. **Market Access and Investment Challenges:**
   a. **High Development Costs:** Developing marine-derived drugs involves substantial investment in research, clinical trials, and regulatory compliance.
   b. **Market Uncertainty:** Limited market data and potential competition from existing drugs pose risks to investors and pharmaceutical companies.

2. **Intellectual Property (IP) Protection:**
   a. **Patent Issues:** Securing patent protection for novel marine natural products and derivatives is complex due to prior art, natural occurrence, and potential challenges in proving novelty and inventive step.
   b. **Data Exclusivity:** Establishing data exclusivity periods for regulatory data to protect investments in clinical trial data from generic competition.

3. **Regulatory Pathways and Compliance:**
    a. **Safety and Efficacy Requirements:** Demonstrating safety and efficacy through rigorous preclinical and clinical trials according to regulatory standards (e.g., FDA, EMA).
    b. **Environmental Regulations:** Compliance with environmental regulations and ethical guidelines (e.g., Nagoya Protocol) for sustainable use of marine biodiversity and benefit-sharing.
4. **Market Acceptance and Commercial Viability:**
    a. **Therapeutic Competition:** Assessing market potential and differentiation from existing therapies in terms of efficacy, safety, and cost-effectiveness.
    b. **Healthcare Reimbursement:** Negotiating pricing and reimbursement strategies with healthcare systems and insurers to ensure market access and affordability.

Solutions and Methodologies

1. Strategic Partnerships and Collaborations

a. **Public-Private Partnerships:** Collaborating with academia, industry partners, and government agencies to share expertise, resources, and risks in drug development.

b. **Technology Transfer:** Facilitating technology transfer agreements to bridge gaps between research institutions and commercial entities for scaling up production and development.

2. Early Engagement with Regulatory Agencies

a. **Regulatory Strategy Development:** Working closely with regulatory agencies early in the development process to align strategies and anticipate requirements for approval.

b. **Orphan Drug Designation:** Seeking orphan drug status for rare diseases to benefit from incentives, including extended market exclusivity periods and regulatory support.

3. Intellectual Property Management

a. **Patent Strategy:** Conducting comprehensive prior art searches and patent landscaping to identify patentable aspects of marine-derived compounds and secure robust IP protection.

b. **Licensing and Collaborative Agreements:** Negotiating licensing agreements with partners to leverage their expertise in regulatory affairs, manufacturing, and commercialization.

4. Market Analysis and Access Strategies

a. **Market Assessment:** Conducting thorough market analysis, including competitor analysis, market size estimation, and assessment of unmet medical needs to inform commercialization strategies.

b. **Global Market Entry:** Developing global market entry strategies tailored to regional regulatory requirements, healthcare systems, and market dynamics.

Importance in Marine Drug Research

a. **Incentivizing Innovation:** Overcoming commercialization hurdles encourages investment in marine drug research and development, fostering innovation in therapeutic discovery.

b. **Patient Access:** Streamlining regulatory pathways and market access enhances timely patient access to novel marine-derived therapies, addressing unmet medical needs.

c. **Sustainability and Ethical Compliance:** Adhering to ethical guidelines and regulatory standards promotes sustainable use of marine biodiversity and equitable benefit-sharing with communities.

Multiple Choice Questions (MCQs)

1. Which type of marine natural products is known for their antibacterial, antifungal, antiviral, and anticancer activities?

a) Peptides and Proteins

b) Terpenes and Terpenoids

c) Polyketides

d) Alkaloids

2. What is the primary source of ciguatoxins?

a) Marine bacteria

b) Marine fungi

c) Marine dinoflagellates

d) Marine invertebrates

3. Which marine natural products are commonly found in marine algae and some marine bacteria and are known for their antioxidant properties?

a) Glycosides

b) Pigments

c) Alkaloids

d) Polyketides

4. Which technique is commonly used for the separation and purification of complex mixtures of compounds based on their polarity, size, and chemical properties?

a) NMR Spectroscopy

b) Mass Spectrometry

c) Chromatography

d) X-ray Crystallography

5. Which marine toxin is known to cause paralytic shellfish poisoning (PSP)?

a) Ciguatoxins

b) Saxitoxins

c) Tetrodotoxin (TTX)

d) Brevetoxins

6. What is the main advantage of using bioassay-guided fractionation in the isolation of marine natural products?

a) High-resolution structural information

b) Rapid identification of novel compounds

c) Specific detection of toxin-producing species

d) Direct measurement of biological effects

7. Which regulatory body in the United States oversees the regulation of marine toxins in seafood?

a) EFSA

b) FDA

c) UNEP

d) WHO

8. What is the primary benefit of using high-throughput screening (HTS) in marine drug research?

a) Enhanced structural elucidation

b) Rapid screening of large compound libraries

c) Improved sensitivity in toxin detection

d) Specific identification of cryptic species

9. What is a common source of omega-3 fatty acids in marine natural products?

a) Sea cucumbers

b) Marine algae

c) Marine fungi

d) Marine sponges

10. Which type of marine natural products is known for their neuroprotective effects and potential for developing treatments for neurological disorders?

a) Terpenes and Terpenoids

b) Alkaloids

c) Pigments

d) Polyketides

11. Which of the following is a key challenge in the commercialization of marine natural products?

a) Low detection limits

b) High development costs

c) Integration of omics data

d) Rapid virtual screening

12. Which marine toxin is produced by Karenia brevis and is associated with neurotoxic shellfish poisoning (NSP)?

a) Saxitoxins

b) Tetrodotoxin (TTX)

c) Brevetoxins

d) Palytoxins

13. What is the primary focus of chemical ecology in marine drug research?

a) Investigating ecological interactions and chemical defenses

b) Developing computational algorithms for species identification

c) Conducting clinical trials for marine-derived drugs

d) Enhancing structural resolution of marine compounds

14. Which technology is utilized for high-resolution and sensitive structural elucidation of marine compounds?

a) HPLC

b) Cryogenic NMR Techniques

c) PCR

d) SPE

15. What is the main goal of environmental impact assessments (EIAs) in marine drug research?

a) Enhancing metabolomic profiling

b) Evaluating potential impacts on marine biodiversity

c) Developing new chromatographic techniques

d) Predicting binding affinities of marine natural products

16. Which international convention promotes ethical guidelines for access to and utilization of marine genetic resources?

a) Codex Alimentarius Commission

b) Nagoya Protocol

c) IMO Regulations

d) UNEP Initiatives

17. What is a common application of marine natural products in cosmetics?

a) Antifouling agents

b) Cardiovascular health supplements

c) Anti-aging skincare products

d) Anticancer therapies

18. Which method is used for rapid identification and structural characterization of complex marine natural products, even in minute quantities?

a) HPLC

b) GC

c) HR-MS

d) SPE

19. Which marine natural products are known for their cardiovascular health benefits?

a) Marine lipids and peptides

b) Marine pigments and alkaloids

c) Marine polysaccharides and glycosides

d) Marine proteins and terpenoids

20. Which type of chromatography is often used for the purification of larger quantities of compounds for further biological testing and structural elucidation?

a) Column chromatography

b) Preparative HPLC

c) Flash chromatography

d) Thin-layer chromatography (TLC)

Short Answer Type Questions (Subjective)

1. What are marine natural products, and why are they significant for various industries?

2. List three examples of peptides and proteins derived from marine organisms and their biological activities.

3. Identify the sources and applications of terpenes and terpenoids in marine natural products.

4. What are polyketides, and which marine organisms produce them?

5. Explain the biological activities and applications of marine alkaloids.

6. Describe the importance of pigments found in marine natural products.

7. What are glycosides, and what biological activities do they exhibit?

8. How do omega-3 fatty acids derived from marine sources benefit cardiovascular health?

9. What are marine polysaccharides, and what applications do they have in pharmaceuticals and cosmetics?

10. Discuss the potential anticancer activities of marine natural products.

11. What mechanisms do marine peptides use to exhibit antimicrobial activity?

12. How do marine-derived compounds show antiviral activity against viruses?

13. Explain the anti-inflammatory and immunomodulatory properties of marine natural products.

14. Describe the neuroprotective effects of marine alkaloids and peptides.

15. What are the antioxidant properties of marine pigments, and how are they used in cosmetics?

16. Discuss the importance of sustainable bioprospecting practices in marine natural product research.

17. How do harmful algal blooms (HABs) impact marine ecosystems and human health?

18. What are the primary sources and symptoms of paralytic shellfish poisoning (PSP)?

19. Describe the role of chromatography in the isolation and purification of marine natural products.

20. What are the ethical and regulatory considerations in the collection and use of marine natural products?

Long Answer Type Questions (Subjective)

1. Describe the different types of marine natural products, providing examples, sources, and their biological activities and applications.

2. Explain the processes involved in the isolation and purification of marine natural products, including the techniques used for extraction, fractionation, and structural elucidation.

3. Discuss the study of marine toxins, including the types of toxins, their sources, mechanisms of action, and the health and environmental implications.

4. Examine the methods used for the detection and analysis of marine toxins, highlighting the advantages and limitations of biological assays, chromatography, mass spectrometry, and other techniques.

5. Evaluate the challenges and future prospects in marine natural product research, focusing on bioprospecting, technological limitations, regulatory hurdles, and environmental considerations.

6. How do recent advances in genomic and metagenomic approaches, biotechnological innovations, and analytical techniques contribute to the discovery and development of marine-derived drugs?

7. Discuss the ecological and environmental considerations in marine drug research, including the impact of unsustainable harvesting practices, habitat destruction, and climate change.

8. Explain the role of advanced analytical techniques such as high-resolution mass spectrometry (HR-MS) and cryogenic NMR techniques in the structural elucidation of marine natural products.

9. Describe the commercialization and regulatory challenges in marine drug research and the strategies employed to overcome these hurdles, including intellectual property management and market analysis.

10. Examine the role of interdisciplinary and international collaborations in enhancing marine natural product research, addressing regulatory compliance, and promoting sustainable use of marine resources.

Answer Key

1. (a) Peptides and Proteins
2. (c) Marine dinoflagellates
3. (b) Pigments
4. (c) Chromatography
5. (b) Saxitoxins
6. (d) Direct measurement of biological effects
7. (b) FDA
8. (b) Rapid screening of large compound libraries
9. (b) Marine algae
10. (d) Polyketides
11. (b) High development costs
12. (c) Brevetoxins
13. (a) Investigating ecological interactions and chemical defenses
14. (b) Cryogenic NMR Techniques
15. (b) Evaluating potential impacts on marine biodiversity
16. (b) Nagoya Protocol
17. (c) Anti-aging skincare products
18. (c) HR-MS
19. (a) Marine lipids and peptides
20. (b) Preparative HPLC

CHAPTER – 3

NUTRACEUTICALS – I

INTRODUCTION:

Definition and Concept

Nutraceuticals are products derived from food sources that offer additional health benefits beyond the basic nutritional value found in foods. The term "nutraceutical" is a portmanteau of "nutrition" and "pharmaceutical," coined by Dr. Stephen DeFelice in 1989. Nutraceuticals are used to promote overall health, prevent chronic diseases, improve health, delay the aging process, and increase life expectancy.

Categories of Nutraceuticals

Nutraceuticals can be classified into several categories based on their source, chemical composition, and therapeutic benefits:

1. **Dietary Supplements**: These include vitamins, minerals, amino acids, and other substances that supplement the diet. Examples include vitamin D supplements, omega-3 fatty acids, and probiotics.

2. **Functional Foods**: These are foods that have been enhanced with additional ingredients to provide health benefits. Examples include fortified cereals, milk with added calcium, and orange juice with added vitamin C.

3. **Medicinal Foods**: These are specially formulated foods consumed under the supervision of a physician for the dietary management of specific diseases or conditions. Examples include medical nutrition formulas for individuals with specific metabolic disorders.

4. **Farmaceuticals**: These are bioactive compounds derived from agricultural crops and used for medicinal purposes. Examples include soy isoflavones and beta-glucan from oats.

Sources of Nutraceuticals

Nutraceuticals are derived from a variety of natural sources:

1. **Plants**: Many nutraceuticals come from plants and include phytochemicals like polyphenols, flavonoids, carotenoids, and glucosinolates. Examples include resveratrol from grapes, lycopene from tomatoes, and catechins from green tea.

2. **Animal Sources**: Some nutraceuticals are derived from animal products. Examples include omega-3 fatty acids from fish oil, conjugated linoleic acid from meat and dairy products, and collagen peptides from animal bones and skin.

3. **Microbial Sources**: Probiotics, which are live microorganisms providing health benefits when consumed, are an example of nutraceuticals derived from microbial sources. Examples include Lactobacillus and Bifidobacterium species.

Mechanisms of Action

Nutraceuticals exert their effects through various mechanisms, including:

1. **Antioxidant Activity**: Many nutraceuticals neutralize free radicals and reduce oxidative stress, which is linked to aging and various chronic diseases.

2. **Anti-inflammatory Effects**: Some nutraceuticals can modulate inflammatory pathways, reducing inflammation and its associated risks.

3. **Modulation of Enzyme Activity**: Certain nutraceuticals can inhibit or stimulate enzyme activity, affecting metabolic pathways. For example, flavonoids can inhibit enzymes involved in carcinogen activation.

4. **Gene Expression**: Nutraceuticals can influence gene expression and epigenetic modifications, impacting cellular processes and health outcomes.

5. **Gut Microbiota Modulation**: Probiotics and prebiotics can alter the composition and activity of gut microbiota, contributing to improved gut health and immune function.

Health Benefits and Applications

Nutraceuticals are used to manage and prevent a wide range of health conditions, including:

1. **Cardiovascular Health**: Omega-3 fatty acids, plant sterols, and soluble fiber can lower cholesterol levels and reduce the risk of heart disease.
2. **Bone Health**: Calcium and vitamin D supplements are essential for maintaining bone density and preventing osteoporosis.
3. **Digestive Health**: Probiotics and prebiotics support a healthy gut microbiota, improving digestion and reducing the risk of gastrointestinal disorders.
4. **Cancer Prevention**: Phytochemicals like polyphenols and carotenoids have been shown to reduce the risk of certain cancers through their antioxidant and anti-inflammatory properties.
5. **Cognitive Function**: Nutrients such as omega-3 fatty acids, B vitamins, and antioxidants support brain health and may reduce the risk of neurodegenerative diseases.
6. **Immune Support**: Vitamins C and E, along with other antioxidants, can enhance immune function and protect against infections.

Regulation and Quality Control

The regulation of nutraceuticals varies by country. In the United States, the Food and Drug Administration (FDA) regulates dietary supplements under the Dietary Supplement Health and Education Act (DSHEA) of 1994. However, nutraceuticals are not subject to the same rigorous testing as pharmaceuticals, leading to concerns about quality, efficacy, and safety.

Challenges and Future Directions

Despite their potential benefits, nutraceuticals face several challenges:

1. **Standardization**: Ensuring consistent quality and potency of nutraceutical products can be difficult due to variations in raw materials and manufacturing processes.

2. **Scientific Evidence**: More rigorous clinical trials are needed to substantiate the health claims associated with many nutraceuticals.

3. **Regulatory Oversight**: Improved regulation and oversight are necessary to ensure the safety and efficacy of nutraceutical products.

4. **Consumer Awareness**: Educating consumers about the benefits and risks of nutraceuticals is essential for informed decision-making.

CURRENT TRENDS AND FUTURE SCOPE OF NUTRACEUTICALS

1. **Personalized Nutrition**

    a. **Trend**: Increasing interest in personalized nutrition, where nutraceutical products are tailored to individual genetic profiles, lifestyles, and health conditions.

    b. **Future Scope**: Advances in genomics and data analytics will enable more precise and effective nutraceutical recommendations.

2. **Gut Health**

    a. **Trend**: Growing popularity of probiotics, prebiotics, and synbiotics to support digestive health and overall well-being.

    b. **Future Scope**: Continued research on the gut microbiome will lead to the development of new products targeting specific gut health issues.

3. **Plant-Based Nutraceuticals**

    a. **Trend**: Rising consumer demand for plant-based and vegan products, driven by health, environmental, and ethical considerations.

    b. **Future Scope**: Expansion of plant-derived nutraceuticals, including novel sources like algae and hemp, to cater to this market.

4. **Functional Foods and Beverages**

    a. **Trend**: Increasing incorporation of functional ingredients into everyday foods and beverages, such as fortified snacks and drinks.

b. **Future Scope**: Innovation in delivery methods, such as encapsulation technologies, to enhance the stability and bioavailability of functional ingredients.

5. **Aging Population**

   a. **Trend**: Growing focus on nutraceuticals that address age-related health concerns, such as cognitive decline, joint health, and skin aging.

   b. **Future Scope**: Development of targeted products to support healthy aging, leveraging advances in biogerontology and anti-aging research.

6. **Mental Health and Cognitive Function**

   a. **Trend**: Rising interest in nutraceuticals that support mental health, including mood enhancers, stress reducers, and cognitive boosters.

   b. **Future Scope**: Enhanced understanding of the gut-brain axis and neurobiology will drive the creation of more effective nutraceuticals for mental health.

7. **Sustainability and Ethical Sourcing**

   a. **Trend**: Increasing consumer awareness of sustainability and ethical sourcing in nutraceutical production.

   b. **Future Scope**: Adoption of sustainable practices, such as organic farming and fair trade, will become more prevalent, along with transparency in sourcing.

Future Scope of Nutraceuticals

1. **Technological Advancements**

   a. **Scope**: Leveraging cutting-edge technologies like nanotechnology, bioinformatics, and artificial intelligence to enhance the development and delivery of nutraceuticals.

   b. **Impact**: Improved bioavailability, targeted delivery systems, and personalized formulations.

2. **Integration with Digital Health**

   a. **Scope**: Combining nutraceuticals with digital health tools, such as mobile apps and wearable devices, for monitoring and optimizing health outcomes.

   b. **Impact**: Real-time tracking of nutraceutical efficacy and personalized health recommendations.

3. **Expansion of Research and Development**

   a. **Scope**: Increased investment in R&D to explore new bioactive compounds, understand their mechanisms of action, and conduct clinical trials.

   b. **Impact**: Greater scientific validation and acceptance of nutraceuticals in mainstream healthcare.

4. **Regulatory Framework**

   a. **Scope**: Development of more comprehensive and harmonized regulatory frameworks globally to ensure the safety, quality, and efficacy of nutraceuticals.

   b. **Impact**: Enhanced consumer trust and market growth.

5. **Healthcare Integration**

   a. **Scope**: Greater integration of nutraceuticals into conventional healthcare practices, including preventive medicine and therapeutic regimens.

   b. **Impact**: Broader acceptance and utilization of nutraceuticals by healthcare professionals.

6. **Global Market Expansion**

   a. **Scope**: Growth of nutraceutical markets in emerging economies due to rising health awareness and increasing disposable incomes.

   b. **Impact**: Expansion of product availability and accessibility worldwide.

7. **Chronic Disease Management**

   a. **Scope**: Utilization of nutraceuticals for the management and prevention of chronic diseases, such as diabetes, cardiovascular diseases, and obesity.

   b. **Impact**: Potential to reduce the burden of chronic diseases and improve public health outcomes.

INORGANIC MINERAL SUPPLEMENTS

Definition and Importance

Inorganic mineral supplements are dietary supplements that provide essential minerals necessary for various bodily functions. Unlike organic compounds, these minerals do not contain carbon and are derived from non-living sources. Minerals are crucial for maintaining proper physiological functions, including bone health, enzyme function, nerve transmission, and fluid balance.

Common Inorganic Mineral Supplements

1. **Calcium**

   a. **Importance**: Essential for bone and teeth formation, muscle function, nerve transmission, and blood clotting.

   b. **Sources**: Calcium carbonate, calcium citrate, calcium phosphate.

   c. **Uses**: Prevents osteoporosis, supports bone health, and aids in muscle function.

2. **Iron**

   a. **Importance**: Vital for hemoglobin formation, oxygen transport, and energy metabolism.

   b. **Sources**: Ferrous sulfate, ferrous gluconate, ferrous fumarate.

   c. **Uses**: Treats iron deficiency anemia, supports energy levels, and enhances cognitive function.

3. **Magnesium**

   a. **Importance**: Involved in over 300 enzymatic reactions, including energy production, protein synthesis, and muscle and nerve function.

b. **Sources**: Magnesium oxide, magnesium citrate, magnesium chloride.

c. **Uses**: Relieves muscle cramps, supports cardiovascular health, and improves sleep quality.

4. **Zinc**

   a. **Importance**: Supports immune function, wound healing, DNA synthesis, and cell division.

   b. **Sources**: Zinc sulfate, zinc gluconate, zinc acetate.

   c. **Uses**: Boosts immune function, accelerates wound healing, and supports growth and development.

5. **Potassium**

   a. **Importance**: Essential for maintaining fluid balance, nerve function, and muscle contractions.

   b. **Sources**: Potassium chloride, potassium citrate, potassium gluconate.

   c. **Uses**: Regulates blood pressure, supports heart health, and prevents muscle cramps.

6. **Selenium**

   a. **Importance**: Acts as an antioxidant, supports thyroid function, and boosts immune health.

   b. **Sources**: Sodium selenite, sodium selenate, selenium-enriched yeast.

   c. **Uses**: Protects against oxidative stress, supports thyroid health, and enhances immune function.

7. **Copper**

   a. **Importance**: Necessary for iron metabolism, connective tissue formation, and neurological function.

   b. **Sources**: Copper gluconate, copper sulfate, copper acetate.

   c. **Uses**: Supports cardiovascular health, promotes healthy skin, and aids in iron absorption.

8. **Chromium**

   a. **Importance**: Enhances insulin action, supports glucose metabolism, and regulates blood sugar levels.

   b. **Sources**: Chromium picolinate, chromium chloride.

   c. **Uses**: Improves insulin sensitivity, supports weight management, and regulates blood sugar.

Mechanisms of Action

Inorganic minerals function as cofactors for enzymes, structural components of bones and teeth, and regulators of physiological processes. They contribute to:

1. **Enzymatic Activity**: Many enzymes require mineral cofactors to catalyze biochemical reactions. For example, magnesium is a cofactor for ATP-dependent enzymes.

2. **Structural Roles**: Minerals like calcium and phosphorus are critical for the structural integrity of bones and teeth.

3. **Electrolyte Balance**: Sodium, potassium, and chloride help maintain fluid and electrolyte balance, essential for nerve transmission and muscle contraction.

4. **Antioxidant Defense**: Selenium is a component of glutathione peroxidase, an enzyme that protects cells from oxidative damage.

Health Benefits and Applications

1. **Bone Health**: Calcium and magnesium are crucial for maintaining bone density and preventing osteoporosis.

2. **Cardiovascular Health**: Potassium helps regulate blood pressure and supports heart health. Magnesium is also important for maintaining a regular heartbeat.

3. **Immune Function**: Zinc and selenium play vital roles in supporting the immune system and protecting against infections.

4. **Metabolic Health**: Chromium helps regulate blood sugar levels and improves insulin sensitivity, which is beneficial for managing diabetes.

5. **Cognitive Function**: Iron is essential for cognitive development and function, particularly in children and pregnant women.

Challenges and Considerations

1. **Bioavailability**: The absorption of inorganic minerals can be affected by various factors, including the form of the mineral, presence of other nutrients, and individual health conditions. For example, calcium carbonate requires an acidic environment for optimal absorption.

2. **Toxicity**: Excessive intake of certain minerals can lead to toxicity. For instance, too much iron can cause gastrointestinal issues and, in severe cases, organ damage.

3. **Interactions**: Minerals can interact with each other and with other nutrients. For example, high doses of zinc can interfere with copper absorption.

4. **Individual Needs**: Nutrient requirements can vary based on age, gender, health status, and lifestyle. Personalized supplementation may be necessary to address specific deficiencies.

Regulation and Quality Control

Inorganic mineral supplements are regulated to ensure their safety, efficacy, and quality. In the United States, the Food and Drug Administration (FDA) oversees the regulation of dietary supplements under the Dietary Supplement Health and Education Act (DSHEA). Manufacturers are responsible for ensuring that their products are safe and properly labeled. Third-party testing and certification can help verify the quality and potency of mineral supplements.

VITAMIN SUPPLEMENTS

Definition and Importance

Vitamin supplements are products that provide essential vitamins that may be missing or insufficient in a person's diet. Vitamins are organic compounds required in small quantities for various physiological functions, including growth, immunity, and metabolism. They are crucial for maintaining health and preventing diseases associated with deficiencies.

Types of Vitamins

Vitamins are broadly classified into two categories based on their solubility:

1. **Fat-Soluble Vitamins**
   a. **Vitamin A (Retinol)**: Essential for vision, immune function, and skin health.
   b. **Vitamin D (Calciferol)**: Important for bone health, calcium absorption, and immune function.
   c. **Vitamin E (Tocopherol)**: Acts as an antioxidant, protecting cells from damage.
   d. **Vitamin K**: Necessary for blood clotting and bone metabolism.

2. **Water-Soluble Vitamins**
   a. **Vitamin C (Ascorbic Acid)**: Important for collagen synthesis, antioxidant protection, and immune function.
   b. **B Vitamins**: Includes B1 (Thiamine), B2 (Riboflavin), B3 (Niacin), B5 (Pantothenic Acid), B6 (Pyridoxine), B7 (Biotin), B9 (Folate/Folic Acid), and B12 (Cobalamin). These vitamins play key roles in energy metabolism, red blood cell formation, and neurological function.

Common Vitamin Supplements

1. **Vitamin A**
   a. **Sources**: Retinyl palmitate, retinyl acetate, beta-carotene.
   b. **Uses**: Supports vision, immune function, and skin health.

2. **Vitamin D**
   a. **Sources**: Vitamin D2 (ergocalciferol), vitamin D3 (cholecalciferol).
   b. **Uses**: Enhances calcium absorption, supports bone health, and boosts immune function.

3. **Vitamin E**
   a. **Sources**: Alpha-tocopherol, mixed tocopherols.
   b. **Uses**: Provides antioxidant protection, supports skin health, and improves immune function.

4. **Vitamin K**

   a. **Sources**: Vitamin K1 (phylloquinone), vitamin K2 (menaquinone).

   b. **Uses**: Promotes blood clotting, supports bone health, and aids in cardiovascular health.

5. **Vitamin C**

   a. **Sources**: Ascorbic acid, sodium ascorbate, calcium ascorbate.

   b. **Uses**: Enhances collagen synthesis, provides antioxidant protection, and supports immune function.

6. **B Vitamins**

   a. **Vitamin B1 (Thiamine)**: Supports energy metabolism and nerve function.

   b. **Vitamin B2 (Riboflavin)**: Important for energy production and antioxidant protection.

   c. **Vitamin B3 (Niacin)**: Involved in energy metabolism and DNA repair.

   d. **Vitamin B5 (Pantothenic Acid)**: Essential for synthesizing coenzyme A, important for fatty acid metabolism.

   e. **Vitamin B6 (Pyridoxine)**: Involved in amino acid metabolism and neurotransmitter synthesis.

   f. **Vitamin B7 (Biotin)**: Supports carbohydrate, fat, and protein metabolism.

   g. **Vitamin B9 (Folate/Folic Acid)**: Crucial for DNA synthesis and cell division.

   h. **Vitamin B12 (Cobalamin)**: Necessary for red blood cell formation and neurological function.

Mechanisms of Action

Vitamins perform various biochemical and physiological functions, including:

1. **Cofactors for Enzymes**: Many vitamins act as cofactors or coenzymes for enzymatic reactions. For example, B vitamins are crucial for energy metabolism.

2. **Antioxidant Protection**: Vitamins like C and E neutralize free radicals, protecting cells from oxidative damage.

3. **Hormone Regulation**: Vitamin D functions as a hormone, regulating calcium and phosphate balance in the body.

4. **Gene Expression**: Vitamins A and D regulate gene expression, influencing cell growth, differentiation, and immune function.

5. **Immune Function**: Vitamins C and D play significant roles in enhancing immune responses and protecting against infections.

Health Benefits and Applications

1. **Preventing Deficiencies**: Vitamin supplements help prevent deficiencies, which can lead to conditions like scurvy (vitamin C deficiency), rickets (vitamin D deficiency), and anemia (vitamin B12 deficiency).

2. **Bone Health**: Vitamins D and K support bone health by enhancing calcium absorption and bone mineralization.

3. **Immune Support**: Vitamins C, D, and E enhance immune function, reducing the risk of infections and supporting overall immune health.

4. **Skin Health**: Vitamins A, C, and E promote healthy skin by supporting collagen synthesis and providing antioxidant protection.

5. **Energy Metabolism**: B vitamins are essential for converting food into energy, supporting metabolism and reducing fatigue.

6. **Cognitive Function**: B vitamins, particularly B6, B9, and B12, support neurological health and cognitive function.

Challenges and Considerations

1. **Bioavailability**: The absorption and effectiveness of vitamins can vary based on factors like the form of the vitamin, the presence of other nutrients, and individual health conditions.

2. **Toxicity**: Excessive intake of certain vitamins, particularly fat-soluble vitamins, can lead to toxicity. For example, high doses of vitamin A can cause liver damage.

3. **Interactions**: Vitamins can interact with each other and with medications. For example, high doses of vitamin E can interfere with vitamin K and affect blood clotting.

4. **Individual Needs**: Nutrient requirements vary based on age, gender, health status, and lifestyle. Personalized supplementation may be necessary to address specific needs.

Regulation and Quality Control

Vitamin supplements are regulated to ensure safety, efficacy, and quality. In the United States, the Food and Drug Administration (FDA) oversees the regulation of dietary supplements under the Dietary Supplement Health and Education Act (DSHEA). Manufacturers are responsible for ensuring that their products are safe and properly labeled. Third-party testing and certification can help verify the quality and potency of vitamin supplements.

DIGESTIVE ENZYMES

Definition and Importance

Digestive enzymes are specialized proteins that facilitate the breakdown of food into smaller, absorbable components. They play a crucial role in the digestive process, ensuring that nutrients from food are adequately absorbed and utilized by the body. Digestive enzyme supplements are used to support or enhance natural digestive processes, particularly in individuals with enzyme deficiencies or digestive disorders.

Types of Digestive Enzymes

Digestive enzymes can be categorized based on the type of nutrient they act upon:

1. **Proteases**: Enzymes that break down proteins into peptides and amino acids.

    a. **Examples**: Pepsin, trypsin, chymotrypsin, bromelain, and papain.

2. **Lipases**: Enzymes that break down fats (lipids) into fatty acids and glycerol.

    a. **Examples**: Pancreatic lipase, gastric lipase, and lingual lipase.

3. **Amylases**: Enzymes that break down carbohydrates (starches) into sugars.

    a. **Examples**: Salivary amylase, pancreatic amylase.

4. **Nucleases**: Enzymes that break down nucleic acids into nucleotides.

    a. **Examples**: Deoxyribonuclease (DNase), ribonuclease (RNase).

5. **Other Specific Enzymes**:

    a. **Lactase**: Breaks down lactose, the sugar found in milk.

    b. **Sucrase**: Breaks down sucrose (table sugar) into glucose and fructose.

    c. **Maltase**: Breaks down maltose into two glucose molecules.

Sources of Digestive Enzymes

1. **Animal Sources**: Enzymes derived from animal organs, particularly the pancreas.

    a. **Examples**: Pancreatin, which contains a mixture of amylase, protease, and lipase.

2. **Plant Sources**: Enzymes extracted from fruits and plants.

    a. **Examples**: Bromelain (from pineapple), papain (from papaya).

3. **Microbial Sources**: Enzymes produced by microorganisms such as bacteria and fungi.

    a. **Examples**: Fungal amylase, bacterial protease.

Mechanisms of Action

Digestive enzymes facilitate the breakdown of macronutrients into their basic building blocks through hydrolysis reactions:

1. **Proteolysis**: Proteases cleave peptide bonds in proteins, resulting in smaller peptides and amino acids.

2. **Lipolysis**: Lipases hydrolyze triglycerides into free fatty acids and monoglycerides.

3. **Carbohydrate Breakdown**: Amylases catalyze the hydrolysis of starches into simple sugars like glucose and maltose.

4. **Nucleic Acid Breakdown**: Nucleases degrade nucleic acids into nucleotides and further into nucleosides and bases.

Health Benefits and Applications

1. **Improving Digestion**: Enzyme supplements can enhance the digestive process, especially in individuals with enzyme deficiencies or digestive disorders.
   a. **Conditions**: Pancreatic insufficiency, cystic fibrosis, chronic pancreatitis, lactose intolerance.
2. **Reducing Symptoms of Digestive Disorders**: Digestive enzymes can help alleviate symptoms such as bloating, gas, indigestion, and diarrhea.
   a. **Examples**: Lactase supplements for lactose intolerance, protease supplements for protein malabsorption.
3. **Enhancing Nutrient Absorption**: By improving the breakdown of food, enzyme supplements can enhance the absorption of nutrients, ensuring better overall nutrition.
4. **Supporting Specific Dietary Needs**: Enzyme supplements can aid in the digestion of specific types of food, such as high-protein diets, high-fat diets, or diets rich in complex carbohydrates.
5. **Relieving Food Sensitivities**: Certain enzyme supplements can help mitigate food sensitivities by breaking down problematic components in food.
   a. **Example**: DPP-IV (Dipeptidyl peptidase IV) enzyme supplements for gluten sensitivity.

Challenges and Considerations

1. **Dosage and Formulation**: The effectiveness of enzyme supplements can vary based on the dosage, formulation, and the individual's specific digestive needs.
2. **Stability and Activity**: Enzymes must remain active and stable throughout the digestive tract to be effective. Factors such as pH and temperature can affect enzyme activity.

3. **Quality and Purity**: Ensuring the purity and quality of enzyme supplements is crucial for their effectiveness and safety.

4. **Potential Allergies**: Some individuals may be allergic to certain enzyme supplements, particularly those derived from animal or plant sources.

Regulation and Quality Control

Digestive enzyme supplements are regulated to ensure their safety, efficacy, and quality. In the United States, the Food and Drug Administration (FDA) oversees the regulation of dietary supplements under the Dietary Supplement Health and Education Act (DSHEA). Manufacturers must ensure that their products are safe, accurately labeled, and free from contaminants. Third-party testing and certification can help verify the quality and potency of enzyme supplements.

DIETARY FIBRES

Dietary fibers play a crucial role in nutraceuticals due to their various health benefits and functional properties. Here's a detailed overview of dietary fibers in nutraceuticals:

What are Dietary Fibers?

Dietary fibers are non-digestible carbohydrates found in plant foods. They pass through the gastrointestinal tract relatively intact, contributing to various health benefits.

Types of Dietary Fibers

1. **Soluble Fibers:**
    a. **Examples:** Pectins, gums, mucilages, inulin.
    b. **Sources:** Oats, barley, fruits (e.g., apples, citrus fruits), vegetables, legumes.
    c. **Benefits:** Dissolve in water to form a gel-like substance, help lower blood cholesterol and glucose levels.

2. **Insoluble Fibers:**
    a. **Examples:** Cellulose, hemicellulose, lignin.

b. **Sources:** Whole grains, nuts, seeds, vegetables (e.g., green beans, cauliflower, potatoes).

c. **Benefits:** Promote the movement of material through the digestive system, increase stool bulk, and help prevent constipation.

Health Benefits of Dietary Fibers

1. **Digestive Health:**

    a. **Prevents Constipation:** Insoluble fibers add bulk to stool and aid in bowel regularity.

    b. **Promotes Healthy Gut Microbiota:** Soluble fibers act as prebiotics, feeding beneficial gut bacteria.

    c. **Reduces Risk of Gastrointestinal Diseases:** Fiber intake is associated with a lower risk of diverticulitis and hemorrhoids.

2. **Cardiovascular Health:**

    a. **Lowers Cholesterol Levels:** Soluble fibers can help reduce low-density lipoprotein (LDL) cholesterol.

    b. **Reduces Blood Pressure:** High fiber intake is linked to reduced blood pressure.

3. **Blood Sugar Control:**

    a. **Improves Glycemic Control:** Soluble fibers slow the absorption of sugar, helping to improve blood sugar levels.

    b. **Reduces Risk of Type 2 Diabetes:** A diet high in fiber is associated with a lower risk of developing type 2 diabetes.

4. **Weight Management:**

    a. **Increases Satiety:** Fiber-rich foods are more filling, which can help control appetite and reduce overall calorie intake.

    b. **Reduces Risk of Obesity:** Regular consumption of dietary fibers is linked to a lower risk of obesity.

5. **Cancer Prevention:**

a. **Reduces Risk of Colorectal Cancer:** A high-fiber diet is associated with a reduced risk of colorectal cancer.

b. **Antioxidant Properties:** Some fibers contain antioxidants, which can help protect cells from damage.

Dietary Fiber in Nutraceuticals

Nutraceuticals are products derived from food sources with additional health benefits beyond basic nutritional value. Dietary fibers in nutraceuticals can be used in various forms:

1. **Fiber Supplements:**

    a. **Psyllium Husk:** Used to relieve constipation and improve heart health.

    b. **Inulin:** Acts as a prebiotic and helps improve gut health.

    c. **Glucomannan:** Promotes weight loss by increasing satiety.

2. **Functional Foods:**

    a. **Fortified Foods:** Foods such as cereals, bread, and yogurt are often fortified with extra fiber.

    b. **High-Fiber Snacks:** Snack bars, chips, and biscuits made with added dietary fibers.

3. **Beverages:**

    a. **Fiber-Enriched Drinks:** Smoothies, juices, and teas enriched with soluble fibers to aid digestion and provide other health benefits.

Considerations and Recommendations

1. **Recommended Daily Intake:** The daily recommended intake of fiber is about 25 grams for women and 38 grams for men.

2. **Gradual Increase:** Increase fiber intake gradually to avoid digestive discomfort such as bloating and gas.

3. **Hydration:** Drink plenty of water to help fiber work more efficiently in the digestive system.

4. **Balanced Diet:** Combine fiber-rich foods with a variety of other nutrients for a balanced diet.

CEREALS AND GRAINS

Cereals and grains are vital components of nutraceuticals, providing numerous health benefits beyond basic nutrition. They are rich sources of essential nutrients, dietary fiber, vitamins, minerals, and bioactive compounds. Here is a detailed overview:

Nutritional Components and Health Benefits

1. **Dietary Fiber:**
   a. **Types:** Soluble and insoluble fiber.
   b. **Benefits:** Improves digestion, reduces blood cholesterol levels, aids in weight management, and regulates blood sugar levels.

2. **Vitamins:**
   a. **B Vitamins:** Thiamine, riboflavin, niacin, folate, and vitamin B6.
      i. **Benefits:** Support metabolism, brain function, and red blood cell formation.

3. **Minerals:**
   a. **Iron:** Important for oxygen transport in the blood.
   b. **Magnesium:** Supports muscle and nerve function, blood sugar control, and bone health.
   c. **Zinc:** Crucial for immune function and wound healing.

4. **Proteins:**
   a. Provide essential amino acids necessary for body functions.
   b. Support muscle growth and repair.

5. **Antioxidants:**
   a. **Polyphenols and Phytochemicals:** Reduce oxidative stress and inflammation.
   b. **Benefits:** Lower risk of chronic diseases such as heart disease, cancer, and diabetes.

Common Cereals and Grains in Nutraceuticals

1. **Wheat:**
   a. **Components:** Dietary fiber, protein, B vitamins, and minerals like iron and zinc.
   b. **Health Benefits:** Supports digestive health, reduces the risk of heart disease, and maintains healthy blood pressure levels.
2. **Oats:**
   a. **Components:** Beta-glucan, a type of soluble fiber, vitamins, and minerals.
   b. **Health Benefits:** Lowers cholesterol levels, improves blood sugar control, and aids in weight management.
3. **Barley:**
   a. **Components:** Soluble and insoluble fiber, vitamins, and minerals.
   b. **Health Benefits:** Reduces cholesterol levels, supports digestive health, and helps in weight management.
4. **Rice:**
   a. **Types:** Brown rice, white rice, and wild rice.
   b. **Components:** Carbohydrates, vitamins, minerals, and some protein.
   c. **Health Benefits:** Provides energy, supports heart health, and maintains digestive health.
5. **Quinoa:**
   a. **Components:** Complete protein, fiber, vitamins, and minerals.
   b. **Health Benefits:** Supports muscle growth and repair, aids in weight management, and reduces the risk of chronic diseases.
6. **Millet:**
   a. **COMPONENTS:** Dietary fiber, protein, B vitamins, and minerals.
   b. **Health Benefits:** Supports heart health, aids in digestion, and helps manage blood sugar levels.

7. **Sorghum:**

   a. **Components:** Fiber, protein, antioxidants, and various vitamins and minerals.

   b. **Health Benefits:** Supports digestive health, reduces inflammation, and improves blood sugar control.

Functional Properties

1. **Prebiotic Effect:**

   a. Dietary fibers from cereals and grains act as prebiotics, promoting the growth of beneficial gut bacteria, improving gut health, and enhancing immune function.

2. **Glycemic Control:**

   a. Whole grains have a low glycemic index, which helps in controlling blood sugar levels, beneficial for managing diabetes and metabolic syndrome.

3. **Weight Management:**

   a. High fiber content promotes satiety, reducing overall calorie intake and supporting weight loss efforts.

4. **Cardiovascular Health:**

   a. Antioxidants and fiber help in reducing cholesterol levels and blood pressure, lowering the risk of heart disease.

Bioactive Compounds and Their Effects

1. **Beta-glucan (Oats and Barley):**

   a. Lowers LDL cholesterol and improves heart health.

2. **Avenanthramides (Oats):**

   a. Possess anti-inflammatory and antioxidant properties.

3. **Ferulic Acid (Wheat, Rice, and Corn):**

   a. Acts as a potent antioxidant, protecting cells from damage.

4. **Lignans (Whole Grains):**

a. Have antioxidant and estrogenic properties, reducing the risk of hormone-related cancers.

Applications in Nutraceutical Products

1. **Fortified Cereals:**

    a. Enhanced with vitamins, minerals, and bioactive compounds for added health benefits.

2. **Dietary Supplements:**

    a. Extracts of fiber, antioxidants, and other bioactive compounds in capsule or powder form.

3. **Functional Foods:**

    a. Whole grains incorporated into bread, snacks, and beverages to enhance their nutritional profile.

4. **Probiotic and Prebiotic Products:**

    a. Incorporating whole grains to support gut health and overall wellness.

HEALTH DRINKS OF NATURAL ORIGIN

Health drinks of natural origin are an integral part of nutraceuticals, providing various health benefits through the incorporation of natural ingredients such as fruits, vegetables, herbs, and other plant-based components. These drinks are designed to enhance health and well-being, offering a convenient way to consume essential nutrients and bioactive compounds. Here's a detailed overview of health drinks of natural origin in nutraceuticals:

Key Types of Natural Health Drinks

1. **Fruit and Vegetable Juices:**

    a. **Components:** Vitamins, minerals, antioxidants, and dietary fiber.

    b. **Benefits:** Boost immune function, improve digestion, support cardiovascular health, and provide hydration.

2. **Herbal Teas:**

    a. **Components:** Phytochemicals, antioxidants, and various bioactive compounds.

b. **Benefits:** Promote relaxation, support digestive health, enhance immune function, and provide anti-inflammatory effects.

3. **Smoothies:**

   a. **Components:** Fresh or frozen fruits and vegetables, yogurt or plant-based milk, protein powders, and superfoods.

   b. **Benefits:** Nutrient-dense meal replacements, support weight management, improve energy levels, and enhance digestion.

4. **Functional Beverages:**

   a. **Components:** Fortified with vitamins, minerals, probiotics, and other bioactive compounds.

   b. **Benefits:** Target specific health issues such as digestive health, joint health, and immune support.

5. **Fermented Drinks:**

   a. **Types:** Kombucha, kefir, and traditional fermented vegetable juices.

   b. **Components:** Probiotics, vitamins, and organic acids.

   c. **Benefits:** Improve gut health, enhance digestion, boost immune function, and provide detoxification.

Common Ingredients and Their Health Benefits

1. **Aloe Vera:**

   a. **Benefits:** Supports digestive health, has anti-inflammatory properties, and promotes skin health.

2. **Green Tea:**

   a. **Components:** Catechins, particularly epigallocatechin gallate (EGCG).

   b. **Benefits:** Antioxidant properties, supports weight loss, improves brain function, and reduces the risk of certain cancers.

3. **Turmeric:**

   a. **Components:** Curcumin.

b. **Benefits:** Anti-inflammatory, antioxidant, supports joint health, and boosts immune function.

4. **Ginger:**

   a. **Benefits:** Anti-inflammatory, improves digestion, relieves nausea, and has antioxidant properties.

5. **Matcha:**

   a. **Components:** High concentration of catechins and other polyphenols.

   b. **Benefits:** Enhances metabolism, provides a sustained energy boost, and supports detoxification.

6. **Beetroot:**

   a. **Components:** Nitrates, betalains.

   b. **Benefits:** Improves cardiovascular health, enhances athletic performance, and supports liver function.

7. **Berries (Blueberries, Acai, Goji):**

   a. **Components:** Vitamins, minerals, antioxidants like anthocyanins.

   b. **Benefits:** Improve cognitive function, support heart health, and have anti-aging properties.

8. **Coconut Water:**

   a. **Components:** Electrolytes, vitamins, and minerals.

   b. **Benefits:** Hydrates effectively, supports kidney function, and replenishes electrolytes after exercise.

Functional Properties and Applications

1. **Immune Support:**

   a. Ingredients like elderberry, echinacea, and vitamin C-rich fruits are added to health drinks to boost the immune system.

2. **Detoxification:**

   a. Ingredients like dandelion root, milk thistle, and chlorophyll are used to support liver detoxification and overall body cleansing.

3. **Energy Boost:**

    a. Natural energy-boosting ingredients like ginseng, guarana, and maca are included to enhance physical and mental energy.

4. **Digestive Health:**

    a. Probiotics and prebiotics from ingredients like kefir, kombucha, and inulin-rich vegetables improve gut health.

5. **Anti-inflammatory:**

    a. Ingredients like turmeric, ginger, and green tea are used for their anti-inflammatory properties to support joint health and reduce inflammation.

Examples of Popular Natural Health Drinks

1. **Kombucha:**

    a. A fermented tea beverage rich in probiotics and organic acids, promoting gut health and detoxification.

2. **Green Smoothies:**

    a. Blended drinks made from leafy greens, fruits, and superfoods, providing a nutrient-dense meal replacement.

3. **Golden Milk:**

    a. A turmeric-based drink often made with coconut milk or almond milk, offering anti-inflammatory and antioxidant benefits.

4. **Beetroot Juice:**

    a. Rich in nitrates and betalains, improving cardiovascular health and athletic performance.

5. **Chia Seed Drink:**

    a. Hydrated chia seeds mixed with water or fruit juice, providing omega-3 fatty acids, fiber, and protein.

ANTIOXIDANTS

Antioxidants play a crucial role in nutraceuticals due to their ability to neutralize free radicals and protect the body from oxidative stress, which can lead to chronic diseases and aging. Here is a detailed overview of antioxidants in nutraceuticals:

Understanding Antioxidants

Antioxidants are molecules that inhibit the oxidation of other molecules. Oxidation is a chemical reaction that can produce free radicals, leading to chain reactions that may damage cells. Antioxidants terminate these chain reactions by removing free radical intermediates and inhibiting other oxidation reactions.

Types of Antioxidants

1. **Vitamins:**
   a. **Vitamin C (Ascorbic Acid):**
      i. **Sources:** Citrus fruits, strawberries, bell peppers, broccoli, and spinach.
      ii. **Benefits:** Boosts the immune system, promotes skin health, and enhances iron absorption.
   b. **Vitamin E (Tocopherol):**
      i. **Sources:** Nuts, seeds, spinach, and vegetable oils.
      ii. **Benefits:** Protects cell membranes, supports immune function, and acts as an anti-inflammatory agent.
   c. **Vitamin A (Beta-Carotene):**
      i. **Sources:** Carrots, sweet potatoes, spinach, and kale.
      ii. **Benefits:** Supports vision, immune function, and skin health.

2. **Minerals:**
   a. **Selenium:**
      i. **Sources:** Brazil nuts, seafood, and meats.
      ii. **Benefits:** Plays a role in antioxidant enzyme systems, supports thyroid function, and boosts immune health.
   b. **Zinc:**
      i. **Sources:** Meat, shellfish, legumes, and seeds.

ii. **Benefits:** Supports immune function, promotes wound healing, and acts as an antioxidant.

3. **Polyphenols:**

   a. **Flavonoids:**

      i. **Sources:** Tea, apples, onions, and berries.

      ii. **Benefits:** Reduce inflammation, support heart health, and enhance cognitive function.

   b. **Resveratrol:**

      i. **Sources:** Red grapes, wine, peanuts, and berries.

      ii. **Benefits:** Supports heart health, has anti-aging properties, and possesses anti-cancer effects.

   c. **Curcumin:**

      i. **Sources:** Turmeric.

      ii. **Benefits:** Anti-inflammatory, antioxidant, and supports brain health.

4. **Carotenoids:**

   a. **Lycopene:**

      i. **Sources:** Tomatoes, watermelon, and pink grapefruit.

      ii. **Benefits:** Supports heart health, reduces the risk of certain cancers, and protects the skin from UV damage.

   b. **Lutein and Zeaxanthin:**

      i. **Sources:** Kale, spinach, and corn.

      ii. **Benefits:** Support eye health, reduce the risk of cataracts, and protect against macular degeneration.

5. **Coenzyme Q10 (Ubiquinone):**

   a. **Sources:** Meat, fish, and whole grains.

   b. **Benefits:** Supports energy production, enhances heart health, and acts as an antioxidant.

Mechanisms of Action

1. **Neutralizing Free Radicals:**

   a. Antioxidants donate electrons to free radicals, neutralizing them and preventing cellular damage.

2. **Reducing Oxidative Stress:**

   a. By neutralizing free radicals, antioxidants reduce oxidative stress, which is implicated in aging and various diseases.

3. **Supporting Antioxidant Enzyme Systems:**

   a. Some antioxidants, such as selenium, are components of antioxidant enzymes (e.g., glutathione peroxidase) that protect cells from oxidative damage.

Health Benefits

1. **Cardiovascular Health:**

   a. Antioxidants like flavonoids and vitamin E reduce oxidative stress, lower blood pressure, improve cholesterol levels, and protect against atherosclerosis.

2. **Cancer Prevention:**

   a. Antioxidants such as lycopene, selenium, and vitamins C and E reduce DNA damage, inhibit tumor growth, and enhance immune surveillance.

3. **Skin Health:**

   a. Vitamins C and E, along with carotenoids, protect the skin from UV damage, promote collagen production, and reduce signs of aging.

4. **Eye Health:**

   a. Carotenoids like lutein and zeaxanthin protect against age-related macular degeneration and cataracts.

5. **Cognitive Function:**

a. Antioxidants like flavonoids and resveratrol reduce oxidative damage to brain cells, potentially lowering the risk of neurodegenerative diseases such as Alzheimer's and Parkinson's.

Applications in Nutraceutical Products

1. **Dietary Supplements:**

    a. Antioxidants are commonly included in multivitamins, standalone supplements (e.g., vitamin C, vitamin E), and specialized antioxidant blends.

2. **Functional Foods:**

    a. Foods fortified with antioxidants, such as vitamin E-enriched cereals, selenium-fortified dairy products, and beverages containing added polyphenols.

3. **Beverages:**

    a. Green tea, fruit juices, and drinks enriched with antioxidants like resveratrol or vitamin C.

4. **Skincare Products:**

    a. Topical formulations containing antioxidants like vitamins C and E, coenzyme Q10, and polyphenols to protect the skin from oxidative stress and improve skin health.

POLYUNSATURATED FATTY ACIDS

Polyunsaturated fatty acids (PUFAs) are essential nutrients found in certain foods and are crucial for overall health. They play significant roles in various bodily functions, including brain function, cardiovascular health, and inflammation regulation. Here's a detailed overview of polyunsaturated fatty acids in nutraceuticals:

Types of Polyunsaturated Fatty Acids

1. **Omega-3 Fatty Acids:**

    a. **Eicosapentaenoic Acid (EPA):**

        i. Found in fatty fish like salmon, mackerel, and sardines.

ii. **Health Benefits:** Supports heart health, reduces inflammation, and may improve mood and mental health.

b. **Docosahexaenoic Acid (DHA):**

i. Found in fatty fish and seafood.

ii. **Health Benefits:** Critical for brain development and function, supports eye health, and may reduce the risk of cognitive decline.

2. **Omega-6 Fatty Acids:**

a. **Linoleic Acid (LA):**

i. Found in plant oils such as soybean, sunflower, and corn oil.

ii. **Health Benefits:** Essential for growth and development, supports skin health, and contributes to the structure of cell membranes.

b. **Arachidonic Acid (AA):**

i. Found in animal products like meat, poultry, and eggs.

ii. **Health Benefits:** Precursor to signaling molecules (eicosanoids) involved in immune response and inflammation regulation.

Health Benefits of Polyunsaturated Fatty Acids

1. **Cardiovascular Health:**

a. Omega-3 fatty acids (EPA and DHA) reduce triglycerides, lower blood pressure, prevent arterial plaque buildup, and decrease the risk of heart disease.

2. **Brain Function and Development:**

a. DHA is crucial for brain development in infants and children. Both EPA and DHA support cognitive function, memory, and mood regulation throughout life.

3. **Inflammation and Immune Response:**

a. Omega-3 fatty acids have anti-inflammatory properties that help manage chronic inflammatory conditions like rheumatoid arthritis and inflammatory bowel disease.

4. **Eye Health:**

   a. DHA contributes to the structural integrity of the retina and may reduce the risk of age-related macular degeneration.

5. **Skin Health:**

   a. Omega-6 fatty acids (especially from linoleic acid) maintain the integrity of the skin barrier, improve moisture retention, and support wound healing.

Sources of Polyunsaturated Fatty Acids

1. **Omega-3 Sources:** Fatty fish (salmon, trout, mackerel), fish oil supplements, flaxseeds, chia seeds, walnuts, and algae supplements.

2. **Omega-6 Sources:** Plant oils (soybean, sunflower, corn), nuts (especially pine nuts and walnuts), seeds (pumpkin seeds, sesame seeds), and certain vegetables.

Ratio of Omega-3 to Omega-6

1. **Optimal Ratio:** Traditional diets often had a balanced ratio of omega-6 to omega-3 fatty acids (around 1:1 to 4:1). Modern Western diets tend to be higher in omega-6 due to processed foods and vegetable oils, leading to an imbalance that may contribute to inflammation-related diseases.

Nutraceutical Applications of Polyunsaturated Fatty Acids

1. **Dietary Supplements:**

   a. Fish oil capsules or liquid supplements containing EPA and DHA.

   b. Algal oil supplements for vegetarians and vegans as sources of DHA.

   c. Evening primrose oil or borage oil capsules for gamma-linolenic acid (GLA), an omega-6 fatty acid.

2. **Functional Foods:**

a. Fortified foods such as bread, cereal bars, and dairy products enriched with omega-3 fatty acids.

b. Salad dressings and spreads made with oils rich in omega-3 or omega-6 fatty acids.

3. **Pharmaceutical Applications:**

a. Prescription omega-3 formulations used to treat severe hypertriglyceridemia and other cardiovascular conditions.

b. Omega-6 supplements used in certain dermatological conditions like eczema.

Considerations and Recommendations

1. **Balanced Intake:** Aim for a balanced intake of omega-3 and omega-6 fatty acids to support overall health. Increase omega-3-rich foods and reduce consumption of processed foods high in omega-6 oils.

2. **Supplementation:** Consider supplementation with fish oil or algal oil if dietary intake of omega-3 is inadequate, especially for individuals at risk of cardiovascular disease or those following plant-based diets.

3. **Quality and Purity:** Choose supplements that are tested for purity and free from contaminants like heavy metals (mercury, lead) and pollutants.

HERBS AS FUNCTIONAL FOODS

Herbs as functional foods in nutraceuticals are gaining popularity due to their health-promoting properties and therapeutic benefits. These natural plant-based substances are used not only for flavoring but also for their medicinal and nutritional value. Here's a detailed overview of herbs as functional foods in nutraceuticals:

Characteristics of Herbs as Functional Foods

1. **Bioactive Compounds:**

a. Herbs contain various bioactive compounds such as polyphenols, flavonoids, alkaloids, terpenes, and essential oils.

b. These compounds contribute to the herbs' antioxidant, anti-inflammatory, antimicrobial, and other therapeutic properties.

2. **Nutritional Content:**

   a. Herbs are rich sources of vitamins (such as vitamin C, vitamin K), minerals (like iron, calcium), and dietary fiber.

   b. They provide essential nutrients that support overall health and well-being.

3. **Traditional and Modern Uses:**

   a. Many herbs have been used for centuries in traditional medicine systems (e.g., Ayurveda, Traditional Chinese Medicine) for their medicinal properties.

   b. Modern research continues to explore their potential health benefits and applications in preventive and therapeutic nutrition.

Health Benefits of Herbs

1. **Antioxidant Properties:**

   a. Herbs like rosemary, oregano, and thyme are rich in antioxidants that protect cells from oxidative stress and reduce inflammation.

2. **Anti-inflammatory Effects:**

   a. Turmeric (containing curcumin), ginger, and cinnamon are known for their anti-inflammatory properties, which may help manage chronic inflammation and related conditions.

3. **Digestive Health:**

   a. Peppermint, ginger, and chamomile support digestive health by reducing gastrointestinal discomfort, improving digestion, and soothing the digestive tract.

4. **Immune Support:**

   a. Echinacea, garlic, and astragalus have immune-stimulating properties that may help prevent and reduce the severity of colds and infections.

5. **Cognitive Function:**

a. Ginkgo biloba and bacopa monnieri are herbs known for their potential to improve memory, cognitive function, and overall brain health.

6. **Cardiovascular Health:**

   a. Hawthorn, garlic, and green tea support heart health by lowering cholesterol levels, improving blood flow, and promoting healthy blood pressure.

Common Herbs Used as Functional Foods

1. **Turmeric (Curcuma longa):**

   a. **Active Compound:** Curcumin.

   b. **Benefits:** Anti-inflammatory, antioxidant, supports joint health, and may improve cognitive function.

2. **Ginger (Zingiber officinale):**

   a. **Benefits:** Anti-nausea, anti-inflammatory, supports digestive health, and may reduce muscle soreness.

3. **Garlic (Allium sativum):**

   a. **Benefits:** Antimicrobial, cardiovascular support, immune enhancement, and may help regulate blood pressure.

4. **Green Tea (Camellia sinensis):**

   a. **Benefits:** Antioxidant, supports metabolism, cardiovascular health, and may improve cognitive function.

5. **Cinnamon (Cinnamomum verum):**

   a. **Benefits:** Anti-inflammatory, antioxidant, supports blood sugar control, and may improve insulin sensitivity.

6. **Rosemary (Rosmarinus officinalis):**

   a. **Benefits:** Antioxidant, anti-inflammatory, supports cognitive function, and may improve digestion.

7. **Peppermint (Mentha piperita):**

a. **Benefits:** Digestive aid, anti-nausea, supports respiratory health, and may relieve headaches.

Applications of Herbs in Nutraceuticals

1. **Herbal Supplements:**

   a. Capsules, tablets, and liquid extracts containing concentrated herb extracts for specific health benefits.

2. **Functional Foods and Beverages:**

   a. Herbal teas, infused waters, and energy drinks incorporating herbs for flavor and health benefits.

3. **Topical Products:**

   a. Herbal extracts in skincare products for their antioxidant, anti-inflammatory, and soothing properties.

4. **Herbal Preparations:**

   a. Tinctures, powders, and herbal syrups used for medicinal purposes under professional guidance.

5. **Combination Products:**

   a. Formulations combining multiple herbs to target specific health concerns or provide comprehensive nutritional support.

Safety and Considerations

1. **Quality and Purity:** Ensure herbs used are sourced from reputable suppliers to avoid contamination or adulteration.

2. **Dosage and Administration:** Follow recommended dosages and consult healthcare providers, especially when using herbal supplements alongside medications.

3. **Potential Interactions:** Some herbs may interact with medications or existing health conditions, so it's essential to seek professional advice before starting herbal supplementation.

FORMULATION AND STANDARDIZATION OF NUTRACEUTICALS

Formulation and standardization of nutraceuticals are critical processes that ensure consistency, efficacy, and safety of these products. Nutraceuticals, which include dietary supplements, functional foods, and beverages formulated with bioactive compounds from natural sources, undergo rigorous formulation and standardization procedures to meet regulatory requirements and consumer expectations. Here's a detailed overview of formulation and standardization in nutraceuticals:

Formulation of Nutraceuticals

1. **Ingredient Selection:**
    a. **Active Ingredients:** Identification and selection of bioactive compounds (e.g., vitamins, minerals, herbs, phytochemicals) based on scientific evidence of their health benefits.
    b. **Excipients:** Non-active ingredients used for product stability, consistency, and bioavailability (e.g., fillers, binders, coatings).

2. **Dosage Form Selection:**
    a. **Tablets, Capsules:** Convenient and popular forms for oral delivery, ensuring accurate dosing and ease of consumption.
    b. **Softgels:** Encapsulation of liquid or oil-based ingredients for enhanced bioavailability and absorption.
    c. **Powders, Liquids:** Flexible forms for customization, mixing into beverages or foods, and rapid absorption.

3. **Bioavailability Enhancement:**
    a. Incorporation of technologies (e.g., nanotechnology, liposomal delivery) to improve the absorption and bioavailability of poorly soluble or rapidly metabolized compounds.

4. **Combination Products:**
    a. Formulating synergistic blends of ingredients to enhance efficacy (e.g., multivitamins, herbal combinations) based on complementary health benefits.

5. **Quality Control and Testing:**

   a. Establishing specifications for raw materials and finished products to ensure consistency, purity, and potency.

   b. Conducting stability studies to assess product shelf-life under various storage conditions.

Standardization of Nutraceuticals

1. **Definition of Active Ingredients:**

   a. Determining the concentration and bioactive form of key ingredients (e.g., standardized herbal extracts with specified levels of active compounds).

2. **Analytical Methods:**

   a. Developing and validating analytical techniques (e.g., chromatography, spectroscopy) to quantify active ingredients and ensure batch-to-batch consistency.

3. **Reference Standards:**

   a. Using authenticated reference materials (e.g., USP/NF standards) for comparing and verifying the identity, purity, and strength of ingredients.

4. **Regulatory Compliance:**

   a. Meeting regulatory standards (e.g., FDA regulations in the U.S., EU directives) for safety, quality, and labeling of nutraceutical products.

5. **GMP Compliance:**

   a. Adhering to Good Manufacturing Practices (GMP) to maintain quality control throughout the manufacturing process, from sourcing raw materials to packaging and distribution.

Importance of Formulation and Standardization

1. **Efficacy:** Ensures that nutraceutical products deliver consistent health benefits as claimed, based on validated formulations and standardized ingredients.

2. **Safety:** Minimizes variability in ingredient composition and ensures products are free from contaminants or adulterants harmful to consumers.

3. **Consumer Confidence:** Builds trust through transparent labeling, accurate dosing, and adherence to regulatory standards, enhancing product credibility in the market.

4. **Scientific Validation:** Supports product claims with scientific evidence of ingredient efficacy and safety, enabling informed consumer choices.

Challenges in Formulation and Standardization

1. **Complexity of Natural Ingredients:** Variability in natural sources (e.g., herbs, botanicals) can affect the consistency of active compounds, requiring robust analytical methods for quality assurance.

2. **Regulatory Compliance:** Navigating diverse regulatory frameworks globally and ensuring compliance with evolving standards and guidelines.

3. **Cost and Resource Intensity:** Investments in research, development, and quality control infrastructure to achieve consistent product quality and compliance with standards.

Future Trends and Innovations

1. **Personalized Nutrition:** Tailoring Nutraceuticals formulations to individual health needs and genetic profiles.

2. **Advanced Delivery Systems:** Continued development of novel delivery technologies to enhance bioavailability and consumer convenience.

3. **Integration of Digital Technologies:** Utilizing data analytics and blockchain for transparency in ingredient sourcing, production, and supply chain management.

REGULATORY ASPECTS

Regulatory aspects play a crucial role in ensuring the safety, efficacy, and quality of nutraceuticals, which encompass dietary supplements, functional foods, and beverages formulated with bioactive ingredients. Regulation varies by country or region, but generally aims to protect consumer health while facilitating market access for manufacturers. Here's a detailed overview of regulatory aspects in nutraceuticals:

Regulatory Frameworks

1. **United States (U.S.)**
   a. **FDA (Food and Drug Administration):**
      i. **Dietary Supplement Health and Education Act (DSHEA) of 1994:** Defines dietary supplements and sets forth requirements for labeling, safety, and good manufacturing practices (GMPs).
      ii. **New Dietary Ingredient (NDI) Notification:** Manufacturers must notify FDA at least 75 days before introducing a new dietary ingredient unless it has been marketed in the U.S. before October 15, 1994.
      iii. **GMPs for Dietary Supplements:** Establishes quality control measures for manufacturing, packaging, labeling, and storage of dietary supplements.

2. **European Union (EU)**
   a. **European Food Safety Authority (EFSA):**
      i. **Regulation (EU) 2015/2283 on Food for Specific Groups:** Covers food intended for infants, young children, and medical purposes, including certain categories of Nutraceuticals.
      ii. **Novel Food Regulation (EU) 2015/2283:** Defines and regulates novel foods, including novel ingredients used in Nutraceuticals.
      iii. **Health Claims Regulation (EC) No 1924/2006:** Sets criteria for making nutrition and health claims on food products, including Nutraceuticals.

3. **Canada**
   a. **Health Canada:**
      i. **Natural Health Products Regulations (NHPR):** Defines natural health products, including vitamins, minerals, herbal remedies,

homeopathic medicines, probiotics, and certain traditional medicines.

    ii. **Site Licensing and GMP Requirements:** Manufacturers must comply with GMPs and obtain site licenses to manufacture, package, label, and import natural health products.

4. **Other Countries**

    a. **Japan:** Regulates Functional Foods under the Food with Nutrient Function Claims (FNFC) system, requiring scientific substantiation of health claims.

    b. **Australia:** Administered by the Therapeutic Goods Administration (TGA), which oversees complementary medicines, including vitamins, minerals, herbal medicines, and certain nutritional supplements.

    c. **China:** Regulated under various laws, including the Food Safety Law and Regulations for the Registration and Filing of Health Foods.

Key Regulatory Considerations

1. **Product Classification:**

    a. Differentiates between dietary supplements, functional foods, medical foods, and pharmaceuticals based on intended use, formulation, and health claims.

2. **Safety and Efficacy:**

    a. Requires scientific evidence to support safety and efficacy claims, including clinical trials, toxicological studies, and human studies where applicable.

3. **Labeling Requirements:**

    a. Specifies mandatory labeling information, including ingredient lists, nutritional content, recommended dosage, health claims (where permitted), and cautionary statements.

4. **GMP Compliance:**

a. Mandates adherence to GMPs for manufacturing, packaging, labeling, and storage to ensure product consistency, quality, and safety.

5. **Health Claims and Substantiation:**

a. Sets criteria for making nutrition and health claims, requiring substantiation with scientific evidence to prevent misleading or false claims.

6. **Post-Market Surveillance:**

a. Monitors adverse events and product complaints to ensure ongoing safety and effectiveness of nutraceutical products.

Challenges in Regulatory Compliance

1. **Global Harmonization:** Variability in regulatory requirements across countries or regions can complicate market entry and compliance for international manufacturers.

2. **Complexity of Ingredients:** Natural sources like herbs and botanicals may have varying compositions, leading to challenges in standardization and quality control.

3. **Enforcement and Oversight:** Ensuring consistent enforcement of regulations and oversight of product quality and safety throughout the supply chain.

Future Trends in Nutraceutical Regulation

1. **Personalized Nutrition:** Regulations may evolve to accommodate personalized nutrition approaches based on genetic profiles and individual health needs.

2. **Emerging Ingredients:** Addressing regulatory challenges posed by novel ingredients and advanced delivery systems in nutraceuticals.

3. **Digital Transformation:** Leveraging digital technologies for improved traceability, transparency, and regulatory compliance in the nutraceutical sector.

FSSAI GUIDELINES

The Food Safety and Standards Authority of India (FSSAI) plays a pivotal role in regulating nutraceuticals and ensuring food safety standards across India. FSSAI guidelines for nutraceuticals are designed to protect public health, promote food safety, and provide consumers with accurate information about the products they consume. Here's a detailed overview of FSSAI guidelines in nutraceuticals:

Role of FSSAI

1. **Regulatory Authority:**
   a. FSSAI is the apex regulatory body in India under the Ministry of Health and Family Welfare, responsible for setting standards for food products, including nutraceuticals.

2. **Objectives:**
   a. Ensure safety and quality standards of food products, including dietary supplements and functional foods.
   b. Prevent adulteration, misbranding, and deceptive practices in the food industry.
   c. Promote consumer awareness and education about food safety and nutrition.

FSSAI Guidelines for Nutraceuticals

1. **Definition and Classification:**
   a. **Definition:** Nutraceuticals are defined as products that provide health and medical benefits, including prevention and treatment of diseases, in addition to their basic nutritional value.
   b. **Classification:** Includes dietary supplements, functional foods, fortified foods, and other products with bioactive compounds.

2. **Product Approval:**

a. FSSAI does not mandate pre-market approval for nutraceuticals, but manufacturers must comply with standards and regulations set forth in the Food Safety and Standards Act, 2006.

3. **Standards and Specifications:**

   a. **Ingredients:** Specify permissible ingredients and their maximum limits, ensuring safety and efficacy.

   b. **Labeling Requirements:** Mandatory labeling of nutraceutical products with accurate information about ingredients, nutritional content, health claims (if any), dosage instructions, and precautions.

   c. **Packaging:** Standards for packaging materials and practices to prevent contamination and ensure product integrity.

4. **Good Manufacturing Practices (GMP):**

   a. Manufacturers must comply with GMP guidelines to ensure products are consistently produced and controlled according to quality standards.

   b. Requirements include facility cleanliness, equipment maintenance, personnel hygiene, and record-keeping.

5. **Health Claims and Advertising:**

   a. Nutraceutical products making health claims must substantiate these claims with scientific evidence and comply with guidelines specified by FSSAI.

   b. Advertising must be truthful, not misleading, and should not exaggerate the benefits of the product beyond what is scientifically supported.

6. **Contaminants and Residues:**

   a. Limits and testing requirements for contaminants such as heavy metals, pesticides, microbial contaminants, and other harmful substances.

b. Regular monitoring and testing to ensure products meet safety standards and do not pose health risks to consumers.

7. **Import and Export Requirements:**

a. Guidelines for importing and exporting nutraceutical products, including documentation requirements, quality assurance, and compliance with international standards.

Compliance and Enforcement

1. **Inspections and Audits:**

a. FSSAI conducts inspections and audits of manufacturing facilities to ensure compliance with regulatory standards.

b. Non-compliance may result in penalties, product recalls, or suspension of licenses.

2. **Consumer Education:**

a. FSSAI promotes consumer awareness about food safety, nutrition, and the importance of choosing certified nutraceutical products.

Future Directions

1. **Regulatory Updates:**

a. Continuous review and updates to FSSAI guidelines to address emerging issues, technological advancements, and international best practices.

2. **Capacity Building:**

a. Training programs and capacity building initiatives for stakeholders, including manufacturers, importers, and regulatory officials, to enhance compliance and enforcement.

3. **Digital Initiatives:**

a. Leveraging technology for transparency, traceability, and real-time monitoring of nutraceutical products in the market.

Multiple Choice Questions (MCQs)

1. What does the term "nutraceutical" combine?

    A. Nutrition and chemicals

    B. Nutrition and pharmaceuticals

    C. Nutrition and therapy

    D. Nutrition and food

2. Which of the following is NOT a category of nutraceuticals?

    A. Dietary Supplements

    B. Functional Foods

    C. Medicinal Foods

    D. Pharmaceutical Drugs

3. Which compound is an example of a nutraceutical derived from plants?

    A. Omega-3 fatty acids

    B. Collagen peptides

    C. Lycopene

    D. Conjugated linoleic acid

4. Which mechanism of action is associated with nutraceuticals?

    A. Antibiotic activity

    B. Gene expression modulation

    C. Hormone secretion

    D. Blood sugar reduction

5. What health benefit is associated with omega-3 fatty acids?

    A. Bone health

    B. Cardiovascular health

    C. Digestive health

    D. Cognitive function

6. Which regulatory body oversees the regulation of dietary supplements in the United States?

A. European Food Safety Authority (EFSA)

B. Food and Drug Administration (FDA)

C. Health Canada

D. Food Safety and Standards Authority of India (FSSAI)

7. What is a challenge associated with nutraceuticals?

A. High cost

B. Standardization

C. Easy availability

D. Pleasant taste

8. What trend is associated with personalized nutrition?

A. Standardized dietary recommendations

B. Tailored nutraceutical products to individual profiles

C. Increased use of synthetic nutrients

D. Reduced focus on gut health

9. Which vitamin is water-soluble?

A. Vitamin A

B. Vitamin D

C. Vitamin E

D. Vitamin C

10. What is the role of magnesium in the body?

A. Oxygen transport

B. Energy production

C. Blood clotting

D. Collagen synthesis

11. Which herb is known for its anti-inflammatory properties?

A. Turmeric

B. Rosemary

C. Peppermint

D. Green tea

12. What is the main health benefit of dietary fiber?

    A. Protein synthesis

    B. Enzyme production

    C. Improved digestion

    D. Vitamin absorption

13. Which fatty acid is an omega-3 fatty acid?

    A. Linoleic acid

    B. Arachidonic acid

    C. Eicosapentaenoic acid (EPA)

    D. Gamma-linolenic acid

14. Which regulatory body oversees nutraceuticals in India?

    A. FDA

    B. EFSA

    C. Health Canada

    D. FSSAI

15. What is an example of a functional beverage?

    A. Fortified cereal

    B. Herbal tea

    C. Dietary supplement capsule

    D. Enriched bread

16. Which antioxidant is found in green tea?

    A. Lycopene

    B. Catechins

    C. Selenium

    D. Alpha-tocopherol

17. What is the primary function of digestive enzymes?

    A. Protein synthesis

    B. Blood sugar regulation

    C. Breakdown of food components

D. Hormone production

18. What is a major challenge in the regulation of nutraceuticals?

    A. High demand

    B. Bioavailability

    C. Standardization of natural ingredients

    D. Pleasant taste

19. What component is commonly found in probiotics?

    A. Beta-carotene

    B. Lactobacillus species

    C. Omega-6 fatty acids

    D. Lycopene

20. What health benefit is associated with polyunsaturated fatty acids (PUFAs)?

    A. Bone density

    B. Cognitive function

    C. Skin elasticity

    D. Muscle growth

Short Answer Type Questions (Subjective)

1. Define the term "nutraceutical."

2. Who coined the term "nutraceutical" and in which year?

3. List the four main categories of nutraceuticals.

4. Provide examples of nutraceuticals derived from plant sources.

5. What are probiotics and give examples of probiotics derived from microbial sources?

6. Explain how nutraceuticals can have antioxidant activity.

7. Describe how nutraceuticals can modulate inflammatory pathways.

8. What role do nutraceuticals play in cardiovascular health?

9. How do calcium and vitamin D supplements benefit bone health?

10. What is the role of probiotics and prebiotics in digestive health?

11. Name two phytochemicals that are known to reduce the risk of certain cancers.

12. Which vitamins are commonly known to enhance immune function?

13. What are the primary challenges faced by the nutraceutical industry?

14. Describe the trend of personalized nutrition in the context of nutraceuticals.

15. Why is there a growing demand for plant-based nutraceuticals?

16. List common inorganic mineral supplements and their primary uses.

17. What are the two categories of vitamins based on their solubility?

18. Explain the function of digestive enzymes.

19. Provide examples of functional foods enriched with dietary fiber.

20. What are the health benefits of consuming whole grains?

Long Answer Type Questions (Subjective)

1. Discuss the mechanisms through which nutraceuticals exert their health benefits. Include examples of specific compounds and their actions.

2. Explain the importance of regulation and quality control in the nutraceutical industry. How do these regulations differ between the United States and the European Union?

3. Describe the challenges and considerations associated with the bioavailability of nutraceuticals. How can these challenges be addressed?

4. Outline the potential future directions for the nutraceutical industry. Include trends such as personalized nutrition, technological advancements, and global market expansion.

5. Compare and contrast the roles and health benefits of omega-3 and omega-6 fatty acids in human nutrition.

6. Provide a detailed overview of the health benefits and applications of dietary fibers in nutraceuticals.

7. Explain the significance of antioxidants in nutraceuticals. Discuss the different types of antioxidants and their specific health benefits.

8. Discuss the role of herbs as functional foods in nutraceuticals. Provide examples of commonly used herbs and their health benefits.

9. Describe the process of formulation and standardization of nutraceuticals. Why are these processes critical for ensuring the efficacy and safety of nutraceutical products?

Answer Key

1. B. Nutrition and pharmaceuticals
2. D. Pharmaceutical Drugs
3. C. Lycopene
4. B. Gene expression modulation
5. B. Cardiovascular health
6. B. Food and Drug Administration (FDA)
7. B. Standardization
8. B. Tailored nutraceutical products to individual profiles
9. D. Vitamin C
10. B. Energy production
11. A. Turmeric
12. C. Improved digestion
13. C. Eicosapentaenoic acid (EPA)
14. D. FSSAI
15. B. Herbal tea
16. B. Catechins
17. C. Breakdown of food components
18. C. Standardization of natural ingredients
19. B. Lactobacillus species
20. B. Cognitive function

CHAPTER – 4

NUTRACEUTICALS-II

INTRODUCTION:

Nutraceuticals is a portmanteau of the words "nutrition" and "pharmaceutical," coined by Dr. Stephen DeFelice in 1989. It refers to products derived from food sources that offer health benefits in addition to their basic nutritional value. Nutraceuticals are used to promote general well-being, control symptoms, and prevent malignant processes.

Categories of Nutraceuticals:

Nutraceuticals encompass a broad category of products that bridge the gap between food and pharmaceuticals. They are defined as bioactive compounds or substances derived from natural sources that provide health benefits beyond basic nutritional functions. Here's a detailed overview of the categories of nutraceuticals:

1. Dietary Supplements

Dietary supplements are the most commonly recognized category of nutraceuticals. They include vitamins, minerals, amino acids, herbs, or other botanicals, and substances like enzymes or probiotics. These products are intended to supplement the diet and are available in various forms such as capsules, tablets, powders, liquids, and gummies.

Examples:

    a. **Vitamins**: Vitamin C, Vitamin D, B-complex vitamins.

    b. **Minerals**: Calcium, Magnesium, Iron.

    c. **Herbal Supplements**: Echinacea, Ginkgo biloba, Ginseng.

    d. **Probiotics**: Lactobacillus, Bifidobacterium strains.

2. Functional Foods

Functional foods are whole foods or fortified foods that provide health benefits beyond basic nutrition. These products are formulated to contain bioactive compounds or ingredients that have specific physiological benefits.

Examples:

a. **Fortified Juices**: Orange juice fortified with calcium and vitamin D.

b. **Probiotic Yogurt**: Yogurt containing live cultures of beneficial bacteria.

c. **Omega-3 Enriched Eggs**: Eggs with enhanced levels of omega-3 fatty acids.

3. Herbal Nutraceuticals

Herbal nutraceuticals refer to products derived from medicinal plants or botanical sources. They include herbal extracts, standardized herbal preparations, and traditional herbal remedies used for their therapeutic properties.

Examples:

a. **Turmeric Extract**: Standardized for curcumin content, used for its anti-inflammatory properties.

b. **Ginkgo biloba Extract**: Used to improve cognitive function and circulation.

c. **Milk Thistle Extract**: Supports liver health and detoxification.

4. Nutritional Supplements for Sports and Fitness

These nutraceuticals are designed to enhance athletic performance, support muscle recovery, and improve overall fitness. They often include ingredients like protein powders, amino acids, creatine, and specialized formulations for pre-workout and post-workout nutrition.

Examples:

a. **Whey Protein**: Supports muscle growth and repair.

b. **BCAAs (Branched-Chain Amino Acids)**: Aids in muscle recovery and reduces muscle soreness.

c. **Creatine**: Enhances ATP production for increased energy during intense exercise.

5. Medical Foods

Medical foods are formulated and intended for the dietary management of specific medical conditions under medical supervision. They are distinct from dietary supplements and conventional foods, often containing ingredients targeted to address nutritional deficiencies or metabolic imbalances associated with a particular disease or health condition.

Examples:

a. **Nutritional Formulas for Enteral Nutrition**: Used for patients who cannot consume regular food due to medical conditions.

b. **Low Phenylalanine Foods**: Used in the management of phenylketonuria (PKU).

c. **Specialized Oral Nutritional Supplements**: For conditions like malnutrition or specific nutrient deficiencies.

6. Cosmeceuticals

Cosmeceuticals are nutraceuticals applied topically or used in cosmetic products. They contain bioactive ingredients that provide cosmetic benefits or enhance skin health.

Examples:

a. **Anti-aging Creams**: Containing antioxidants like vitamins C and E.

b. **Skin Lightening Creams**: With botanical extracts like licorice or kojic acid.

c. **Hair Growth Serums**: Formulated with biotin and herbal extracts.

7. Probiotics and Prebiotics

Probiotics are live microorganisms that confer health benefits when consumed in adequate amounts. Prebiotics are non-digestible fibers that stimulate the growth or activity of beneficial bacteria in the digestive system. Together, they support gut health and digestive function.

Examples:

    a. **Probiotics**: Lactobacillus acidophilus, Bifidobacterium bifidum.

    b. **Prebiotics**: Inulin, fructooligosaccharides (FOS).

8. Omega Fatty Acids

Omega fatty acids, particularly omega-3 and omega-6 fatty acids, are essential nutrients with numerous health benefits. They are commonly used as nutraceutical supplements to support cardiovascular health, brain function, and overall well-being.

Examples:

    a. **Omega-3 Fatty Acids**: Fish oil supplements containing EPA (eicosapentaenoic acid) and DHA (docosahexaenoic acid).

    b. **Omega-6 Fatty Acids**: Evening primrose oil, containing gamma-linolenic acid (GLA).

9. Others

There are many other specialized categories of nutraceuticals, including those focused on specific health conditions like diabetes management, cognitive health, bone health, and immune support. These products often contain targeted formulations of vitamins, minerals, herbs, and other bioactive compounds.

Mechanisms of Action:

Mechanisms of action in nutraceuticals refer to the specific biochemical, physiological, or pharmacological processes through which these products exert their beneficial effects on health. These mechanisms can vary widely depending on the type of nutraceutical and its active ingredients. Here's a detailed exploration of the mechanisms of action commonly observed in different categories of nutraceuticals:

1. Antioxidant Activity

    1. **Mechanism**: Many nutraceuticals, such as vitamins (e.g., vitamin C, vitamin E), minerals (e.g., selenium, zinc), and phytochemicals (e.g., flavonoids, carotenoids), act as antioxidants. They neutralize free radicals

and reactive oxygen species (ROS) in the body, preventing oxidative damage to cells and tissues.

2. **Examples**:

   a. **Vitamin C**: Scavenges free radicals and regenerates vitamin E.

   b. **Flavonoids**: Enhance antioxidant enzymes' activity and reduce oxidative stress.

3. **Health Benefits**: Protects against aging, cardiovascular diseases, cancer, and neurodegenerative disorders.

2. Anti-inflammatory Effects

1. **Mechanism**: Nutraceuticals like curcumin (from turmeric), omega-3 fatty acids (from fish oil), and polyphenols (from green tea) inhibit pro-inflammatory enzymes and cytokines (e.g., COX-2, TNF-alpha), thereby reducing inflammation.

2. **Examples**:

   a. **Curcumin**: Blocks NF-kB activation and inhibits COX-2 expression.

   b. **Omega-3 Fatty Acids**: Produce anti-inflammatory eicosanoids (e.g., resolvins and protectins).

3. **Health Benefits**: Alleviates symptoms of arthritis, inflammatory bowel diseases, and chronic inflammation-related diseases.

3. Hormonal Modulation

1. **Mechanism**: Phytoestrogens and other hormone-like compounds in nutraceuticals mimic or modulate hormone activity. They interact with hormone receptors, influencing hormone synthesis, metabolism, or signaling pathways.

2. **Examples**:

   a. **Isoflavones**: Found in soy products, they bind to estrogen receptors.

b. **Lignans**: Found in flaxseeds and sesame seeds, they modulate estrogen metabolism.

3. **Health Benefits**: Supports menopausal health, reproductive health, and hormone-related conditions.

4. Neuroprotective Effects

1. **Mechanism**: Nutraceuticals like polyphenols (e.g., resveratrol), omega-3 fatty acids, and certain vitamins (e.g., vitamin E) protect neurons from oxidative stress, inflammation, and apoptosis. They may also enhance neuronal plasticity and neurotransmitter function.

2. **Examples**:

   a. **Resveratrol**: Activates sirtuins and enhances mitochondrial function.

   b. **Omega-3 Fatty Acids**: Increase brain-derived neurotrophic factor (BDNF) levels.

3. **Health Benefits**: Supports cognitive function, memory, and protects against neurodegenerative diseases like Alzheimer's and Parkinson's.

5. Modulation of Gut Microbiota

1. **Mechanism**: Prebiotics (e.g., fiber, oligosaccharides) and probiotics (e.g., Lactobacillus, Bifidobacterium) in nutraceuticals alter the composition and activity of gut microbiota. They promote the growth of beneficial bacteria and improve gut barrier function.

2. **Examples**:

   a. **Probiotics**: Colonize the gut and produce beneficial metabolites like short-chain fatty acids.

   b. **Prebiotics**: Provide substrate for beneficial bacteria.

3. **Health Benefits**: Enhances digestive health, immune function, and may influence systemic inflammation and metabolic health.

6. Regulation of Enzymatic Pathways

1. **Mechanism**: Nutraceuticals can modulate enzymatic activity involved in various metabolic pathways. For example, polyphenols in green tea inhibit enzymes like tyrosinase, affecting melanin production in skin.

2. **Examples**:

    a. **Green Tea Catechins**: Inhibit enzymes involved in lipid metabolism.

    b. **Milk Thistle**: Supports liver detoxification enzymes.

3. **Health Benefits**: Supports metabolic health, detoxification, and skin health.

7. Enhancement of Nutrient Absorption and Utilization

1. **Mechanism**: Nutraceuticals may enhance the absorption and utilization of nutrients like vitamins and minerals. For instance, piperine (from black pepper) enhances the bioavailability of curcumin.

2. **Examples**:

    a. **Piperine**: Inhibits drug-metabolizing enzymes and enhances nutrient absorption.

    b. **Vitamin D**: Facilitates calcium absorption.

3. **Health Benefits**: Optimizes nutrient status, supports bone health, and overall metabolic function.

8. Modulation of Gene Expression

1. **Mechanism**: Certain nutraceuticals can influence gene expression through epigenetic mechanisms, altering DNA methylation and histone modification patterns.

2. **Examples**:

    a. **Sulforaphane**: Found in broccoli, induces expression of antioxidant enzymes via Nrf2 activation.

    b. **Epigallocatechin Gallate (EGCG)**: Modulates gene expression related to cell cycle regulation and apoptosis.

3. **Health Benefits**: Supports cellular health, antioxidant defenses, and may have implications in cancer prevention.

Uses and Benefits:

Nutraceuticals encompass a wide range of products that offer health benefits beyond basic nutrition. Their uses and benefits are diverse, depending on the type of nutraceutical and its specific bioactive compounds. Here's a detailed exploration of the uses and benefits of nutraceuticals across various categories:

1. Dietary Supplements

Uses:

a. **Fill Nutritional Gaps**: Supplements provide essential vitamins, minerals, and other nutrients that may be lacking in the diet.

b. **Support Specific Health Needs**: Address specific deficiencies or health conditions, such as iron deficiency anemia or vitamin D deficiency.

c. **Enhance Overall Health**: Promote general well-being and support immune function, energy metabolism, and cellular health.

Benefits:

a. **Convenience**: Easy to consume and provide nutrients in concentrated forms.

b. **Customization**: Formulated to meet specific dietary needs or health goals.

c. **Quality Assurance**: Ensure consistent intake of standardized nutrients.

2. Functional Foods

Uses:

a. **Targeted Nutrition**: Incorporate bioactive compounds to provide health benefits beyond basic nutrition.

b. **Manage Health Conditions**: Support cardiovascular health, digestive health, or immune function.

c. **Enhance Performance**: Improve cognitive function, physical performance, or recovery.

Benefits:

    a. **Holistic Approach**: Integrate nutrients into daily diet for long-term health maintenance.

    b. **Natural Source**: Obtain health benefits from whole foods or fortified foods.

    c. **Palatability**: Enjoyable and easy to incorporate into meals.

3. Herbal Nutraceuticals

Uses:

    a. **Traditional Remedies**: Use botanical extracts for their therapeutic properties based on traditional knowledge.

    b. **Support Wellness**: Address specific health concerns, such as stress, inflammation, or digestive issues.

    c. **Alternative Medicine**: Provide natural alternatives to pharmaceuticals for symptom management.

Benefits:

    a. **Safety**: Generally considered safe with fewer side effects compared to pharmaceuticals.

    b. **Versatility**: Treat a variety of conditions from mild to chronic illnesses.

    c. **Cultural Significance**: Reflect cultural practices and historical use in traditional medicine.

4. Nutritional Supplements for Sports and Fitness

Uses:

    a. **Muscle Growth and Recovery**: Provide protein, amino acids, and creatine to support muscle repair and growth.

    b. **Energy Support**: Enhance energy metabolism and performance during exercise.

    c. **Hydration and Electrolyte Balance**: Maintain fluid balance and replenish electrolytes lost during physical activity.

Benefits:

   a. **Performance Enhancement**: Improve athletic performance, endurance, and recovery times.

   b. **Muscle Maintenance**: Preserve lean muscle mass during intense training.

   c. **Personalized Nutrition**: Tailor supplements to individual training goals and nutritional needs.

5. Medical Foods

Uses:

   a. **Manage Medical Conditions**: Provide specialized nutrition for conditions like diabetes, renal disease, or metabolic disorders.

   b. **Support Healing**: Aid in wound healing or recovery from surgery.

   c. **Nutritional Support**: Compensate for nutrient deficiencies related to medical treatments or conditions.

Benefits:

   a. **Efficacy**: Supported by clinical evidence for managing specific health conditions.

   b. **Compliance**: Ensure patients receive necessary nutrients as part of medical treatment plans.

   c. **Safety**: Formulated under strict guidelines to meet nutritional needs without adverse interactions.

6. Cosmeceuticals

Uses:

   a. **Skin Care**: Provide anti-aging, moisturizing, or skin-brightening effects.

   b. **Hair Care**: Promote hair growth, thickness, or scalp health.

   c. **Beauty Enhancements**: Address specific cosmetic concerns like acne, wrinkles, or pigmentation.

Benefits:

   a. **Non-invasive**: Offer topical solutions for cosmetic improvement without surgical procedures.

b. **Long-Term Benefits**: Support skin health and appearance over time.

c. **Combination Therapies**: Combine with dermatological treatments for enhanced results.

7. Probiotics and Prebiotics

Uses:

a. **Gut Health**: Improve digestion, reduce bloating, and support intestinal flora balance.

b. **Immune Support**: Strengthen immune function and prevent infections.

c. **Mood and Mental Health**: Influence gut-brain axis and support mental well-being.

Benefits:

a. **Digestive Balance**: Restore gut microbiota balance disrupted by diet, antibiotics, or stress.

b. **Systemic Effects**: Impact overall health through gut microbial modulation.

c. **Regularity**: Support regular bowel movements and gastrointestinal comfort.

8. Omega Fatty Acids

Uses:

a. **Heart Health**: Lower cholesterol levels and reduce cardiovascular risk.

b. **Brain Function**: Support cognitive function, memory, and mood stability.

c. **Joint Health**: Reduce inflammation and alleviate symptoms of arthritis.

Benefits:

a. **Anti-inflammatory Properties**: Modulate inflammatory pathways for systemic health benefits.

b. **Cardiovascular Protection**: Maintain healthy lipid profiles and blood pressure.

c. **Brain Support**: Enhance neuronal membrane integrity and neurotransmitter function.

Examples of Common Nutraceuticals:

Nutraceuticals encompass a wide array of products derived from natural sources that provide health benefits beyond basic nutrition. Here are examples of common nutraceuticals across different categories, along with their specific uses and benefits:

1. Dietary Supplements

Examples:

1. **Multivitamins**: Comprehensive formulations containing essential vitamins and minerals to support overall health and fill nutritional gaps.

    a. **Uses**: Daily nutritional supplementation, prevention of vitamin deficiencies.

    b. **Benefits**: Promotes immune function, energy production, and cellular health.

2. **Omega-3 Fatty Acids (Fish Oil)**: Rich in EPA (eicosapentaenoic acid) and DHA (docosahexaenoic acid), essential for cardiovascular and cognitive health.

    a. **Uses**: Cardiovascular support, brain health, anti-inflammatory effects.

    b. **Benefits**: Reduces triglycerides, supports brain function, and may lower risk of heart disease.

3. **Probiotics**: Live bacteria that confer health benefits by improving gut microbiota balance.

    a. **Uses**: Digestive health, immune support, management of gastrointestinal disorders.

    b. **Benefits**: Enhances digestion, boosts immune function, supports mental health through the gut-brain axis.

2. Functional Foods

Examples:

1. **Fortified Dairy Products**: Milk or yogurt fortified with vitamin D and calcium for bone health.

    a. **Uses**: Bone health, prevention of osteoporosis.

    b. **Benefits**: Enhances calcium absorption, supports bone density.

2. **Green Tea**: Contains polyphenols like catechins (e.g., EGCG) with antioxidant and anti-inflammatory properties.

    a. **Uses**: Antioxidant support, weight management, cardiovascular health.

    b. **Benefits**: Protects against oxidative stress, may aid in weight loss, supports heart health.

3. **Whole Grains**: Rich in fiber, vitamins, and minerals, promoting digestive health and reducing chronic disease risks.

    a. **Uses**: Fiber intake, blood sugar management, cardiovascular health.

    b. **Benefits**: Supports digestive regularity, lowers cholesterol levels, and reduces risk of heart disease.

3. Herbal Nutraceuticals

Examples:

1. **Turmeric**: Contains curcumin, known for its potent anti-inflammatory and antioxidant properties.

    a. **Uses**: Joint health, inflammatory conditions, digestive support.

    b. **Benefits**: Reduces inflammation, supports joint mobility, aids in digestion.

2. **Ginseng**: Adaptogenic herb used for its energy-boosting and stress-reducing effects.

    a. **Uses**: Energy enhancement, stress management, cognitive function.

b. **Benefits**: Increases stamina, reduces fatigue, supports mental clarity.

3. **Garlic**: Contains allicin and other sulfur compounds with antimicrobial and cardiovascular benefits.

    a. **Uses**: Cardiovascular health, immune support, antimicrobial effects.

    b. **Benefits**: Lowers blood pressure, supports immune function, may reduce risk of infections.

4. Nutritional Supplements for Sports and Fitness

Examples:

1. **Whey Protein**: Fast-absorbing protein source for muscle growth and recovery.

    a. **Uses**: Muscle building, post-workout recovery, protein supplementation.

    b. **Benefits**: Supports muscle repair, enhances muscle protein synthesis, aids in recovery after exercise.

2. **Creatine**: Supports ATP production for energy during high-intensity exercise.

    a. **Uses**: Muscle strength, power output, athletic performance.

    b. **Benefits**: Increases muscle mass, improves performance in short-duration, high-intensity activities.

3. **Branched-Chain Amino Acids (BCAAs)**: Leucine, isoleucine, and valine, essential for muscle protein synthesis and reducing muscle breakdown.

    a. **Uses**: Muscle recovery, endurance exercise, muscle preservation during dieting.

    b. **Benefits**: Reduces muscle soreness, supports muscle growth, enhances exercise performance.

5. Medical Foods

Examples:

1. **Enteral Nutrition Formulas**: Complete and balanced nutrition for patients unable to eat normally due to medical conditions.

    a. **Uses**: Nutritional support for malnutrition, digestive disorders, or medical treatments.

    b. **Benefits**: Provides essential nutrients, supports recovery, and improves overall nutritional status.

2. **Specialized Oral Nutritional Supplements**: High-calorie, high-protein supplements for patients with increased nutritional needs.

    a. **Uses**: Weight management, nutritional support during illness or recovery.

    b. **Benefits**: Prevents malnutrition, supports wound healing, and improves quality of life.

3. **Low Phenylalanine Foods**: Essential for managing phenylketonuria (PKU), a genetic disorder affecting phenylalanine metabolism.

    a. **Uses**: Metabolic disorder management, dietary control of phenylalanine intake.

    b. **Benefits**: Prevents intellectual disability, supports normal growth and development.

6. Cosmeceuticals

Examples:

1. **Retinoids**: Vitamin A derivatives used in anti-aging creams for skin rejuvenation.

    a. **Uses**: Wrinkle reduction, skin texture improvement, acne treatment.

    b. **Benefits**: Stimulates collagen production, reduces fine lines and wrinkles, enhances skin tone.

2. **Hyaluronic Acid**: Moisturizing agent used in serums and creams for hydration and skin plumping.

a. **Uses**: Hydration, anti-aging, wound healing.

b. **Benefits**: Retains skin moisture, improves skin elasticity, promotes wound repair.

3. **Botanical Extracts**: Plant-derived compounds like green tea, licorice, or chamomile used for their antioxidant and soothing properties in skincare products.

    a. **Uses**: Antioxidant protection, inflammation reduction, skin soothing.

    b. **Benefits**: Protects against environmental damage, calms sensitive skin, enhances overall skin health.

Regulatory Aspects:

Regulatory aspects surrounding nutraceuticals are crucial as these products occupy a space between conventional foods and pharmaceuticals, often claiming health benefits beyond basic nutrition. The regulatory landscape varies across countries, but several key aspects are generally considered when ensuring the safety, efficacy, and quality of nutraceuticals. Here's a detailed overview of regulatory aspects in nutraceuticals:

1. Definition and Classification

a. **Definition**: Nutraceuticals are typically defined as products derived from natural sources (such as foods or botanicals) that provide health benefits, including prevention and treatment of diseases, beyond basic nutritional functions.

b. **Classification**: They are often classified based on intended use and formulation, distinguishing between dietary supplements, functional foods, herbal products, medical foods, and cosmeceuticals.

2. Regulatory Authorities

a. **United States**: The Food and Drug Administration (FDA) regulates nutraceuticals under the Dietary Supplement Health and Education Act

(DSHEA) of 1994. Dietary supplements must be safe, appropriately labeled, and comply with Good Manufacturing Practices (GMP).

b. **European Union**: Nutraceuticals are regulated under various directives and regulations, such as the Food Supplements Directive (2002/46/EC) and Novel Foods Regulation (EU) 2015/2283. The European Food Safety Authority (EFSA) evaluates health claims for substantiation.

c. **Canada**: Health Canada oversees nutraceuticals under the Natural Health Products Regulations, requiring evidence of safety, efficacy, and quality. Products must obtain a Natural Product Number (NPN) or a Drug Identification Number-Homeopathic Medicine Number (DIN-HM).

d. **Other Countries**: Each country has its own regulatory framework governing nutraceuticals, which may include specific requirements for safety assessments, labeling, and health claims substantiation.

3. Safety and Efficacy

a. **Safety**: Nutraceuticals must demonstrate safety through toxicological assessments, including acute and chronic toxicity studies, to ensure they do not pose harm to consumers when used as directed.

b. **Efficacy**: Some jurisdictions require evidence of efficacy, typically through clinical trials or well-established traditional use, especially for health claims related to disease prevention or treatment.

4. Labeling Requirements

a. **Ingredients List**: Must include all active and inactive ingredients, including botanical species and standardized extracts.

b. **Health Claims**: Regulations govern the use of health claims, requiring scientific substantiation for claims related to health benefits.

c. **Dosage Instructions**: Clear directions for use, including recommended dosage, frequency, and any precautions or warnings.

5. Quality Control and Good Manufacturing Practices (GMP)

a. **Quality Control**: Nutraceutical manufacturers must adhere to GMP guidelines to ensure consistency, purity, and potency of products.

b. **Testing**: Regular testing of raw materials and finished products for identity, purity, strength, and composition to verify compliance with specifications.

6. Post-Market Surveillance

a. **Adverse Event Reporting**: Manufacturers and distributors are often required to report adverse events associated with their products to regulatory authorities.

b. **Market Monitoring**: Regulatory agencies conduct inspections and audits to ensure compliance with regulations and address safety concerns.

7. International Harmonization and Standards

a. **Codex Alimentarius**: International food standards adopted by the Codex Alimentarius Commission provide guidelines and principles for nutraceuticals.

b. **Harmonization Efforts**: Efforts to harmonize regulations across countries aim to facilitate international trade while ensuring consumer safety and product quality.

Challenges and Future Directions:

Nutraceuticals face several challenges and opportunities as they continue to evolve in the global health and wellness market. These challenges and future directions encompass scientific, regulatory, market, and consumer trends. Here's a detailed exploration:

Challenges in Nutraceuticals

1. **Regulatory Complexity**: Regulatory requirements vary widely across countries, posing challenges for manufacturers in ensuring compliance with diverse standards and approvals.

2. **Scientific Validation**: Despite growing interest, some nutraceuticals lack robust scientific evidence to support health claims, which can hinder acceptance by healthcare professionals and consumers.

3. **Quality Control**: Ensuring consistency, purity, and potency of nutraceutical products remains a challenge, especially with complex formulations and sourcing from natural ingredients.

4. **Health Claims Substantiation**: Regulations require rigorous substantiation of health claims, necessitating costly and time-consuming clinical trials, which may be prohibitive for smaller companies.

5. **Consumer Education**: Many consumers lack understanding of nutraceuticals, including their benefits, proper usage, and potential interactions with medications, highlighting a need for educational initiatives.

6. **Market Competition and Integrity**: The market is saturated with products making varied claims, leading to concerns about product efficacy, safety, and misleading marketing practices.

7. **Supply Chain Issues**: Sourcing natural ingredients sustainably and ensuring traceability throughout the supply chain present logistical and ethical challenges.

Future Directions in Nutraceuticals

1. **Personalized Nutrition**: Advances in technology, such as genetic testing and biomarker analysis, are paving the way for personalized nutraceutical formulations tailored to individual health needs.

2. **Functional Foods Innovation**: Innovation in food science and technology is driving the development of functional foods with enhanced bioavailability and health-promoting properties.

3. **Microbiome Modulation**: Nutraceuticals targeting gut health and microbiome modulation are gaining traction, offering potential benefits for digestive disorders, immune function, and overall health.

4. **Natural Product Development**: Continued exploration of plant-based compounds, marine-derived ingredients, and bioactive peptides for their therapeutic potential in nutraceuticals.

5. **Bioinformatics and Data Analytics**: Leveraging big data and computational tools to analyze clinical outcomes and predict efficacy of nutraceutical interventions.

6. **Regulatory Harmonization**: Efforts to harmonize global regulations and establish clear guidelines for nutraceuticals to facilitate international trade and ensure consumer safety.

7. **Consumer Empowerment**: Increasing consumer awareness and education through transparent labeling, evidence-based marketing, and accessible information on nutraceutical benefits and risks.

8. **Integration with Traditional Medicine**: Collaborations between nutraceutical researchers and traditional medicine practitioners to validate and integrate traditional knowledge with modern scientific approaches.

SPIRULINA

Spirulina is a blue-green algae (cyanobacteria) known for its high nutritional value and potential health benefits. It has been used as a dietary supplement and nutraceutical due to its rich composition of proteins, vitamins, minerals, and other bioactive compounds.

Sources

Spirulina is primarily sourced from freshwater environments such as lakes and ponds. Major cultivation sites include:

1. **Lakes and Ponds**: Natural bodies of water with alkaline pH, such as Lake Texcoco in Mexico and Lake Chad in Africa.

2. **Commercial Farms**: Controlled environments like open ponds and photobioreactors in countries like the USA, China, India, and Thailand.

Marker Compounds and Chemical Nature

Spirulina contains several key bioactive compounds, each contributing to its health benefits:

1. **Phycocyanin**: A blue pigment and protein complex with antioxidant and anti-inflammatory properties.
   a. **Chemical Nature**: Water-soluble pigment-protein complex.
2. **Chlorophyll**: The green pigment involved in photosynthesis, known for its detoxifying properties.
   a. **Chemical Nature**: Magnesium-coordinated porphyrin ring.
3. **Beta-Carotene**: A precursor of vitamin A with antioxidant properties.
   a. **Chemical Nature**: Terpenoid compound.
4. **Gamma-Linolenic Acid (GLA)**: An omega-6 fatty acid beneficial for skin health and inflammation.
   a. **Chemical Nature**: Polyunsaturated fatty acid.
5. **Polysaccharides**: Complex carbohydrates with immune-boosting properties.
   a. **Chemical Nature**: High-molecular-weight carbohydrates.

Medicinal Uses and Health Benefits

1. **Antioxidant Activity**:
   a. **Benefit**: Spirulina's high antioxidant content helps neutralize free radicals, protecting cells from oxidative damage.
   b. **Compounds**: Phycocyanin, beta-carotene, and chlorophyll.
2. **Anti-inflammatory Effects**:
   a. **Benefit**: Reduces inflammation, potentially benefiting conditions like arthritis and asthma.
   b. **Compounds**: Phycocyanin and GLA.
3. **Immune System Support**:
   a. **Benefit**: Enhances immune response and increases the production of antibodies.
   b. **Compounds**: Polysaccharides and phycocyanin.

4. **Detoxification**:
   a. **Benefit**: Helps in detoxifying heavy metals and other toxins from the body.
   b. **Compounds**: Chlorophyll and polysaccharides.
5. **Cardiovascular Health**:
   a. **Benefit**: Lowers cholesterol levels, blood pressure, and reduces the risk of cardiovascular diseases.
   b. **Compounds**: GLA, beta-carotene, and other antioxidants.
6. **Anti-Cancer Potential**:
   a. **Benefit**: Some studies suggest that spirulina can inhibit the growth of cancer cells.
   b. **Compounds**: Phycocyanin and beta-carotene.
7. **Anti-Viral and Anti-Bacterial Properties**:
   a. **Benefit**: Spirulina has been shown to inhibit the replication of certain viruses and bacteria.
   b. **Compounds**: Polysaccharides and phycocyanin.
8. **Improving Gut Health**:
   a. **Benefit**: Acts as a prebiotic, promoting the growth of beneficial gut bacteria.
   b. **Compounds**: Polysaccharides.
9. **Supporting Eye Health**:
   a. **Benefit**: High levels of beta-carotene and other carotenoids support vision and overall eye health.
   b. **Compounds**: Beta-carotene and chlorophyll.
10. **Enhancing Physical Performance**:
    a. **Benefit**: Provides high protein content and essential amino acids, aiding in muscle repair and growth.
    b. **Compounds**: Proteins and amino acids.

SOYA BEAN

Soya bean (Glycine max) is a legume widely recognized for its high protein content and numerous health benefits. It is a staple in many diets and is used as a nutraceutical due to its rich composition of bioactive compounds.

Sources

Soya beans are primarily cultivated in:

1. **United States**: Major producer with vast areas dedicated to soybean farming.
2. **Brazil**: Another leading producer with extensive cultivation.
3. **Argentina**: Significant exporter of soy products.
4. **China**: Both a producer and major consumer of soybeans.
5. **India**: Increasing production and consumption of soy-based products.

Marker Compounds and Chemical Nature

1. **Isoflavones**: Phytoestrogens with antioxidant properties.
    a. **Chemical Nature**: Polyphenolic compounds. Key isoflavones include genistein, daidzein, and glycitein.
2. **Proteins**: High-quality plant proteins.
    a. **Chemical Nature**: Complex molecules composed of amino acids. Key proteins include glycinin and beta-conglycinin.
3. **Saponins**: Compounds with cholesterol-lowering properties.
    a. **Chemical Nature**: Glycosides with a steroid or triterpenoid structure.
4. **Phytosterols**: Plant sterols that help lower cholesterol.
    a. **Chemical Nature**: Steroid compounds similar to cholesterol.
5. **Lecithin**: Phospholipid with emulsifying properties.
    a. **Chemical Nature**: Phosphatidylcholine, a major component of cell membranes.
6. **Vitamins and Minerals**: Rich in vitamins (B complex, vitamin E) and minerals (calcium, iron, magnesium).

a. **Chemical Nature**: Various chemical forms such as tocopherols for vitamin E and chelated minerals.

Medicinal Uses and Health Benefits

1. **Cardiovascular Health**:
   a. **Benefit**: Soy protein helps reduce LDL cholesterol levels and improve heart health.
   b. **Compounds**: Proteins, saponins, and phytosterols.

2. **Bone Health**:
   a. **Benefit**: Isoflavones like genistein help maintain bone density and reduce the risk of osteoporosis.
   b. **Compounds**: Isoflavones and calcium.

3. **Hormonal Balance**:
   a. **Benefit**: Isoflavones act as phytoestrogens, which can alleviate menopausal symptoms and improve hormonal balance.
   b. **Compounds**: Genistein and daidzein.

4. **Anti-Cancer Properties**:
   a. **Benefit**: Isoflavones have been shown to reduce the risk of certain cancers, particularly breast and prostate cancer.
   b. **Compounds**: Genistein and daidzein.

5. **Antioxidant Activity**:
   a. **Benefit**: Reduces oxidative stress and protects cells from damage.
   b. **Compounds**: Isoflavones, saponins, and vitamin E.

6. **Weight Management**:
   a. **Benefit**: High protein content aids in satiety and weight control.
   b. **Compounds**: Proteins and fiber.

7. **Diabetes Management**:
   a. **Benefit**: Improves insulin sensitivity and regulates blood sugar levels.
   b. **Compounds**: Proteins and isoflavones.

8. **Digestive Health**:

a. **Benefit**: Lecithin and dietary fiber promote healthy digestion and gut health.

b. **Compounds**: Lecithin and fiber.

9. **Immune Support**:

a. **Benefit**: Enhances immune function and reduces inflammation.

b. **Compounds**: Proteins, saponins, and isoflavones.

GINSENG

Ginseng is one of the most well-known and widely used herbs in traditional medicine and modern nutraceuticals. Here's a detailed overview of its sources, marker compounds, chemical nature, medicinal uses, and health benefits:

Sources

Ginseng is primarily sourced from the roots of plants in the genus Panax. The two main types are:

1. **Asian Ginseng (Panax ginseng)**

2. **American Ginseng (Panax quinquefolius)**

Both species are native to different regions: Panax ginseng is found in China, Korea, and Siberia, while Panax quinquefolius is native to North America.

Marker Compounds and Chemical Nature

The primary active compounds in ginseng are **ginsenosides**, a class of steroid glycosides and triterpene saponins. There are over 100 different ginsenosides identified, but some of the most important ones include:

1. Rb1

2. Rb2

3. Rc

4. Rd

5. Re

6. Rf

7. Rg1

8. Rg3

9. Rh1

These ginsenosides have diverse structures and can be categorized into two major types based on their chemical nature:

1. **Protopanaxadiol (PPD) ginsenosides**: Such as Rb1, Rb2, Rc, and Rd.

2. **Protopanaxatriol (PPT) ginsenosides**: Such as Re, Rf, and Rg1.

Medicinal Uses and Health Benefits

Ginseng has a broad spectrum of medicinal uses and health benefits attributed to its bioactive compounds, primarily ginsenosides:

1. **Adaptogenic Effects**: Ginseng is known as an adaptogen, helping the body resist stress and maintain homeostasis.

2. **Immune System Enhancement**: Ginseng boosts the immune system, increasing resistance to infections and diseases.

3. **Antioxidant Properties**: Ginsenosides have potent antioxidant effects, protecting cells from damage caused by free radicals.

4. **Anti-inflammatory Effects**: Ginseng reduces inflammation and may be beneficial in managing inflammatory conditions.

5. **Cognitive Function**: Ginseng is believed to improve cognitive function, memory, and concentration. It may be helpful in managing neurodegenerative diseases like Alzheimer's.

6. **Energy and Stamina**: Ginseng is used to enhance physical performance, reduce fatigue, and increase energy levels.

7. **Blood Sugar Regulation**: Ginseng can help regulate blood sugar levels, making it beneficial for people with diabetes.

8. **Cardiovascular Health**: Ginseng improves blood circulation, reduces blood pressure, and has protective effects on the heart.

9. **Anti-cancer Properties**: Some studies suggest that ginsenosides have anti-cancer properties, inhibiting the growth and spread of cancer cells.

10. **Sexual Health**: Ginseng is used to improve sexual performance and treat erectile dysfunction.

Mechanism of Action

The health benefits of ginseng are primarily due to its interaction with various cellular pathways:

1. **Modulation of Immune Response**: Ginsenosides modulate the immune system by enhancing the activity of natural killer cells, macrophages, and T-lymphocytes.

2. **Antioxidant Defense**: Ginsenosides increase the expression of antioxidant enzymes like superoxide dismutase (SOD) and catalase (CAT), reducing oxidative stress.

3. **Anti-inflammatory Pathways**: Ginsenosides inhibit the production of pro-inflammatory cytokines and enzymes like COX-2 and iNOS.

4. **Neuroprotective Effects**: Ginsenosides promote neuroprotection by enhancing the production of neurotrophic factors and reducing apoptosis in neuronal cells.

5. **Metabolic Regulation**: Ginseng affects glucose metabolism by enhancing insulin sensitivity and promoting glucose uptake in cells.

GARLIC

Garlic (Allium sativum) is a widely recognized and utilized herb in both culinary and medicinal contexts. Here's a detailed overview of its sources, marker compounds, chemical nature, medicinal uses, and health benefits:

Sources

Garlic is sourced from the bulb of the Allium sativum plant, which is part of the Allium genus. It is cultivated globally, with significant production in China, India, South Korea, Egypt, and Russia.

Marker Compounds and Chemical Nature

Garlic contains several biologically active compounds, with the most significant being sulfur-containing compounds. The primary marker compounds include:

1. **Allicin**: Formed when garlic is crushed or chopped, it is responsible for garlic's distinct aroma and many of its health benefits.
2. **Diallyl Disulfide (DADS)**
3. **Diallyl Trisulfide (DATS)**
4. **S-allyl-cysteine (SAC)**
5. **Ajoene**: Formed from allicin and is known for its anti-thrombotic properties.

These compounds are highly reactive and can exert multiple beneficial effects on health. Allicin, for instance, is not present in raw garlic but is produced when garlic is chopped or crushed, catalyzed by the enzyme alliinase from alliin.

Medicinal Uses and Health Benefits

Garlic has been used medicinally for thousands of years and continues to be popular in modern nutraceuticals due to its wide range of health benefits:

1. **Cardiovascular Health**: Garlic helps reduce blood pressure, cholesterol levels (total and LDL), and prevents atherosclerosis, thereby supporting heart health.
2. **Antimicrobial Properties**: Garlic has broad-spectrum antimicrobial activity against bacteria, viruses, fungi, and parasites.
3. **Antioxidant Effects**: Garlic contains antioxidants that protect cells against oxidative damage, which is linked to aging and several diseases.
4. **Anti-inflammatory Properties**: The sulfur compounds in garlic can reduce inflammation, beneficial in conditions like arthritis.
5. **Immune System Boost**: Garlic enhances immune function, making the body more resistant to infections and diseases.
6. **Anti-cancer Effects**: Studies suggest garlic can reduce the risk of certain cancers, including stomach and colorectal cancers.
7. **Detoxification**: Garlic promotes detoxification by enhancing liver enzyme function and flushing out toxins.
8. **Blood Sugar Regulation**: Garlic can improve insulin sensitivity and help regulate blood sugar levels, beneficial for people with diabetes.

9. **Improvement in Digestion**: Garlic stimulates digestion and has been used to treat various gastrointestinal issues.

Mechanism of Action

The health benefits of garlic are primarily due to the action of its sulfur-containing compounds:

1. **Cardiovascular Effects**: Garlic lowers blood pressure by promoting vasodilation through the production of hydrogen sulfide (H2S). It also inhibits platelet aggregation, reducing the risk of thrombus formation.

2. **Antimicrobial Activity**: Allicin and other sulfur compounds disrupt microbial cell membranes and inhibit enzyme activities essential for microbial growth.

3. **Antioxidant Mechanisms**: Garlic increases the activity of antioxidant enzymes like glutathione peroxidase and superoxide dismutase, neutralizing free radicals.

4. **Anti-inflammatory Actions**: Garlic reduces the production of pro-inflammatory cytokines and inhibits enzymes like cyclooxygenase (COX) involved in inflammation.

5. **Immune Modulation**: Garlic enhances the activity of immune cells like macrophages, lymphocytes, and natural killer cells.

6. **Anti-cancer Pathways**: Garlic compounds induce apoptosis (programmed cell death) in cancer cells, inhibit cell proliferation, and interfere with cancer cell signaling pathways.

BROCCOLI

Broccoli (Brassica oleracea var. italica) is a highly nutritious vegetable widely studied and utilized in nutraceuticals for its health benefits. Here's a detailed overview of its sources, marker compounds, chemical nature, medicinal uses, and health benefits:

Sources

Broccoli is a cruciferous vegetable belonging to the Brassicaceae family. It is cultivated worldwide, with significant production in China, India, the United States, and Italy. The most commonly consumed parts are the flower heads and stalks.

Marker Compounds and Chemical Nature

Broccoli contains several bioactive compounds, with glucosinolates being the primary marker compounds. Upon hydrolysis, these glucosinolates produce biologically active isothiocyanates. Key compounds include:

1. **Sulforaphane**: A major isothiocyanate derived from glucoraphanin, known for its potent antioxidant and anti-cancer properties.
2. **Indole-3-carbinol (I3C)**: Formed from glucobrassicin, it has been studied for its anti-cancer effects.
3. **Vitamin C**: An essential antioxidant vitamin.
4. **Kaempferol**: A flavonoid with anti-inflammatory and antioxidant properties.
5. **Quercetin**: Another flavonoid with antioxidant and anti-inflammatory effects.

Medicinal Uses and Health Benefits

Broccoli's rich composition of vitamins, minerals, fiber, and phytochemicals contributes to its wide range of medicinal uses and health benefits:

1. **Cancer Prevention**: Sulforaphane and indole-3-carbinol have been shown to inhibit the growth of cancer cells and reduce the risk of various cancers, including breast, prostate, and colorectal cancers.
2. **Detoxification**: Sulforaphane activates phase II detoxification enzymes, enhancing the body's ability to eliminate harmful substances.
3. **Antioxidant Effects**: The high vitamin C content and presence of flavonoids like kaempferol and quercetin help neutralize free radicals, protecting cells from oxidative damage.
4. **Anti-inflammatory Properties**: Broccoli's bioactive compounds can reduce inflammation, beneficial in managing conditions like arthritis.

5. **Heart Health**: Broccoli consumption is linked to reduced risk factors for cardiovascular diseases, such as high blood pressure and cholesterol levels.

6. **Digestive Health**: The high fiber content in broccoli aids in digestion, promotes regular bowel movements, and supports gut health.

7. **Bone Health**: Broccoli contains calcium, vitamin K, and magnesium, essential for maintaining healthy bones.

8. **Immune Support**: The vitamins and minerals in broccoli, particularly vitamin C, boost immune function.

9. **Eye Health**: Broccoli is rich in beta-carotene, lutein, and zeaxanthin, which are important for maintaining healthy vision and protecting against age-related eye disorders.

Mechanism of Action

The health benefits of broccoli are attributed to the synergistic action of its various bioactive compounds:

1. **Cancer Prevention**: Sulforaphane promotes the production of detoxifying enzymes and induces apoptosis in cancer cells. Indole-3-carbinol modulates estrogen metabolism and inhibits the growth of hormone-sensitive cancers.

2. **Detoxification**: Sulforaphane enhances the activity of phase II detoxification enzymes, such as glutathione S-transferase, aiding in the elimination of toxins.

3. **Antioxidant Defense**: Vitamin C and flavonoids like kaempferol and quercetin scavenge free radicals, reducing oxidative stress and preventing cellular damage.

4. **Anti-inflammatory Actions**: Bioactive compounds in broccoli inhibit the production of pro-inflammatory cytokines and enzymes like COX-2, reducing inflammation.

5. **Cardiovascular Protection**: Sulforaphane and other compounds in broccoli improve endothelial function, reduce oxidative stress, and lower cholesterol levels, supporting heart health.

6. **Gut Health**: Dietary fiber in broccoli promotes the growth of beneficial gut bacteria and enhances digestive function.

7. **Bone Health**: Calcium, vitamin K, and magnesium in broccoli contribute to bone mineralization and strength.

8. **Immune Enhancement**: Vitamin C boosts the production and function of white blood cells, enhancing the immune response.

9. **Eye Protection**: Carotenoids like lutein and zeaxanthin protect the eyes from oxidative damage and reduce the risk of age-related macular degeneration.

GREEN AND HERBAL TEA

Green and herbal teas are widely recognized for their numerous health benefits and are popular components of nutraceuticals. Here's a detailed overview of their sources, marker compounds, chemical nature, medicinal uses, and health benefits:

Sources

1. **Green Tea**: Green tea is made from the leaves of the Camellia sinensis plant. It is minimally processed, allowing it to retain its green color and active compounds. Major producers include China, Japan, and India.

2. **Herbal Tea**: Herbal teas are made from various plant materials, including leaves, flowers, seeds, and roots. Unlike green tea, they do not come from the Camellia sinensis plant. Popular herbal teas include chamomile, peppermint, hibiscus, ginger, and rooibos.

Marker Compounds and Chemical Nature

Green Tea:

1. **Catechins**: These are the primary active compounds, including epigallocatechin gallate (EGCG), epicatechin (EC), epicatechin gallate (ECG), and epigallocatechin (EGC).

2. **Caffeine**: A natural stimulant found in varying amounts.

3. **Theanine**: An amino acid known for its calming effects.

4. **Polyphenols**: Including flavonoids, which have strong antioxidant properties.

Herbal Tea:

1. **Essential Oils**: Found in teas like peppermint and chamomile, contributing to their aroma and therapeutic effects.
2. **Flavonoids**: Such as quercetin, kaempferol, and luteolin, which provide antioxidant benefits.
3. **Tannins**: Present in teas like rooibos, known for their astringent properties.
4. **Polysaccharides**: Found in teas like ginger, contributing to immune-boosting effects.

Medicinal Uses and Health Benefits

Green Tea:

1. **Antioxidant Properties**: Catechins, particularly EGCG, are powerful antioxidants that protect cells from damage by free radicals.
2. **Cardiovascular Health**: Regular consumption of green tea is linked to reduced risk of heart disease, lower LDL cholesterol levels, and improved blood vessel function.
3. **Weight Management**: Green tea can boost metabolism and increase fat burning, aiding in weight loss.
4. **Cancer Prevention**: Some studies suggest that the catechins in green tea may help prevent certain types of cancer, including breast, prostate, and colorectal cancers.
5. **Brain Health**: The combination of caffeine and theanine in green tea can improve brain function, enhance mood, and protect against neurodegenerative diseases.
6. **Blood Sugar Regulation**: Green tea can help regulate blood sugar levels and improve insulin sensitivity, beneficial for people with diabetes.
7. **Anti-inflammatory Effects**: Green tea's polyphenols can reduce inflammation and may help manage inflammatory conditions.

Herbal Tea:

1. **Digestive Health**: Teas like peppermint and ginger are well-known for their ability to soothe digestive issues, reduce nausea, and relieve bloating.

2. **Relaxation and Sleep**: Chamomile and valerian root teas have calming effects, promoting relaxation and improving sleep quality.

3. **Immune Support**: Herbal teas like echinacea and ginger can boost the immune system, helping to ward off infections.

4. **Anti-inflammatory Properties**: Many herbal teas contain compounds that reduce inflammation, aiding in the management of conditions like arthritis.

5. **Antioxidant Benefits**: Herbal teas such as hibiscus and rooibos are rich in antioxidants, which help protect against oxidative stress and cellular damage.

6. **Hydration**: Herbal teas are a good way to stay hydrated and can be a healthier alternative to sugary drinks.

Mechanism of Action

Green Tea:

1. **Antioxidant Mechanism**: Catechins scavenge free radicals and enhance the activity of antioxidant enzymes, reducing oxidative stress.

2. **Cardiovascular Effects**: Catechins improve endothelial function, reduce LDL oxidation, and inhibit platelet aggregation, protecting against cardiovascular disease.

3. **Metabolic Boost**: Caffeine and catechins synergistically enhance thermogenesis and fat oxidation, promoting weight loss.

4. **Neuroprotective Actions**: EGCG and theanine protect neurons, reduce brain inflammation, and modulate neurotransmitter levels, improving cognitive function.

Herbal Tea:

1. **Digestive Aid**: Essential oils in peppermint and ginger stimulate digestive enzymes and reduce gastrointestinal spasms, aiding digestion.

2. **Calming Effects**: Compounds in chamomile and valerian bind to GABA receptors in the brain, promoting relaxation and sleep.

3. **Immune Modulation**: Polysaccharides and flavonoids in herbal teas enhance immune cell activity, increasing resistance to infections.

4. **Anti-inflammatory Actions**: Flavonoids and essential oils inhibit the production of pro-inflammatory cytokines and enzymes like COX-2, reducing inflammation.

FLAX SEEDS

Flax seeds (Linum usitatissimum) are highly valued in nutraceuticals for their rich nutrient profile and numerous health benefits. Here's a detailed overview of their sources, marker compounds, chemical nature, medicinal uses, and health benefits:

Sources

Flax seeds are harvested from the flax plant (Linum usitatissimum), which is cultivated globally, with significant production in Canada, China, India, and the United States. Flax seeds come in two varieties: brown and golden, both of which offer similar nutritional benefits.

Marker Compounds and Chemical Nature

Flax seeds are known for their unique composition of bioactive compounds, which include:

1. **Alpha-linolenic Acid (ALA)**: An essential omega-3 fatty acid.

2. **Lignans (Secoisolariciresinol Diglucoside - SDG)**: Phytoestrogens with antioxidant properties.

3. **Dietary Fiber**: Both soluble and insoluble fiber.

4. **Proteins**: High-quality plant-based proteins.

5. **Mucilage Gums**: Polysaccharides that provide a gel-forming soluble fiber.

Medicinal Uses and Health Benefits

Flax seeds offer a wide range of medicinal uses and health benefits, largely due to their rich content of omega-3 fatty acids, lignans, and fiber:

1. **Cardiovascular Health**:
   a. **Omega-3 Fatty Acids**: ALA helps reduce inflammation, lower blood pressure, and decrease the risk of cardiovascular diseases.
   b. **Lignans**: These phytoestrogens have antioxidant properties that help lower LDL cholesterol levels and improve overall heart health.
   c. **Fiber**: Soluble fiber in flax seeds helps reduce blood cholesterol levels.
2. **Digestive Health**:
   a. **Dietary Fiber**: Flax seeds are high in both soluble and insoluble fiber, promoting healthy bowel movements and preventing constipation.
   b. **Mucilage Gums**: The gel-forming fiber helps soothe the digestive tract and can be beneficial for conditions like irritable bowel syndrome (IBS).
3. **Anti-inflammatory Effects**:
   a. **ALA**: The omega-3 fatty acids in flax seeds help reduce inflammation, which can be beneficial for conditions like rheumatoid arthritis and other inflammatory diseases.
4. **Cancer Prevention**:
   a. **Lignans**: Flax seeds are one of the richest sources of lignans, which have been shown to have anti-cancer properties, particularly in hormone-related cancers like breast and prostate cancer.
5. **Hormonal Balance**:
   a. **Phytoestrogens**: Lignans in flax seeds can help balance hormones, which may alleviate symptoms of menopause and improve reproductive health.
6. **Weight Management**:
   a. **Fiber**: The high fiber content promotes a feeling of fullness, reducing overall calorie intake and aiding in weight management.
7. **Skin Health**:

a. **Omega-3 Fatty Acids**: ALA helps maintain skin health by keeping it hydrated and reducing inflammation that can lead to skin conditions like acne and eczema.

8. **Blood Sugar Regulation**:

   a. **Fiber and Lignans**: The fiber in flax seeds helps stabilize blood sugar levels, making it beneficial for people with diabetes.

Mechanism of Action

1. **Cardiovascular Protection**:

   a. **ALA** reduces inflammatory markers and decreases triglyceride levels.

   b. **Lignans** act as antioxidants, preventing oxidative damage to blood vessels and lowering LDL cholesterol.

   c. **Soluble Fiber** forms a gel in the digestive tract that can bind to cholesterol and bile acids, facilitating their excretion.

2. **Digestive Health**:

   a. **Insoluble Fiber** adds bulk to stool, promoting regular bowel movements.

   b. **Soluble Fiber and Mucilage Gums** form a gel that slows down digestion, promoting nutrient absorption and soothing the digestive tract.

3. **Anti-inflammatory Effects**:

   a. **ALA** is converted into eicosapentaenoic acid (EPA) and docosahexaenoic acid (DHA), which are potent anti-inflammatory agents.

   b. **Lignans** inhibit the production of pro-inflammatory cytokines.

4. **Cancer Prevention**:

   a. **Lignans** modulate hormone metabolism and inhibit the growth of hormone-dependent cancer cells.

   b. **Antioxidant Properties** of lignans protect cells from DNA damage.

5. **Hormonal Balance**:

a. **Phytoestrogens** in lignans mimic estrogen, balancing hormone levels and alleviating menopausal symptoms.

6. **Weight Management**:

    a. **Fiber** promotes satiety, reducing overall food intake and aiding in weight control.

7. **Skin Health**:

    a. **ALA** maintains skin barrier function and reduces inflammation.

8. **Blood Sugar Regulation**:

    a. **Soluble Fiber** slows carbohydrate digestion and absorption, stabilizing blood sugar levels.

BLACK COHOSH

Black cohosh (Actaea racemosa, formerly known as Cimicifuga racemosa) is a plant commonly used in nutraceuticals for its potential benefits in managing menopausal symptoms and other health conditions. Here's a detailed overview of its sources, marker compounds, chemical nature, medicinal uses, and health benefits:

Sources

Black cohosh is a perennial herb native to North America, particularly found in woodland areas. It has been used traditionally by Native American tribes and is now widely cultivated for medicinal purposes.

Marker Compounds and Chemical Nature

Black cohosh contains several bioactive compounds, with the most significant being:

1. **Triterpene Glycosides**:

    a. **Actein**

    b. **27-Deoxyactein**

2. **Phenolic Acids**:

    a. **Ferulic Acid**

    b. **Caffeic Acid**

3. **Flavonoids**:

   a. **Quercetin**

   b. **Kaempferol**

4. **Alkaloids**:

   a. **N-Methylcytisine**

5. **Resins** and **Tannins**: Contributing to the overall bioactivity of the plant.

Medicinal Uses and Health Benefits

Black cohosh has been extensively studied for its medicinal properties, particularly in relation to women's health. Its primary uses and health benefits include:

1. **Menopausal Symptom Relief**:

   a. **Hot Flashes and Night Sweats**: Black cohosh is commonly used to reduce the frequency and severity of hot flashes and night sweats in menopausal women.

   b. **Mood Swings and Anxiety**: It can help alleviate mood disturbances and anxiety associated with menopause.

   c. **Sleep Disturbances**: It has been reported to improve sleep quality in menopausal women.

2. **Premenstrual Syndrome (PMS)**:

   a. **Menstrual Cramps**: Black cohosh can reduce the severity of menstrual cramps.

   b. **Mood Swings and Irritability**: It may help in managing mood swings and irritability during the premenstrual period.

3. **Anti-inflammatory Effects**:

   a. **Arthritis and Musculoskeletal Pain**: The anti-inflammatory properties of black cohosh make it useful in managing arthritis and muscle pain.

4. **Bone Health**:

a. **Osteoporosis Prevention**: Black cohosh may help prevent bone loss in postmenopausal women, thereby reducing the risk of osteoporosis.

5. **Antioxidant Properties**:

a. **Cell Protection**: The antioxidant compounds in black cohosh help protect cells from oxidative stress and damage.

Mechanism of Action

1. **Estrogenic Activity**:

a. **Phytoestrogens**: Black cohosh contains compounds that mimic estrogen, which can bind to estrogen receptors and help balance hormone levels, alleviating menopausal symptoms.

2. **Serotonergic Effects**:

a. **Neurotransmitter Modulation**: Black cohosh may influence serotonin levels, which can improve mood and reduce anxiety.

3. **Anti-inflammatory Mechanism**:

a. **Inhibition of Inflammatory Mediators**: The compounds in black cohosh can inhibit the production of pro-inflammatory cytokines and enzymes like COX-2, reducing inflammation.

4. **Antioxidant Activity**:

a. **Scavenging Free Radicals**: The phenolic acids and flavonoids in black cohosh neutralize free radicals, protecting cells from oxidative damage.

TURMERIC

Turmeric (Curcuma longa) is a widely studied herb and spice known for its medicinal properties and health benefits. Here's a detailed overview of its sources, marker compounds, chemical nature, medicinal uses, and health benefits:

Sources

Turmeric is derived from the rhizomes (underground stems) of the Curcuma longa plant, which is native to South Asia. India is the largest producer and exporter of turmeric globally.

Marker Compounds and Chemical Nature

Turmeric contains several bioactive compounds, with the most notable being:

1. **Curcuminoids**:
   a. **Curcumin**: The primary curcuminoid responsible for most of turmeric's biological effects.
   b. **Demethoxycurcumin**
   c. **Bisdemethoxycurcumin**
2. **Turmerones**: Aromatic compounds found in turmeric oil.
3. **Curcumin** is the most extensively studied compound in turmeric and is known for its potent antioxidant, anti-inflammatory, and anticancer properties.

Medicinal Uses and Health Benefits

Turmeric has been used in traditional medicine for centuries and is now widely recognized for its numerous health benefits:

1. **Anti-inflammatory Effects**:
   a. Turmeric's curcuminoids possess strong anti-inflammatory properties, helping to reduce inflammation and symptoms of inflammatory conditions such as arthritis and inflammatory bowel diseases.
2. **Antioxidant Properties**:
   a. Curcumin acts as a powerful antioxidant, scavenging free radicals and reducing oxidative stress, which can protect cells and tissues from damage.
3. **Pain Relief**:
   a. Turmeric has analgesic properties and is used to alleviate pain, particularly in conditions like arthritis and muscle soreness.
4. **Digestive Health**:

a. Turmeric aids digestion and may help alleviate symptoms of indigestion, bloating, and gas.

5. **Liver Health**:

a. It supports liver function and may help protect the liver from toxins and damage.

6. **Heart Health**:

a. Curcumin may improve endothelial function, reduce cholesterol levels, and inhibit platelet aggregation, thereby supporting cardiovascular health.

7. **Cognitive Health**:

a. Turmeric may have neuroprotective effects and could potentially help in the prevention or management of neurodegenerative diseases like Alzheimer's disease.

8. **Anti-cancer Properties**:

a. Curcumin has been studied for its potential role in cancer prevention and treatment, with research showing its ability to inhibit cancer cell growth and induce apoptosis (cell death) in various types of cancer.

9. **Immune Modulation**:

a. Turmeric may help modulate the immune system, enhancing its ability to fight infections and diseases.

Mechanism of Action

1. **Anti-inflammatory Mechanism**:

a. Curcumin inhibits the activity of inflammatory enzymes and mediators, such as cyclooxygenase-2 (COX-2) and prostaglandins, thereby reducing inflammation.

2. **Antioxidant Activity**:

a. Curcumin neutralizes free radicals and enhances the activity of antioxidant enzymes in the body, protecting cells and tissues from oxidative damage.

3. **Pain Relief**:

   a. Turmeric's analgesic effects may involve modulation of pain perception pathways and reduction of inflammatory pain.

4. **Digestive Benefits**:

   a. Turmeric stimulates bile production, which aids in fat digestion, and exhibits anti-inflammatory effects in the gastrointestinal tract.

5. **Liver Protection**:

   a. Curcumin supports liver detoxification pathways and may help prevent liver damage caused by toxins and diseases.

6. **Heart Health Effects**:

   a. Curcumin improves endothelial function, which enhances blood vessel dilation and reduces blood pressure. It also inhibits the oxidation of LDL cholesterol, thereby reducing cardiovascular risk.

7. **Neuroprotective Actions**:

   a. Curcumin crosses the blood-brain barrier and may help reduce oxidative damage, inflammation, and beta-amyloid plaques associated with Alzheimer's disease and other neurodegenerative disorders.

8. **Anti-cancer Mechanisms**:

   a. Curcumin interferes with multiple cell signaling pathways involved in cancer development and progression, including those regulating cell proliferation, apoptosis, and angiogenesis (formation of new blood vessels).

MCQs

1. Who coined the term "Nutraceuticals"?

   a) Dr. John Smith

   b) Dr. Stephen DeFelice

   c) Dr. Jane Doe

d) Dr. Robert Brown

2. What is the primary source of omega-3 fatty acids in nutraceuticals?

   a) Vitamin C

   b) Probiotics

   c) Fish oil supplements

   d) Calcium

3. Which category of nutraceuticals includes live microorganisms that confer health benefits?

   a) Functional Foods

   b) Probiotics

   c) Herbal Nutraceuticals

   d) Medical Foods

4. Which compound in turmeric is responsible for its potent antioxidant properties?

   a) Lignans

   b) Curcumin

   c) Allicin

   d) Sulforaphane

5. Which nutraceutical is known for its ability to alleviate menopausal symptoms?

   a) Spirulina

   b) Black cohosh

   c) Garlic

   d) Broccoli

6. What is the major isothiocyanate derived from glucoraphanin in broccoli?

   a) Indole-3-carbinol

   b) Curcumin

   c) Sulforaphane

   d) Phycocyanin

7. Which component of green tea is primarily responsible for its antioxidant activity?

   a) Theanine

   b) Catechins

   c) Polyphenols

   d) Caffeine

8. Which plant is primarily used to produce flax seeds?

   a) Curcuma longa

   b) Allium sativum

   c) Panax ginseng

   d) Linum usitatissimum

9. What is the primary active compound in garlic responsible for its health benefits?

   a) Beta-Carotene

   b) Allicin

   c) Curcumin

   d) Actein

10. Which nutraceutical is recognized for its ability to reduce blood pressure and cholesterol levels?

   a) Spirulina

   b) Black cohosh

   c) Garlic

   d) Soya bean

11. What is the primary health benefit of consuming dietary fiber from flax seeds?

   a) Enhancing cognitive function

   b) Promoting digestive health

   c) Reducing inflammation

   d) Supporting cardiovascular health

12. Which compound in soybeans is known for its antioxidant properties?

   a) Actein

   b) Curcumin

   c) Isoflavones

   d) Sulforaphane

13. Which nutraceutical contains triterpene glycosides as one of its significant compounds?

   a) Spirulina

   b) Black cohosh

   c) Garlic

   d) Broccoli

14. Which of the following is NOT a category of nutraceuticals?

   a) Dietary Supplements

   b) Functional Foods

   c) Prescription Drugs

   d) Medical Foods

15. Which compound in Spirulina contributes to its anti-inflammatory properties?

   a) Chlorophyll

   b) Beta-Carotene

   c) Phycocyanin

   d) Polysaccharides

16. Which nutrient in soybeans helps in maintaining bone density?

   a) Vitamin C

   b) Isoflavones

   c) Allicin

   d) Curcumin

17. Which flavonoid is found in black cohosh and contributes to its overall bioactivity?

a) Quercetin

b) Theanine

c) Catechins

d) Piperine

18. Which component of herbal teas like peppermint aids in digestion?

a) Polyphenols

b) Essential Oils

c) Tannins

d) Polysaccharides

19. What is the primary health benefit of sulforaphane in broccoli?

a) Enhancing muscle growth

b) Reducing blood sugar levels

c) Cancer prevention

d) Supporting eye health

20. Which compound in turmeric has been studied for its potential role in cancer prevention?

a) Beta-Carotene

b) Chlorophyll

c) Curcumin

d) Isoflavones

Short Answer Type Questions

1. Who coined the term "Nutraceuticals" and in what year?

2. What are dietary supplements, and can you provide three examples?

3. Describe functional foods and give two examples.

4. What are herbal nutraceuticals? Name two examples.

5. What are the main uses of nutritional supplements for sports and fitness?

6. Define medical foods and provide one example.

7. What are cosmeceuticals and how are they used?

8. Explain the difference between probiotics and prebiotics.

9. What are the benefits of omega fatty acids in nutraceuticals?

10. How do antioxidants in nutraceuticals benefit health?

11. What is the role of anti-inflammatory nutraceuticals? Provide one example.

12. How do nutraceuticals support hormonal modulation?

13. Describe the neuroprotective effects of nutraceuticals.

14. Explain how nutraceuticals can modulate gut microbiota.

15. How can nutraceuticals enhance nutrient absorption and utilization?

16. What is the significance of gene expression modulation by nutraceuticals?

17. Provide two benefits of dietary supplements.

18. What is the primary health benefit of functional foods?

19. How do herbal nutraceuticals support wellness?

20. What are the main health benefits of consuming flax seeds?

Long Answer Type Questions

1. Describe the various categories of nutraceuticals and provide examples for each.

2. Explain the mechanisms of action through which nutraceuticals exert their beneficial effects on health.

3. Discuss the regulatory aspects of nutraceuticals in the United States, European Union, and Canada.

4. What are the challenges faced by the nutraceutical industry, and what are the potential future directions for the sector?

5. Explain the sources, marker compounds, chemical nature, medicinal uses, and health benefits of Spirulina.

6. Describe the health benefits of soybeans and the bioactive compounds responsible for these benefits.

7. Discuss the medicinal uses and health benefits of ginseng, including its mechanism of action.

8. Explain how garlic contributes to cardiovascular health and its other medicinal uses.

9. Describe the bioactive compounds in broccoli and their role in health promotion.

10. Discuss the health benefits of green and herbal teas, including their mechanisms of action and examples of popular herbal teas.

Answer Key

1. (b) Dr. Stephen DeFelice

2. (c) Fish oil supplements

3. (b) Probiotics

4. (b) Curcumin

5. (b) Black cohosh

6. (c) Sulforaphane

7. (b) Catechins

8. (d) Linum usitatissimum

9. (b) Allicin

10. (c) Garlic

11. (b) Promoting digestive health

12. (c) Isoflavones

13. (b) Black cohosh

14. (c) Prescription Drugs

15. (c) Phycocyanin

16. (b) Isoflavones

17. (a) Quercetin

18. (b) Essential Oils

19. (c) Cancer prevention

20. (c) Curcumin

CHAPTER – 5

PHYTOPHARMACEUTICALS

INTRODUCTION;

Phytopharmaceuticals are medicinal products derived from plants, which have been used for centuries in traditional medicine systems worldwide. These natural compounds are valued for their therapeutic properties and are often developed into pharmaceutical drugs or dietary supplements. Here's an introduction to phytopharmaceuticals in detail:

1. **Natural Origin**: Phytopharmaceuticals are derived from various parts of plants, including leaves, roots, bark, flowers, and fruits. They contain biologically active compounds such as alkaloids, flavonoids, terpenoids, and polyphenols, which contribute to their medicinal properties.

2. **Traditional and Modern Use**: Many phytopharmaceuticals have been used traditionally for treating various ailments like infections, inflammation, pain, and digestive disorders. Modern research aims to validate these traditional uses and explore new therapeutic applications.

3. **Drug Development**: Phytopharmaceuticals serve as sources for developing pharmaceutical drugs. Examples include aspirin (derived from willow bark), digoxin (from foxglove), and artemisinin (from sweet wormwood), which have been successfully developed into effective medications.

4. **Safety and Efficacy**: While phytopharmaceuticals are generally considered natural and safe, their efficacy and safety profiles vary widely. Standardization of active ingredients and quality control are essential to ensure consistency and minimize potential side effects.

5. **Research and Innovation**: Ongoing research focuses on identifying new phytopharmaceuticals, understanding their mechanisms of action, and

optimizing their therapeutic benefits. This includes studying synergistic effects of plant compounds and exploring novel delivery systems.

6. **Regulation**: Regulatory agencies worldwide oversee the safety, efficacy, and quality of phytopharmaceuticals. Standards and regulations ensure that these products meet pharmaceutical quality standards and are safe for consumer use.

Phytopharmaceuticals represent a fascinating intersection of traditional knowledge and modern scientific exploration, offering potential benefits for healthcare through natural plant-based remedies.

CAROTENOIDS

1. α and β-Carotene:

Occurrence:

a. **Sources:** α and β-carotene are abundant in various fruits and vegetables, particularly those with vibrant orange, yellow, and red colors. Examples include carrots, sweet potatoes, pumpkins, and spinach.

Isolation and Characteristic Features:

a. **Chemical Nature:** α and β-carotene are carotenoids, which are tetraterpenoids consisting of eight isoprene units. They are hydrocarbons with conjugated double bonds, imparting their characteristic color and antioxidant properties.

b. **Isolation:** Extraction methods involve solvent extraction from plant tissues followed by purification using techniques like chromatography.

Uses in Pharmacy:

a. **Pharmaceutical Applications:** α and β-carotene are primarily used as dietary supplements and as precursors for vitamin A synthesis in the body. They are included in formulations for their antioxidant properties and potential health benefits.

Medicinal and Health Benefits:

a. **Antioxidant Activity:** Both carotenes exhibit potent antioxidant properties, scavenging free radicals that can damage cells and contribute to chronic diseases.

b. **Provitamin A Activity:** β-carotene is a precursor of vitamin A (retinol), essential for vision, immune function, and skin health.

c. **Potential Anti-cancer Effects:** Some studies suggest that carotenoids may reduce the risk of certain cancers, although more research is needed.

2. Xanthophyll (Lutein):

Occurrence:

a. **Sources:** Lutein is a xanthophyll present in green leafy vegetables like spinach, kale, and broccoli, as well as in egg yolks.

Isolation and Characteristic Features:

a. **Chemical Nature:** Lutein is a xanthophyll carotenoid with hydroxyl groups on each ionone ring. It has a molecular structure similar to β-carotene but with additional oxygen atoms.

b. **Isolation:** Similar to other carotenoids, lutein is extracted from plant sources and purified using chromatographic methods.

Uses in Pharmacy:

a. **Pharmaceutical Applications:** Lutein is commonly used as a dietary supplement, particularly for eye health formulations aimed at reducing the risk of age-related macular degeneration (AMD) and cataracts.

Medicinal and Health Benefits:

a. **Eye Health:** Lutein, along with zeaxanthin (another xanthophyll), accumulates in the retina where they filter blue light and act as antioxidants, protecting against oxidative damage and supporting visual function.

b. **Skin Health:** Some research suggests that lutein may benefit skin health by reducing oxidative stress and inflammation associated with UV radiation exposure.

LIMONOIDS

1. d-Limonene:

Occurrence:

a. **Sources:** d-Limonene is a naturally occurring monoterpene found in the peels of citrus fruits such as oranges, lemons, and limes. It is also present in various other plants, including juniper, peppermint, and rosemary.

Isolation and Characteristic Features:

a. **Chemical Nature:** d-Limonene is a cyclic monoterpene hydrocarbon with a molecular formula $C_{10}H_{16}$. It consists of two isoprene units and has a chiral center, existing in both dextrorotatory (d-) and levorotatory (l-) forms.

b. **Isolation:** It is typically extracted from citrus peel oils through steam distillation or cold-pressing methods. Further purification can be achieved through fractional distillation.

Uses in Pharmacy:

a. **Pharmaceutical Applications:** d-Limonene is utilized in pharmacy for its aromatic properties and potential medicinal benefits. It is also used as a flavoring agent in food and beverages.

b. **Solvent:** It serves as a natural solvent for various substances and is used in formulations for its ability to dissolve oils and as a carrier in topical preparations.

Medicinal and Health Benefits:

a. **Digestive Aid:** d-Limonene is known for its gastroprotective effects and is used to relieve symptoms of heartburn and gastroesophageal reflux disease (GERD).

b. **Antioxidant and Anti-inflammatory:** It exhibits antioxidant properties, scavenging free radicals, and anti-inflammatory effects that may contribute to its therapeutic benefits.

2. α-Terpineol:

Occurrence:

a. **Sources:** α-Terpineol is a monoterpene alcohol naturally found in essential oils of various plants, including pine, eucalyptus, and tea tree.

Isolation and Characteristic Features:

a. **Chemical Nature:** α-Terpineol has the molecular formula $C_{10}H_{18}O$ and belongs to the class of terpene alcohols. It has a hydroxyl group (-OH) attached to a terpene structure, making it water-soluble and aromatic.

b. **Isolation:** It is extracted from plant essential oils through distillation processes, such as steam distillation or solvent extraction, followed by purification.

Uses in Pharmacy:

a. **Pharmaceutical Applications:** α-Terpineol is utilized in pharmaceutical formulations for its pleasant aroma and potential therapeutic effects. It is also used as a fragrance ingredient in cosmetics and personal care products.

b. **Antimicrobial Properties:** It exhibits antimicrobial activity against various pathogens, making it useful in topical applications and as a preservative in formulations.

Medicinal and Health Benefits:

a. **Sedative and Relaxant:** α-Terpineol has calming properties and is used in aromatherapy for its relaxing effects on the central nervous system.

b. **Anti-inflammatory:** It shows potential anti-inflammatory effects, which may be beneficial for reducing inflammation in topical applications.

SAPONINS

1. Shatavarins:

Occurrence:

a. **Sources:** Shatavarins are predominantly found in the roots of *Asparagus racemosus*, a species of asparagus native to India and other parts of Asia. It is widely cultivated for its medicinal properties in Ayurvedic and traditional medicine systems.

Isolation and Characteristic Features:

a. **Chemical Nature:** Shatavarins are steroidal saponins, which are glycosides consisting of a steroidal aglycone (sapogenin) and one or more sugar chains (glycone). The specific structure of shatavarins includes complex glycosidic bonds attached to the steroidal core.

b. **Isolation:** Extraction of shatavarins involves pulverizing the dried roots of *Asparagus racemosus* followed by solvent extraction. Further purification and isolation are achieved through techniques such as chromatography.

Uses in Pharmacy:

a. **Pharmaceutical Applications:** Shatavarins are utilized in pharmacy and herbal medicine formulations due to their various pharmacological activities. They are often included in preparations such as powders, capsules, and extracts.

b. **Adaptogenic Properties:** Shatavarins are classified as adaptogens, substances that help the body adapt to stress and support overall health and well-being.

Medicinal and Health Benefits:

a. **Female Reproductive Health:** In Ayurvedic medicine, shatavarins are traditionally used to support female reproductive health. They are believed to balance hormones, regulate menstrual cycles, and enhance fertility.

b. **Anti-inflammatory and Immunomodulatory:** Shatavarins exhibit anti-inflammatory properties, which can benefit conditions such as arthritis and inflammatory bowel diseases. They also modulate the immune system, enhancing immune response.

c. **Antioxidant Activity:** Shatavarins possess antioxidant properties, scavenging free radicals that contribute to oxidative stress and aging.

d. **Digestive Health:** They may support gastrointestinal health by promoting digestion and soothing digestive discomfort.

FLAVONOIDS

1. **Resveratrol:**

Occurrence:

a. **Sources:** Resveratrol is a polyphenolic compound found in various plants, including grapes (especially in the skin of red grapes), berries (such as blueberries and cranberries), peanuts, and Japanese knotweed (*Polygonum cuspidatum*).

Isolation and Characteristic Features:

a. **Chemical Nature:** Resveratrol belongs to the stilbenoid family of polyphenols. It has a molecular formula $C_{14}H_{12}O_3$ and consists of two phenol rings linked by a styrene double bond.

b. **Isolation:** Extraction methods involve using solvents like ethanol or methanol to extract resveratrol from plant materials. Purification can be achieved through chromatographic techniques.

Uses in Pharmacy:

a. **Pharmaceutical Applications:** Resveratrol is used in dietary supplements and cosmetic formulations due to its antioxidant properties and potential health benefits.

Medicinal and Health Benefits:

a. **Antioxidant and Anti-inflammatory:** Resveratrol exhibits potent antioxidant activity, neutralizing free radicals and reducing oxidative stress. It also has anti-inflammatory effects, which may benefit cardiovascular health and inflammatory conditions.

b. **Cardiovascular Health:** It is studied for its potential to improve cardiovascular function by promoting vasodilation, reducing LDL cholesterol oxidation, and inhibiting platelet aggregation.

c. **Anti-cancer Properties:** Research suggests resveratrol may have anti-cancer effects by interfering with cancer cell proliferation and inducing apoptosis (programmed cell death).

2. **Rutin:**

Occurrence:

a. **Sources:** Rutin, also known as rutoside, is a flavonoid glycoside found in various plants, including citrus fruits (especially in the peel of citrus fruits), buckwheat, asparagus, and tea.

Isolation and Characteristic Features:

a. **Chemical Nature:** Rutin is a flavonol glycoside composed of quercetin and rutinose (a disaccharide consisting of rhamnose and glucose).

b. **Isolation:** It is extracted from plant materials through extraction with water or alcohol followed by purification steps such as crystallization or chromatography.

Uses in Pharmacy:

a. **Pharmaceutical Applications:** Rutin is used in dietary supplements and pharmaceutical formulations for its antioxidant and anti-inflammatory properties.

Medicinal and Health Benefits:

a. **Antioxidant and Anti-inflammatory:** Rutin acts as an antioxidant, protecting cells from oxidative stress. It also has anti-inflammatory effects, which may benefit conditions like arthritis.

b. **Venotonic Effects:** Rutin is known for its venotonic properties, supporting blood vessel health and reducing symptoms of chronic venous insufficiency.

c. **Cardioprotective:** It may help lower blood pressure and reduce the risk of cardiovascular diseases by improving blood vessel function and reducing cholesterol levels.

3. Hesperidin:

Occurrence:

a. **Sources:** Hesperidin is a flavonoid glycoside primarily found in citrus fruits, particularly in the peel and membranes of oranges and lemons.

Isolation and Characteristic Features:

a. **Chemical Nature:** Hesperidin is a flavanone glycoside composed of hesperetin (aglycone) and rutinose (rutinoside).

b. **Isolation:** Extraction methods involve using water or alcohol to extract hesperidin from citrus peels. Further purification is achieved through filtration and chromatography.

Uses in Pharmacy:

a. **Pharmaceutical Applications:** Hesperidin is used in dietary supplements and pharmaceutical formulations for its potential health benefits.

Medicinal and Health Benefits:

a. **Antioxidant Activity:** Hesperidin exhibits antioxidant properties, protecting cells from oxidative damage.

b. **Vascular Health:** It may improve vascular function, reduce inflammation in blood vessels, and support cardiovascular health.

c. **Anti-inflammatory:** Hesperidin shows potential anti-inflammatory effects, which may benefit conditions like allergies and arthritis.

4. Naringin:

Occurrence:

a. **Sources:** Naringin is a flavanone glycoside found in citrus fruits, especially in grapefruit and bitter oranges.

Isolation and Characteristic Features:

a. **Chemical Nature:** Naringin consists of naringenin (aglycone) and a sugar moiety (glycone).

b. **Isolation:** Extraction methods involve using water or alcohol to extract naringin from citrus fruit peels. Purification follows through filtration and chromatography.

Uses in Pharmacy:

a. **Pharmaceutical Applications:** Naringin is used in dietary supplements and pharmaceuticals for its antioxidant properties and potential health benefits.

Medicinal and Health Benefits:

a. **Antioxidant Activity:** Naringin acts as an antioxidant, scavenging free radicals and reducing oxidative stress.

b. **Metabolic Health:** It may help regulate cholesterol levels, improve insulin sensitivity, and support weight management.

c. **Anti-inflammatory:** Naringin exhibits anti-inflammatory effects, which may aid in reducing inflammation in the body.

5. Quercetin:

Occurrence:

a. **Sources:** Quercetin is a flavonoid found in various fruits, vegetables, and grains, including apples, onions, berries, citrus fruits, grapes, broccoli, and leafy greens.

Isolation and Characteristic Features:

a. **Chemical Nature:** Quercetin is a flavonol, characterized by its backbone structure with hydroxyl groups attached to it.

b. **Isolation:** Extraction methods involve using solvents like ethanol or methanol to extract quercetin from plant materials. Purification can be achieved through chromatographic techniques.

Uses in Pharmacy:

a. **Pharmaceutical Applications:** Quercetin is used in dietary supplements, cosmetics, and pharmaceuticals for its antioxidant, anti-inflammatory, and potential therapeutic properties.

Medicinal and Health Benefits:

a. **Antioxidant and Anti-inflammatory:** Quercetin exhibits strong antioxidant activity, protecting cells from oxidative damage. It also has anti-inflammatory effects, which may benefit various inflammatory conditions.

b. **Immune Support:** It supports immune function and may enhance the body's ability to fight infections.

c. **Cardiovascular Health:** Quercetin may improve cardiovascular health by reducing blood pressure, improving endothelial function, and lowering LDL cholesterol levels.

PHENOLIC ACIDS

Ellagic Acid:

Occurrence:

a. **Sources:** Ellagic acid is a naturally occurring polyphenol found in various fruits, nuts, and vegetables. It is particularly abundant in berries such as strawberries, raspberries, blackberries, and pomegranates. It is also found in nuts like walnuts and pecans.

Isolation and Characteristic Features:

a. **Chemical Nature:** Ellagic acid is a polyphenolic compound belonging to the class of hydrolyzable tannins. It has a molecular formula $C_{14}H_6O_8$ and is derived from the oxidative coupling of gallic acid units.

b. **Isolation:** Extraction methods involve using aqueous or alcoholic solvents to extract ellagic acid from plant materials, especially fruit skins and seeds. Purification can be achieved through techniques such as chromatography.

Uses in Pharmacy:

a. **Pharmaceutical Applications:** Ellagic acid is used in dietary supplements, herbal medicines, and cosmetic formulations due to its antioxidant properties and potential health benefits.

Medicinal and Health Benefits:

a. **Antioxidant Activity:** Ellagic acid exhibits strong antioxidant activity, protecting cells from oxidative damage caused by free radicals.

b. **Anti-inflammatory Effects:** It has anti-inflammatory properties, which may help reduce inflammation and associated symptoms.

c. **Anti-cancer Properties:** Research suggests that ellagic acid may have anti-cancer effects by inhibiting the growth of cancer cells, inducing apoptosis (programmed cell death), and preventing the formation of tumors.

d. **Cardiovascular Health:** It may support cardiovascular health by improving blood vessel function, reducing cholesterol levels, and promoting heart health.

e. **Antimicrobial Effects:** Ellagic acid shows antimicrobial activity against various pathogens, suggesting potential benefits for combating infections.

VITAMINS

Vitamins are essential organic compounds that are crucial for various physiological functions in the human body. They can be obtained from various plant sources and are integral to phytopharmaceuticals. Let's explore the occurrence, isolation, characteristic features, uses in pharmacy, and medicinal benefits of some key vitamins found in phytopharmaceuticals:

Vitamins in Phytopharmaceuticals:

i) Vitamin C (Ascorbic Acid):

Vitamin C, also known as ascorbic acid, is a water-soluble vitamin that plays essential roles in human health and is commonly found in phytopharmaceuticals (medicinal products derived from plants). Here's a detailed exploration of vitamin C in phytopharmaceuticals:

Occurrence in Phytopharmaceuticals

a. **Natural Sources**: Vitamin C is abundant in various fruits and vegetables, especially citrus fruits (oranges, lemons), berries (strawberries, raspberries), kiwi, guava, and vegetables such as bell peppers, broccoli, and leafy greens (spinach, kale).

b. **Bioavailability**: The bioavailability of vitamin C from plant-based sources can vary due to factors like cooking methods (which may degrade vitamin C), storage conditions, and individual absorption rates.

Chemical Nature

a. **Chemical Structure**: Ascorbic acid ($C_6H_8O_6$) is a water-soluble vitamin with antioxidant properties. It is a white crystalline solid with a molecular weight of 176.12 g/mol.

Isolation from Plants

a. **Extraction Methods**: Vitamin C can be extracted from plant materials using methods such as:

    i. **Cold Pressing**: Extracting juice from citrus fruits.

ii. **Aqueous Extraction**: Immersing plant tissues in water to release soluble vitamin C.

iii. **Enzymatic Extraction**: Using enzymes to break down plant cell walls and release vitamin C.

b. **Purification**: After extraction, purification techniques like filtration, precipitation, or chromatography are used to isolate and concentrate ascorbic acid from other plant components.

Uses in Pharmacy

a. **Dietary Supplements**: Vitamin C supplements are widely used to prevent and treat vitamin C deficiency, which can lead to scurvy. These supplements come in various forms, including tablets, capsules, and powders.

b. **Topical Formulations**: Vitamin C is incorporated into skin care products such as serums and creams due to its antioxidant properties. It helps protect the skin from oxidative damage caused by free radicals and UV radiation, promotes collagen synthesis, and reduces signs of aging such as wrinkles and fine lines.

c. **Pharmaceutical Applications**: Vitamin C may be used in pharmaceutical formulations to enhance the stability of other active ingredients and improve the bioavailability of certain drugs.

Medicinal Benefits

a. **Antioxidant Activity**: As an antioxidant, vitamin C scavenges free radicals, thereby protecting cells and tissues from oxidative stress. This property is crucial for reducing the risk of chronic diseases like cardiovascular disease and certain cancers.

b. **Immune Support**: Vitamin C supports immune function by enhancing the production and activity of white blood cells, which help defend the body against infections.

c. **Collagen Synthesis**: Vitamin C is essential for collagen formation, a protein that provides structure to skin, bones, cartilage, and blood vessels. Adequate vitamin C intake supports wound healing, tissue repair, and maintaining healthy gums.

d. **Iron Absorption**: Vitamin C enhances the absorption of non-heme iron (from plant-based foods) by reducing it to a more absorbable form in the intestines. This is particularly beneficial for individuals prone to iron deficiency anemia.

Health Benefits

a. **Skin Health**: Topical application of vitamin C helps improve skin hydration, elasticity, and tone. It reduces hyperpigmentation and enhances the skin's natural barrier against environmental stressors.

b. **Cardiovascular Health**: Regular intake of vitamin C may lower the risk of heart disease by improving blood vessel function, reducing inflammation, and lowering blood pressure.

c. **Eye Health**: Vitamin C, along with other antioxidants, supports eye health by protecting against age-related macular degeneration (AMD) and cataracts.

ii) Vitamin E (Tocopherols and Tocotrienols):

Vitamin E encompasses a group of fat-soluble compounds that include tocopherols and tocotrienols, each with unique forms (alpha, beta, gamma, delta) offering distinct health benefits. Found abundantly in phytopharmaceuticals, they are essential for various physiological functions. Here's a detailed exploration of vitamin E in phytopharmaceuticals:

Occurrence in Phytopharmaceuticals

a. **Natural Sources**: Vitamin E is predominantly found in plant-based oils (such as wheat germ oil, sunflower oil, and olive oil), nuts (almonds, hazelnuts), seeds (sunflower seeds, sesame seeds), and green leafy vegetables (spinach, kale).

b. **Variants**: Tocopherols (alpha, beta, gamma, delta) and tocotrienols (alpha, beta, gamma, delta) are the main forms of vitamin E. They differ in the presence of saturated phytyl chain in tocopherols and unsaturated isoprenoid side chain in tocotrienols, influencing their bioavailability and antioxidant properties.

Chemical Nature

a. **Chemical Structure**: Tocopherols and tocotrienols share a similar basic structure consisting of a chromanol ring and a phytyl or isoprenoid side chain. Alpha-tocopherol is the most biologically active form in humans.

b. **Bioavailability**: Tocotrienols, especially delta-tocotrienol, exhibit higher bioavailability and antioxidant activity compared to tocopherols due to their ability to penetrate cell membranes more effectively.

Isolation from Plants

a. **Extraction Methods**: Vitamin E can be extracted from plant sources using techniques such as:

   i. **Cold Pressing**: Extracting oils from seeds or nuts.

   ii. **Solvent Extraction**: Using non-polar solvents like hexane to isolate vitamin E from plant materials.

   iii. **Supercritical Fluid Extraction**: Employing CO_2 to extract vitamin E, which yields high-quality extracts.

b. **Purification**: After extraction, purification methods such as column chromatography or distillation are used to isolate and concentrate tocopherols or tocotrienols.

Uses in Pharmacy

a. **Dietary Supplements**: Vitamin E supplements, often in the form of alpha-tocopherol, are used to prevent vitamin E deficiency and support antioxidant protection in the body.

b. **Topical Formulations**: Tocopherols and tocotrienols are incorporated into skin care products (creams, lotions) for their antioxidant properties, helping to protect against UV damage, reduce wrinkles, and improve skin hydration.

c. **Pharmaceutical Applications**: Vitamin E may be used in pharmaceutical formulations to stabilize sensitive compounds and enhance their bioavailability, especially in lipid-based formulations.

Medicinal Benefits

a. **Antioxidant Activity**: Vitamin E acts as a potent antioxidant, neutralizing free radicals and protecting cell membranes from oxidative damage. This property helps reduce inflammation and oxidative stress associated with chronic diseases.

b. **Cardiovascular Health**: Alpha-tocopherol may help prevent cardiovascular disease by inhibiting LDL oxidation, reducing plaque formation, and improving endothelial function.

c. **Immune Support**: Vitamin E supports immune function by enhancing the activity of immune cells and reducing inflammation, thereby promoting overall immune health.

Health Benefits

a. **Skin Health**: Topical application of vitamin E helps improve skin elasticity, reduce scars, and protect against UV-induced damage, contributing to youthful and healthy skin.

b. **Brain Health**: Tocotrienols, particularly delta-tocotrienol, may protect neurons from oxidative stress and promote cognitive function, potentially reducing the risk of neurodegenerative diseases like Alzheimer's.

c. **Anti-inflammatory Effects**: Vitamin E's antioxidant properties help mitigate inflammation, making it beneficial for conditions like arthritis and inflammatory skin disorders.

iii) Vitamin A (Retinoids and Carotenoids):

Vitamin A encompasses a group of compounds that include retinoids (preformed vitamin A) and carotenoids (provitamin A), each with distinct roles and sources within phytopharmaceuticals. Here's a detailed exploration of vitamin A in phytopharmaceuticals:

Occurrence in Phytopharmaceuticals

a. **Natural Sources**:

1. **Retinoids**: Preformed vitamin A is found in animal sources such as liver, eggs, and dairy products.

2. **Carotenoids**: Provitamin A carotenoids are abundant in various plant-based foods, including:

    i. **Beta-Carotene**: Found in carrots, sweet potatoes, mangoes, and leafy greens.

    ii. **Alpha-Carotene**: Found in carrots, pumpkins, and red peppers.

    iii. **Lycopene**: Found in tomatoes, watermelon, and pink grapefruit.

    iv. **Lutein and Zeaxanthin**: Found in spinach, kale, and other leafy greens.

b. **Bioavailability**: Carotenoids require conversion to retinoids within the body for optimal utilization, with varying efficiencies depending on the specific carotenoid and individual factors.

Chemical Nature

a. **Retinoids**: Retinoids are bioactive forms of vitamin A, including retinol, retinal, and retinoic acid, crucial for vision, growth, immune function, and cellular communication.

b. **Carotenoids**: Provitamin A carotenoids are pigments with antioxidant properties, such as beta-carotene, which the body converts to retinol as needed.

Isolation from Plants

a. **Extraction Methods**: Carotenoids can be extracted from plant sources using methods like:

i. **Solvent Extraction**: Using organic solvents to extract carotenoids from plant tissues.

ii. **Mechanical Extraction**: Cold pressing or grinding to release carotenoids from fruits and vegetables.

iii. **Enzymatic Extraction**: Using enzymes to break down plant cell walls and release carotenoids.

b. **Purification**: After extraction, purification methods like column chromatography or crystallization are employed to isolate and concentrate carotenoids for use in supplements or pharmaceutical formulations.

Uses in Pharmacy

a. **Dietary Supplements**: Vitamin A supplements provide retinoids or carotenoids to prevent deficiency and support various physiological functions, including vision, immune health, and skin integrity.

b. **Topical Formulations**: Retinoids derived from vitamin A are used in dermatological creams and ointments to treat acne, reduce wrinkles, and improve skin texture and tone.

c. **Pharmaceutical Applications**: Retinoids are utilized in pharmaceutical formulations for treating conditions like acne, psoriasis, and certain cancers, owing to their role in regulating cell growth and differentiation.

Medicinal Benefits

a. **Vision Health**: Retinoids are essential for the synthesis of visual pigments in the retina, crucial for low-light and color vision.

b. **Immune Function**: Vitamin A supports immune responses by promoting the production and function of white blood cells, aiding in infection control and immune regulation.

c. **Skin Health**: Retinoids promote skin cell turnover and collagen production, improving skin texture, reducing wrinkles, and treating conditions like acne and photoaging.

Health Benefits

a. **Antioxidant Activity**: Carotenoids, such as beta-carotene, act as antioxidants, protecting cells from oxidative damage caused by free radicals, thus reducing the risk of chronic diseases.

b. **Cancer Prevention**: Carotenoids may help reduce the risk of certain cancers due to their antioxidant properties and potential roles in regulating cell growth and apoptosis.

c. **Cardiovascular Health**: Some carotenoids, like lycopene and lutein/zeaxanthin, support heart health by reducing inflammation, improving cholesterol levels, and protecting blood vessels from damage.

TOCOTRIENOLS AND TOCOPHEROLS

Occurrence:

Tocotrienols and tocopherols, collectively known as vitamin E, are found in phytopharmaceuticals—medicinal products derived from plants—where they play essential roles due to their antioxidant properties and health benefits. Here's a detailed exploration of their occurrence in phytopharmaceuticals:

Occurrence in Plants

a. **Sources of Tocopherols**:

   i. **Vegetable Oils**: Sunflower oil, wheat germ oil, soybean oil, and olive oil are rich sources of alpha-tocopherol, the most biologically active form of vitamin E.

   ii. **Nuts and Seeds**: Almonds, hazelnuts, sunflower seeds, and sesame seeds contain varying amounts of tocopherols.

   iii. **Green Leafy Vegetables**: Spinach, kale, and Swiss chard provide small amounts of tocopherols.

b. **Sources of Tocotrienols**:

   i. **Palm Oil**: Particularly rich in tocotrienols, especially alpha-tocotrienol and gamma-tocotrienol.

   ii. **Rice Bran Oil**: Contains significant amounts of tocotrienols, including alpha-tocotrienol and gamma-tocotrienol.

iii. **Barley and Oats**: Whole grains like barley and oats contain tocotrienols, albeit in lower concentrations compared to oils.

Chemical Nature

a. **Tocopherols**: These are similar in structure to tocotrienols but have a saturated side chain, making them less bioavailable than tocotrienols.

b. **Tocotrienols**: These have an unsaturated isoprenoid side chain, which enhances their penetration into cell membranes and gives them stronger antioxidant properties compared to tocopherols.

Extraction and Isolation

a. **Extraction Methods**: Tocopherols and tocotrienols can be extracted from plant sources using methods such as:

   i. **Solvent Extraction**: Using solvents like hexane to extract vitamin E from seeds, nuts, or plant tissues.

   ii. **Supercritical Fluid Extraction**: Employing CO_2 under high pressure to extract vitamin E, which yields high-quality extracts.

   iii. **Cold Pressing**: Extracting oils from seeds or nuts, which may retain tocopherols and tocotrienols.

b. **Purification**: After extraction, purification techniques like chromatography or crystallization are used to isolate and concentrate tocopherols or tocotrienols from other components of the plant material.

Uses in Phytopharmaceuticals

a. **Dietary Supplements**: Tocopherols and tocotrienols are used in dietary supplements to provide antioxidant support, promote cardiovascular health, and maintain overall well-being.

b. **Topical Formulations**: These compounds are incorporated into skin care products for their antioxidant properties, helping to protect the skin from oxidative stress, reduce signs of aging, and improve skin hydration.

c. **Pharmaceutical Applications**: Tocopherols and tocotrienols may be used in pharmaceutical formulations to enhance the stability of sensitive compounds and improve their bioavailability, especially in lipid-based formulations.

Health Benefits

a. **Antioxidant Activity**: Tocopherols and tocotrienols scavenge free radicals, reducing oxidative damage to cells and tissues, which may contribute to aging and disease development.

b. **Cardiovascular Health**: Alpha-tocopherol, in particular, has been associated with reduced risk of cardiovascular diseases by protecting LDL cholesterol from oxidation and improving endothelial function.

c. **Skin Health**: Topical application of vitamin E can help maintain skin elasticity, reduce inflammation, and protect against UV damage, thereby improving overall skin health.

Isolation and Characteristic Features:

The isolation of tocotrienols and tocopherols from plant sources involves several key steps, including extraction, purification, and concentration. Here's a detailed look at these processes:

1. Extraction Methods

a. **Solvent Extraction**:

    i. **Process**: Plant materials (such as seeds, nuts, or grains) are ground and then mixed with organic solvents like hexane or ethanol. These solvents dissolve the lipophilic (fat-soluble) compounds, including tocopherols and tocotrienols.

    ii. **Advantages**: Efficient for large-scale extraction, relatively simple, and cost-effective.

    iii. **Disadvantages**: Requires removal of solvents from the final product, potential for residual solvent contamination.

b. **Supercritical Fluid Extraction**:

    i. **Process**: Uses supercritical CO_2 (carbon dioxide at high pressure and temperature) to extract tocopherols and tocotrienols from plant materials.

    ii. **Advantages**: Solvent-free, environmentally friendly, produces high-purity extracts.

    iii. **Disadvantages**: Requires specialized equipment and higher initial costs.

c. **Cold Pressing**:

    i. **Process**: Mechanical pressing of oil-rich plant materials (such as nuts and seeds) to extract oils containing tocopherols and tocotrienols.

    ii. **Advantages**: Simple, no solvents required, retains natural properties of the oils.

    iii. **Disadvantages**: Lower yield compared to solvent extraction.

2. Purification Methods

a. **Column Chromatography**:

    i. **Process**: The crude extract is passed through a column packed with a stationary phase (such as silica gel). Different components of the extract separate based on their affinity to the stationary phase, allowing tocopherols and tocotrienols to be collected separately.

    ii. **Advantages**: High resolution, can separate individual tocopherols and tocotrienols.

    iii. **Disadvantages**: Time-consuming, requires skilled operation.

b. **High-Performance Liquid Chromatography (HPLC)**:

    i. **Process**: A high-pressure pump forces the extract through a column filled with a stationary phase. Different components elute at different times, allowing for precise separation and quantification.

ii.   **Advantages**: High precision, suitable for both analytical and preparative purposes.

iii.   **Disadvantages**: Expensive equipment, requires technical expertise.

c. **Crystallization**:

i.   **Process**: The extract is cooled or mixed with a solvent in which tocopherols and tocotrienols have low solubility, causing them to crystallize out.

ii.   **Advantages**: Simple and cost-effective for purifying large quantities.

iii.   **Disadvantages**: Limited to compounds with suitable crystallization properties.

Characteristic Features of Tocotrienols and Tocopherols

Chemical Structure

a. **Tocopherols**:

i.   Structure: Consist of a chromanol ring with a saturated phytyl side chain. They have four forms (alpha, beta, gamma, delta), differing in the number and position of methyl groups on the chromanol ring.

ii.   Example: Alpha-tocopherol (most biologically active form).

b. **Tocotrienols**:

i.   Structure: Similar to tocopherols but with an unsaturated isoprenoid side chain, which includes three double bonds.

ii.   Example: Alpha-tocotrienol (notable for higher antioxidant activity compared to alpha-tocopherol).

Biological Activity

a. **Antioxidant Properties**: Both tocopherols and tocotrienols act as antioxidants, protecting cell membranes from oxidative damage by neutralizing free radicals.

b. **Cardiovascular Health**: Tocotrienols have been shown to lower cholesterol levels and provide neuroprotective effects, whereas tocopherols are primarily associated with preventing the oxidation of LDL cholesterol.

c. **Skin Health**: Topical application of tocopherols and tocotrienols helps protect the skin from UV damage, reduce inflammation, and promote skin healing.

Solubility and Stability

a. **Solubility**: Both tocopherols and tocotrienols are lipophilic, meaning they are soluble in fats and oils but not in water.

b. **Stability**: Tocopherols are generally more stable than tocotrienols, which are more susceptible to oxidation due to their unsaturated side chain. Both require protection from light, heat, and air to maintain their stability during storage and use.

Applications in Phytopharmaceuticals

a. **Dietary Supplements**: Used to prevent vitamin E deficiency and provide antioxidant support.

b. **Topical Formulations**: Included in creams, lotions, and serums for their skin-protective properties.

c. **Pharmaceutical Formulations**: Added to formulations to enhance the stability of active ingredients and improve their bioavailability.

Uses in Pharmacy:

Tocotrienols and tocopherols are two types of vitamin E compounds, each consisting of four isomers (alpha, beta, gamma, and delta). They are important antioxidants found in various foods and have significant uses in pharmacy, particularly in phytopharmaceuticals. Here's a detailed look at their uses:

Tocotrienols

1. Antioxidant Activity

a. **Mechanism:** Tocotrienols have unsaturated side chains, which enhance their ability to penetrate cellular membranes, providing potent antioxidant protection.

b. **Uses:** They help in reducing oxidative stress by neutralizing free radicals, which is beneficial in managing and preventing chronic diseases such as cardiovascular diseases, diabetes, and neurodegenerative disorders.

2. Cardiovascular Health

a. **Mechanism:** Tocotrienols inhibit the enzyme HMG-CoA reductase, which plays a key role in cholesterol synthesis.

b. **Uses:** They are used to lower LDL cholesterol levels and prevent the progression of atherosclerosis. Tocotrienols also help in reducing blood pressure and improving blood vessel function.

3. Neuroprotection

a. **Mechanism:** Tocotrienols protect neurons from oxidative damage and reduce the accumulation of toxic proteins.

b. **Uses:** They are investigated for their potential in preventing and treating neurodegenerative diseases like Alzheimer's and Parkinson's disease.

4. Anti-Cancer Properties

a. **Mechanism:** Tocotrienols induce apoptosis (programmed cell death) in cancer cells and inhibit angiogenesis (the formation of new blood vessels that feed tumors).

b. **Uses:** They are studied for their potential in treating various cancers, including breast, prostate, and pancreatic cancers.

5. Bone Health

a. **Mechanism:** Tocotrienols enhance the differentiation and function of osteoblasts (bone-forming cells) and reduce the activity of osteoclasts (bone-resorbing cells).

b. **Uses:** They are used to prevent osteoporosis and improve bone density.

Tocopherols

1. Antioxidant Activity

a. **Mechanism:** Tocopherols are effective at scavenging lipid peroxyl radicals, protecting cellular membranes from oxidative damage.

b. **Uses:** They are widely used in dietary supplements and skin care products to protect against oxidative stress and maintain skin health.

2. Anti-Inflammatory Properties

a. **Mechanism:** Tocopherols modulate the expression of inflammatory cytokines and enzymes like cyclooxygenase.

b. **Uses:** They help in managing inflammatory conditions such as arthritis and inflammatory bowel disease.

3. Immune System Support

a. **Mechanism:** Tocopherols enhance the function of immune cells and increase the production of antibodies.

b. **Uses:** They are used to boost the immune system, especially in the elderly and immunocompromised individuals.

4. Skin Health

a. **Mechanism:** Tocopherols protect skin cells from UV radiation and environmental pollutants.

b. **Uses:** They are incorporated into topical formulations to prevent and treat skin damage, promote wound healing, and reduce the appearance of scars.

5. Cardiovascular Health

a. **Mechanism:** Tocopherols inhibit lipid peroxidation and improve endothelial function.

b. **Uses:** They help in preventing cardiovascular diseases by reducing oxidative stress and improving blood lipid profiles.

Combined Uses in Phytopharmaceuticals

Phytopharmaceuticals often combine tocotrienols and tocopherols to maximize their therapeutic effects. Their synergistic antioxidant and anti-inflammatory properties make them valuable in:

1. **Anti-Aging Formulations:** Used in supplements and skincare products to protect against age-related oxidative damage.
2. **Nutritional Supplements:** Included in multivitamins and specific vitamin E supplements to support overall health.
3. **Functional Foods:** Added to foods to enhance their nutritional profile and provide health benefits.
4. **Therapeutic Agents:** Investigated for use in various therapeutic applications, including the treatment of chronic diseases, neuroprotection, and cancer therapy.

Medicinal and Health Benefits:

Tocotrienols and tocopherols, both forms of vitamin E, have numerous medicinal and health benefits that make them valuable in phytopharmaceuticals. Here's a detailed overview of their benefits:

Tocotrienols:

1. Cardiovascular Health

   a. **Mechanism:** Tocotrienols inhibit HMG-CoA reductase, reducing cholesterol synthesis and promoting the removal of LDL cholesterol.
   b. **Benefits:** They lower LDL cholesterol levels, reduce arterial plaque formation, and improve blood vessel function, reducing the risk of atherosclerosis and cardiovascular diseases.

2. Neuroprotection

   a. **Mechanism:** Tocotrienols protect neurons from oxidative damage, inhibit neuroinflammation, and reduce the aggregation of toxic proteins.
   b. **Benefits:** They help in preventing neurodegenerative diseases like Alzheimer's and Parkinson's, improve cognitive function, and enhance brain health.

3. Anti-Cancer Properties

    a. **Mechanism:** Tocotrienols induce apoptosis in cancer cells, inhibit angiogenesis, and suppress cancer cell proliferation.

    b. **Benefits:** They show potential in treating various cancers, including breast, prostate, and pancreatic cancers, by slowing tumor growth and enhancing the effectiveness of conventional treatments.

4. Anti-Inflammatory Effects

    a. **Mechanism:** Tocotrienols modulate inflammatory cytokines and pathways.

    b. **Benefits:** They reduce chronic inflammation, which is linked to numerous diseases such as arthritis, cardiovascular diseases, and metabolic syndrome.

5. Bone Health

    a. **Mechanism:** Tocotrienols stimulate osteoblast activity and inhibit osteoclast activity.

    b. **Benefits:** They help in maintaining bone density and preventing osteoporosis, particularly in postmenopausal women.

6. Skin Health

    a. **Mechanism:** Tocotrienols protect skin cells from UV radiation and oxidative stress.

    b. **Benefits:** They improve skin hydration, reduce wrinkles, and promote wound healing and scar reduction.

Tocopherols:

1. Antioxidant Protection

    a. **Mechanism:** Tocopherols scavenge free radicals and prevent lipid peroxidation.

    b. **Benefits:** They protect cells from oxidative damage, reducing the risk of chronic diseases like heart disease, cancer, and age-related macular degeneration.

2. Immune Support

a. **Mechanism:** Tocopherols enhance the function of immune cells and increase antibody production.

b. **Benefits:** They strengthen the immune system, helping to prevent infections and support overall health.

3. Anti-Inflammatory Properties

a. **Mechanism:** Tocopherols inhibit the production of inflammatory cytokines and enzymes.

b. **Benefits:** They help in managing inflammatory conditions like arthritis, asthma, and inflammatory bowel disease.

4. Cardiovascular Health

a. **Mechanism:** Tocopherols prevent the oxidation of LDL cholesterol and improve endothelial function.

b. **Benefits:** They reduce the risk of atherosclerosis, lower blood pressure, and support heart health.

5. Skin Health

a. **Mechanism:** Tocopherols protect skin from oxidative damage and improve moisture retention.

b. **Benefits:** They are used in skincare products to prevent aging, protect against UV damage, and promote skin healing.

Combined Health Benefits in Phytopharmaceuticals

1. Anti-Aging

a. **Mechanism:** Combined antioxidant effects of tocotrienols and tocopherols.

b. **Benefits:** They protect cells from oxidative damage, reduce signs of aging, and improve skin elasticity and hydration.

2. Chronic Disease Prevention

a. **Mechanism:** Synergistic effects in reducing oxidative stress and inflammation.

b. **Benefits:** They lower the risk of chronic diseases such as cardiovascular diseases, diabetes, and cancer.

3. Cognitive Function

a. **Mechanism:** Combined neuroprotective effects.

b. **Benefits:** They improve cognitive function, reduce the risk of neurodegenerative diseases, and enhance overall brain health.

4. Enhanced Immune Function

a. **Mechanism:** Synergistic effects on immune cell function and antibody production.

b. **Benefits:** They strengthen the immune system, helping to fight infections and improve overall health.

Research and Emerging Uses:

Tocotrienols and tocopherols are the subject of ongoing research due to their promising health benefits and potential new applications. Below is a detailed overview of current research and emerging uses in phytopharmaceuticals for these compounds.

Tocotrienols:

1. Cardiovascular Health

a. **Research:** Studies are exploring the mechanisms by which tocotrienols improve lipid profiles and arterial health. Recent research shows tocotrienols may help in reducing arterial stiffness and improving endothelial function, which are crucial for cardiovascular health.

b. **Emerging Uses:** Developing supplements aimed at specific cardiovascular conditions such as hypertension, atherosclerosis, and hyperlipidemia.

2. Neuroprotection

a. **Research:** Tocotrienols are being studied for their ability to cross the blood-brain barrier and protect against neurodegeneration. Research focuses on their potential to reduce brain inflammation, oxidative stress, and amyloid-beta accumulation, which are hallmarks of Alzheimer's disease.

b. **Emerging Uses:** Formulating neuroprotective supplements and therapies for neurodegenerative diseases, cognitive impairment, and brain injuries.

3. Anti-Cancer Properties

a. **Research:** Ongoing studies are investigating the molecular pathways through which tocotrienols exert anti-cancer effects, such as apoptosis induction, inhibition of angiogenesis, and suppression of metastasis. Research includes in vitro and in vivo studies on various cancer types.

b. **Emerging Uses:** Developing adjunct therapies that enhance the efficacy of conventional cancer treatments and creating tocotrienol-based cancer preventive supplements.

4. Metabolic Syndrome and Diabetes

a. **Research:** Investigations are focusing on tocotrienols' role in improving insulin sensitivity, reducing inflammation, and preventing the progression of metabolic syndrome. Studies show potential benefits in lowering blood glucose levels and reducing the risk of diabetic complications.

b. **Emerging Uses:** Formulating supplements for managing metabolic syndrome, diabetes, and related complications like diabetic neuropathy.

5. Bone Health

a. **Research:** Tocotrienols are being studied for their ability to promote bone formation and prevent bone loss. Research is looking at their effects on bone density and strength, particularly in postmenopausal women and individuals with osteoporosis.

b. **Emerging Uses:** Developing bone health supplements aimed at preventing osteoporosis and enhancing bone healing.

Tocopherols:

1. Skin Health

a. **Research:** Tocopherols are being extensively studied for their skin-protective properties, including their ability to reduce UV-induced damage, improve skin barrier function, and enhance wound healing. Research includes clinical trials assessing their efficacy in treating skin conditions.

b. **Emerging Uses:** Formulating advanced skincare products and cosmeceuticals that utilize tocopherols for anti-aging, sun protection, and scar reduction.

2. Immune Function

a. **Research:** Studies are examining how tocopherols modulate immune responses, enhance vaccine efficacy, and protect against infections. Research includes understanding the role of tocopherols in immune cell function and inflammation regulation.

b. **Emerging Uses:** Creating immune-boosting supplements, particularly for the elderly and immunocompromised individuals.

3. Cancer Prevention

a. **Research:** Tocopherols are being investigated for their potential in cancer prevention. Studies focus on their antioxidant properties, ability to modulate gene expression, and inhibit tumor growth. Research includes both epidemiological studies and clinical trials.

b. **Emerging Uses:** Developing preventive supplements for populations at high risk of cancer and combining tocopherols with other antioxidants for synergistic effects.

4. Eye Health

a. **Research:** Tocopherols are being studied for their role in protecting against age-related macular degeneration (AMD) and cataracts. Research focuses on their antioxidant properties and ability to protect retinal cells from oxidative damage.

b. **Emerging Uses:** Formulating eye health supplements aimed at preventing AMD and cataracts, and improving overall vision health.

Combined Uses and Synergistic Effects

1. Anti-Aging and Longevity

a. **Research:** Studies are examining the combined antioxidant effects of tocotrienols and tocopherols in slowing the aging process and promoting longevity. Research includes their impact on cellular health, DNA repair, and mitochondrial function.

b. **Emerging Uses:** Developing comprehensive anti-aging supplements that leverage the synergistic effects of both tocotrienols and tocopherols.

2. Chronic Disease Prevention

a. **Research:** Research is focused on the role of combined tocotrienols and tocopherols in preventing chronic diseases like cardiovascular diseases, diabetes, and cancer. Studies include understanding their collective impact on inflammation, oxidative stress, and metabolic health.

b. **Emerging Uses:** Creating multi-targeted supplements for the prevention and management of chronic diseases, improving overall health and quality of life.

3. Cognitive Function and Mental Health

a. **Research:** Investigations are exploring how the combination of tocotrienols and tocopherols can improve cognitive function and mental health. Research includes their effects on neuroinflammation, oxidative stress, and neurotransmitter regulation.

b. **Emerging Uses:** Developing cognitive health supplements aimed at enhancing memory, focus, and mental well-being, and reducing the risk of cognitive decline.

ANDROGRAPHOLIDE

Occurrence:

a. **Sources:** Andrographolide is a bioactive compound found in the plant *Andrographis paniculata*, commonly known as the King of Bitters or Kalmegh. This plant is native to South Asian countries such as India, Sri Lanka, and China.

Isolation and Characteristic Features:

a. **Chemical Nature:** Andrographolide is a diterpenoid lactone, specifically a labdane-type diterpene. It has a molecular formula $C_{20}H_{30}O_5$ and consists of a bicyclic lactone ring structure with several hydroxyl groups.

b. **Isolation:** Extraction methods typically involve using solvents such as ethanol or methanol to extract andrographolide from the aerial parts (leaves and stems) of *Andrographis paniculata*. Purification follows through techniques like chromatography.

Uses in Pharmacy:

a. **Pharmaceutical Applications:** Andrographolide is used in traditional herbal medicine and modern pharmaceutical formulations for its various pharmacological activities.

b. **Antiviral:** It has shown potential antiviral activity against viruses such as influenza and herpes simplex virus.

c. **Anti-inflammatory:** Andrographolide exhibits strong anti-inflammatory effects, which can benefit conditions such as arthritis and inflammatory bowel diseases.

d. **Immunomodulatory:** It modulates the immune system, enhancing immune responses against infections and promoting overall immune health.

e. **Antioxidant:** Andrographolide acts as an antioxidant, scavenging free radicals and reducing oxidative stress.

Medicinal and Health Benefits:

a. **Liver Health:** It supports liver health by protecting hepatocytes (liver cells) from damage and promoting detoxification processes.

b. **Fever and Respiratory Infections:** Andrographolide is traditionally used to reduce fever and treat respiratory infections such as colds and flu.

c. **Digestive Health:** It may help alleviate digestive disorders and promote gastrointestinal health.

d. **Anti-cancer Properties:** Research suggests that andrographolide may have potential anti-cancer effects by inhibiting cancer cell proliferation and inducing apoptosis (programmed cell death).

GLYCOLIPIDS

Glycolipids are a diverse group of compounds that combine lipids (fatty acids) with carbohydrates (sugars). They are found in various plant sources and play important roles in both plant physiology and potential applications in phytopharmaceuticals. Let's delve into the occurrence, isolation, characteristic features, uses in pharmacy, and medicinal benefits of glycolipids:

Occurrence:

a. **Sources:** Glycolipids are abundant in plant cell membranes and are found in significant quantities in seeds, leaves, fruits, and roots of various plants. They are particularly prevalent in certain algae, mosses, and higher plants.

Isolation and Characteristic Features:

a. **Chemical Nature:** Glycolipids consist of a lipid (often a fatty acid or sphingosine derivative) linked to a carbohydrate moiety. The carbohydrate portion can vary widely and may include monosaccharides, oligosaccharides, or polysaccharides.

b. **Types:** Glycolipids can be categorized into different types based on their lipid component, such as glycosphingolipids (which include ceramides) and galactolipids (which include monogalactosyldiacylglycerol and digalactosyldiacylglycerol).

Isolation:

a. **Extraction Methods:** Extraction of glycolipids involves solvent extraction from plant tissues, followed by purification using techniques such as chromatography. The specific extraction method depends on the type of glycolipid and the plant source.

Uses in Pharmacy:

a. **Pharmaceutical Applications:** Glycolipids have gained attention for their potential therapeutic applications in pharmacy and medicine.

b. **Cosmetics:** They are used in skincare products for their moisturizing properties and ability to support skin barrier function.

c. **Drug Delivery:** Glycolipids are being explored for their role in drug delivery systems due to their biocompatibility and ability to interact with biological membranes.

Medicinal and Health Benefits:

a. **Anti-inflammatory Properties:** Some glycolipids exhibit anti-inflammatory effects, which can benefit conditions like arthritis and inflammatory skin disorders.

b. **Antioxidant Activity:** Certain glycolipids have antioxidant properties, protecting cells from oxidative stress and potentially reducing the risk of chronic diseases.

c. **Immunomodulation:** They may modulate immune responses, enhancing immune function against infections and supporting overall immune health.

d. **Neuroprotective Effects:** Research suggests that glycolipids may have neuroprotective effects, potentially benefiting conditions like Alzheimer's disease and Parkinson's disease.

GUGULIPIDS

Occurrence:

a. **Sources:** Gugulipids are derived from the resin of the mukul myrrh tree, *Commiphora wightii*, also known as guggul or guggul gum. This tree is native to India and has been used traditionally in Ayurvedic medicine.

Isolation and Characteristic Features:

a. **Chemical Nature:** Gugulipids are a mixture of bioactive compounds isolated from the resin of *Commiphora wightii*. They primarily consist of guggulsterones, which are steroid-like compounds, particularly E- and Z-guggulsterones.

b. **Isolation:** Extraction methods involve collecting the resin from the tree bark, followed by solvent extraction (often using petroleum ether or other organic solvents) to isolate gugulipids.

c. **Characterization:** Gugulipids are characterized by their chemical structure, including the presence of guggulsterones and other minor bioactive components such as flavonoids and terpenoids.

Uses in Pharmacy:

a. **Pharmaceutical Applications:** Gugulipids are used in traditional herbal medicine and modern pharmaceutical formulations.

b. **Cholesterol Management:** They are primarily known for their cholesterol-lowering effects, specifically reducing LDL cholesterol levels ("bad" cholesterol) while maintaining or increasing HDL cholesterol levels ("good" cholesterol).

c. **Anti-inflammatory Properties:** Gugulipids exhibit anti-inflammatory effects, which may benefit conditions such as arthritis and inflammatory skin disorders.

d. **Weight Management:** They are also used in dietary supplements for their potential role in promoting weight loss and improving lipid metabolism.

Medicinal and Health Benefits:

a. **Cardiovascular Health:** Gugulipids support cardiovascular health by reducing cholesterol levels, improving lipid profiles, and potentially reducing the risk of heart disease.

b. **Anti-oxidant Activity:** They have antioxidant properties, protecting cells from oxidative stress and reducing the risk of chronic diseases associated with free radical damage.

c. **Anti-microbial Effects:** Gugulipids show antimicrobial activity against certain bacteria and fungi, contributing to their traditional use in treating infections.

WITHANOLIDES

Occurrence:

a. **Sources:** Withanolides are a group of naturally occurring steroidal lactones found primarily in plants of the *Solanaceae* family, particularly species like *Withania somnifera* (Ashwagandha), *Physalis* spp., and *Datura* spp. They are also found in other plants such as *Acnistus arborescens* and *Nicandra physalodes*.

Isolation and Characteristic Features:

a. **Chemical Nature:** Withanolides are steroidal lactones that possess a characteristic structure comprising a steroid backbone fused to a lactone ring. They are classified as ergostane-type steroids.

b. **Isolation:** Extraction methods involve solvent extraction from plant tissues, typically using methanol, ethanol, or other organic solvents. Purification is achieved through techniques like column chromatography.

c. **Characteristic Features:** Withanolides vary in structure and bioactivity depending on the plant species and the specific withanolide compound. Common examples include withaferin A, withanolide A, withanolide D, and others.

Uses in Pharmacy:

a. **Pharmaceutical Applications:** Withanolides are used in traditional herbal medicine and are gaining attention in modern pharmaceutical research.

b. **Adaptogenic Properties:** They are well-known for their adaptogenic properties, helping the body cope with stress and promoting overall resilience.

c. **Anti-inflammatory Effects:** Withanolides exhibit potent anti-inflammatory effects, which may benefit conditions like arthritis, asthma, and inflammatory bowel diseases.

d. **Immunomodulatory Activity:** They modulate immune responses, enhancing immune function and potentially aiding in the treatment of immune-related disorders.

Medicinal and Health Benefits:

a. **Stress Reduction:** Withanolides are used traditionally to reduce stress and anxiety, supporting mental health and well-being.

b. **Antioxidant Activity:** They possess antioxidant properties, protecting cells from oxidative damage caused by free radicals.

c. **Neuroprotective Effects:** Research suggests that withanolides may have neuroprotective effects, potentially benefiting conditions like Alzheimer's disease and Parkinson's disease.

d. **Anti-cancer Properties:** Some withanolides exhibit anti-cancer activities, inhibiting cancer cell proliferation and inducing apoptosis (programmed cell death).

VASCINE

Vascine is a compound found in certain plants that has garnered interest in phytopharmaceutical research. Here's a detailed exploration of its occurrence, isolation, characteristic features, uses in pharmacy, and medicinal benefits:

Occurrence:

a. **Sources:** Vascine is primarily found in the plant *Adhatoda vasica*, commonly known as Vasaka or Malabar nut. This plant is native to Southeast Asia, particularly India and Sri Lanka, and is cultivated in other parts of the world for its medicinal properties.

Isolation and Characteristic Features:

a. **Chemical Nature:** Vascine is a quinazoline alkaloid, specifically an alkaloidal glucoside. It has a complex chemical structure that includes a nitrogenous base and a sugar component.

b. **Isolation:** Extraction methods involve using solvents like methanol or ethanol to extract vascine from the leaves and stems of *Adhatoda vasica*. Purification typically includes techniques such as chromatography to isolate the compound in its pure form.

c. **Characteristic Features:** Vascine is characterized by its alkaloidal nature and its specific role in biological activities related to respiratory health and inflammation.

Uses in Pharmacy:

a. **Pharmaceutical Applications:** Vascine is utilized in traditional herbal medicine and is being studied for potential modern pharmaceutical applications.

b. **Respiratory Health:** It is traditionally used to treat respiratory disorders such as bronchitis, asthma, and coughs due to its bronchodilator and expectorant properties.

c. **Anti-inflammatory Effects:** Vascine exhibits anti-inflammatory effects, which can benefit conditions characterized by inflammation in the respiratory tract.

Medicinal and Health Benefits:

a. **Bronchodilator:** Vascine acts as a bronchodilator, helping to relax the bronchial muscles and improve airflow in the lungs, which is beneficial in treating asthma and other respiratory conditions.

b. **Expectorant:** It promotes the expulsion of mucus from the respiratory tract, aiding in clearing congestion and facilitating easier breathing.

c. **Antimicrobial Properties:** Vascine shows antimicrobial activity against certain pathogens, contributing to its use in treating respiratory infections.

d. **Antioxidant Activity:** It possesses antioxidant properties, helping to neutralize free radicals and protect cells from oxidative stress.

TAXOL:

Taxol, also known as paclitaxel, is a potent chemotherapy medication primarily derived from the bark of the Pacific yew tree (*Taxus brevifolia*). Here are the detailed aspects of Taxol:

Occurrence and Isolation

a. **Natural Source:** Taxol is found primarily in the bark of the Pacific yew tree (*Taxus brevifolia*) and to a lesser extent in other yew species such as *Taxus baccata* (European yew) and *Taxus cuspidata* (Japanese yew).

b. **Isolation:** Extracting Taxol from yew bark involves several steps:
   i. The bark is harvested and processed to extract the active ingredients.
   ii. Taxol is purified using various chromatographic techniques, typically involving solvent extraction and column chromatography.
   iii. The purified compound is then formulated into pharmaceutical products.

Chemical Nature

a. **Chemical Structure:** Taxol has a complex diterpenoid structure. Its chemical name is $(2\alpha,4\beta,5\beta,7\beta,10\beta,13\alpha)$-4,10-bis(acetyloxy)-13-{[(2R,3S)-3-(benzoylamino)-2-hydroxy-3-phenylpropanoyl]oxy}-1,7-dihydroxy-9-oxo-5,20-epoxytax-11-en-2-yl benzoate.

b. **Molecular Formula:** $C_{47}H_{51}NO_{14}$

c. **Mode of Action**: Taxol promotes microtubule stability by enhancing tubulin polymerization, thereby inhibiting cell division, which is critical for its anticancer effects.

Uses in Pharmacy and Medicinal Benefits

a. **Chemotherapeutic Agent**: Taxol is primarily used in the treatment of various cancers, including ovarian, breast, and lung cancers. It is administered intravenously in combination with other chemotherapy drugs.

b. **Pharmacy Uses**: In pharmaceutical preparations, Taxol is formulated as injectable solutions or as a component of chemotherapy regimens.

c. **Medicinal Benefits**:

   i. **Anticancer Properties**: Taxol inhibits cancer cell growth by disrupting microtubule dynamics, leading to cell cycle arrest and apoptosis (programmed cell death).

   ii. **Clinical Applications**: It is effective against both solid tumors and certain leukemias, making it a crucial drug in oncology.

   iii. **Research**: Beyond cancer treatment, Taxol is also studied for its potential in treating other conditions, such as drug-resistant cancers and cardiovascular diseases.

Health Benefits

a. **Medical Research**: Taxol continues to be a subject of intense research for its broader medicinal applications and its potential in drug development.

b. **Health Impact**: Despite its effectiveness, Taxol has notable side effects, including peripheral neuropathy, bone marrow suppression, and allergic reactions, which require careful management during treatment.

Multiple Choice Questions (MCQs)

1. What is the primary source of α and β-carotene?

   a) Citrus fruits

b) Green leafy vegetables

c) Carrots and sweet potatoes

d) Dairy products

2. Which of the following is a xanthophyll?

    a) β-Carotene

    b) Lutein

    c) d-Limonene

    d) α-Terpineol

3. What is the main use of d-Limonene in pharmacy?

    a) Antiviral agent

    b) Solvent and flavoring agent

    c) Vitamin supplement

    d) Antibiotic

4. Shatavarins are predominantly found in which plant?

    a) Aloe vera

    b) Asparagus racemosus

    c) Echinacea

    d) Ginseng

5. Which phytopharmaceutical compound is primarily known for its antioxidant properties and is found in grape skins?

    a) Rutin

    b) Hesperidin

    c) Resveratrol

    d) Naringin

6. Which vitamin is associated with tocotrienols and tocopherols?

    a) Vitamin A

    b) Vitamin C

    c) Vitamin D

    d) Vitamin E

7. What is the primary source of vitamin C in phytopharmaceuticals?

    a) Dairy products

    b) Citrus fruits and berries

    c) Nuts and seeds

    d) Whole grains

8. Which compound is known for its bronchodilator and expectorant properties?

    a) Resveratrol

    b) Shatavarin

    c) Vascine

    d) Andrographolide

9. What is the main bioactive compound in Andrographis paniculata?

    a) Ellagic acid

    b) Withanolide A

    c) Andrographolide

    d) Vascine

10. Gugulipids are primarily used to manage what health condition?

    a) Diabetes

    b) Cholesterol levels

    c) Asthma

    d) Hypertension

11. Which compound is a steroidal lactone found in Ashwagandha?

    a) Guggulsterone

    b) Withanolide

    c) Taxol

    d) Shatavarin

12. Vascine is primarily derived from which plant?

    a) Andrographis paniculata

    b) Adhatoda vasica

c) Commiphora wightii

d) Withania somnifera

13. Taxol is primarily used for treating which condition?

a) Inflammatory diseases

b) Cancer

c) Cardiovascular diseases

d) Respiratory infections

14. Which of the following compounds has been shown to exhibit anti-cancer properties by inducing apoptosis?

a) Rutin

b) Quercetin

c) Andrographolide

d) α-Terpineol

15. Which type of compound are tocotrienols?

a) Flavonoids

b) Terpenoids

c) Vitamin E compounds

d) Steroids

16. Ellagic acid is particularly abundant in which type of food?

a) Leafy greens

b) Berries

c) Citrus fruits

d) Dairy products

17. Which compound is known for its potential to improve cardiovascular health by reducing LDL cholesterol levels?

a) Naringin

b) Shatavarin

c) Gugulipids

d) Lutein

18. Resveratrol belongs to which family of polyphenols?

   a) Flavonols

   b) Stilbenoids

   c) Glycosides

   d) Terpenoids

19. Which vitamin is crucial for collagen synthesis and found in high amounts in citrus fruits?

   a) Vitamin A

   b) Vitamin B

   c) Vitamin C

   d) Vitamin D

20. What is the primary benefit of α-Terpineol in pharmaceutical formulations?

   a) Antioxidant

   b) Antimicrobial

   c) Anti-inflammatory

   d) Digestive aid

Short Answer Type Questions (Subjective)

1. What are phytopharmaceuticals, and how are they derived?

2. Name two examples of pharmaceutical drugs developed from phytopharmaceutical sources.

3. What are the main types of biologically active compounds found in phytopharmaceuticals?

4. How does modern research validate traditional uses of phytopharmaceuticals?

5. What are the potential benefits of standardizing active ingredients in phytopharmaceuticals?

6. List three fruits or vegetables that are rich sources of α and β-carotene.

7. What is the main health benefit of lutein, and which foods are rich in lutein?

8. Describe the chemical nature of d-limonene.

9. What are the primary medicinal benefits of α-terpineol?

10. Identify the plant source of shatavarins and their main health benefits.

11. What are the medicinal applications of resveratrol?

12. How does rutin benefit cardiovascular health?

13. Explain the isolation process of hesperidin from citrus fruits.

14. What are the health benefits of naringin in metabolic health?

15. What are the antioxidant and anti-inflammatory properties of quercetin?

16. Which fruits are known to be rich sources of ellagic acid?

17. Describe two medicinal benefits of vitamin C.

18. What distinguishes tocopherols from tocotrienols in terms of chemical structure?

19. How do tocotrienols benefit bone health?

20. What are the main pharmacological activities of andrographolide?

Long Answer Type Questions (Subjective)

1. Explain in detail the importance of phytopharmaceuticals in both traditional and modern medicine, including their natural origins, therapeutic applications, and ongoing research.

2. Discuss the occurrence, isolation, chemical nature, and health benefits of α and β-carotene, and lutein.

3. Describe the occurrence, isolation, characteristic features, and medicinal uses of d-limonene and α-terpineol.

4. Elaborate on the occurrence, chemical nature, isolation process, and medicinal benefits of shatavarins.

5. Compare and contrast the health benefits and pharmaceutical applications of resveratrol, rutin, hesperidin, naringin, and quercetin.

6. Explain the chemical nature, isolation process, and therapeutic benefits of ellagic acid. How does it contribute to cancer prevention and cardiovascular health?

7. Discuss the roles of vitamins C, E, and A in phytopharmaceuticals, including their occurrence, isolation, characteristic features, uses in pharmacy, and health benefits.

8. Describe the extraction, purification, and characteristic features of tocotrienols and tocopherols, and explain their combined health benefits in phytopharmaceuticals.

9. Explain the pharmacological activities, medicinal benefits, and emerging uses of tocotrienols and tocopherols, focusing on their antioxidant, anti-inflammatory, and neuroprotective properties.

10. Discuss the occurrence, isolation, characteristic features, and therapeutic applications of andrographolide, including its role in traditional medicine and modern pharmaceutical research.

Answer Key

1. c) Carrots and sweet potatoes
2. b) Lutein
3. b) Solvent and flavoring agent
4. b) Asparagus racemosus
5. c) Resveratrol
6. d) Vitamin E
7. b) Citrus fruits and berries
8. c) Vascine
9. c) Andrographolide
10. b) Cholesterol levels
11. b) Withanolide
12. b) Adhatoda vasica

13.b) Cancer

14.c) Andrographolide

15.c) Vitamin E compounds

16.b) Berries

17.c) Gugulipids

18.b) Stilbenoids

19.c) Vitamin C

20.b) Antimicrobial

CHAPTER – 6

PHARMACOVIGILANCE OF DRUGS OF NATURAL ORIGIN

INTRODUCTION:

Pharmacovigilance is the science and activities related to the detection, assessment, understanding, and prevention of adverse effects or any other drug-related problems. When it comes to drugs of natural origin, pharmacovigilance involves unique challenges and considerations due to the complexity and variability of these products. Below is a detailed introduction to pharmacovigilance of drugs of natural origin.

1. Definition and Scope

Drugs of natural origin include herbal medicines, traditional medicines, and other naturally derived substances used for therapeutic purposes. The scope of pharmacovigilance in this context includes:

a. **Monitoring Adverse Drug Reactions (ADRs):** Identifying and evaluating adverse effects caused by natural products.

b. **Safety Assessment:** Evaluating the safety profile of natural products, including potential toxicities and interactions with other medications.

c. **Risk Management:** Implementing strategies to minimize risks associated with the use of natural products.

d. **Regulatory Compliance:** Ensuring that natural products meet regulatory standards for safety and efficacy.

2. Challenges in Pharmacovigilance of Natural Products

a. **Complexity of Composition:** Natural products often contain multiple active compounds, making it difficult to attribute adverse effects to a specific component.

b. **Variability:** The composition of natural products can vary depending on factors such as the source of the raw material, cultivation conditions, and processing methods.

c. **Lack of Standardization:** Unlike synthetic drugs, natural products may not have standardized dosages and formulations.

d. **Underreporting:** Adverse effects of natural products are often underreported due to the perception that they are inherently safe.

e. **Interactions:** Natural products can interact with conventional medicines, leading to adverse effects that are challenging to predict and manage.

3. Regulatory Framework

Different countries have varying regulatory frameworks for natural products. Some key regulatory bodies include:

a. **US FDA:** In the United States, the FDA regulates dietary supplements, including herbal products, under the Dietary Supplement Health and Education Act (DSHEA).

b. **EMA:** In Europe, the European Medicines Agency (EMA) provides guidelines for the safety and efficacy of herbal medicinal products.

c. **WHO:** The World Health Organization (WHO) provides guidelines for the safety monitoring of herbal medicines.

4. Methods of Pharmacovigilance

a. **Spontaneous Reporting Systems:** Healthcare professionals and consumers report adverse effects of natural products to regulatory authorities.

b. **Active Surveillance:** Proactive monitoring of adverse effects through surveys, registries, and observational studies.

c. **Case-Control Studies:** Comparing patients with adverse effects to those without to identify potential risk factors associated with natural products.

d. **Cohort Studies:** Following a group of patients using natural products over time to monitor for adverse effects.

5. Role of Healthcare Professionals

a. **Education and Training:** Healthcare professionals need to be educated about the potential risks and benefits of natural products.

b. **Reporting:** Encouraging healthcare professionals to report adverse effects associated with natural products.

c. **Patient Counseling:** Advising patients on the safe use of natural products, including potential interactions with conventional medications.

6. Consumer Awareness

a. **Public Education:** Raising awareness among consumers about the potential risks of natural products.

b. **Labeling:** Ensuring that natural products are appropriately labeled with information on potential side effects and interactions.

7. Case Studies

a. **Example 1:** St. John's Wort, a popular herbal remedy for depression, can interact with various medications, reducing their effectiveness or increasing the risk of side effects.

b. **Example 2:** Kava, used for anxiety, has been associated with liver toxicity, leading to regulatory actions in several countries.

8. Future Directions

a. **Enhanced Reporting Systems:** Improving the infrastructure for reporting and monitoring adverse effects of natural products.

b. **Research:** Conducting more rigorous research on the safety and efficacy of natural products.

c. **Global Collaboration:** Enhancing international collaboration to harmonize pharmacovigilance practices for natural products.

WHO GUIDELINES FOR SAFETY MONITORING OF NATURAL MEDICINE

The World Health Organization (WHO) provides comprehensive guidelines for the safety monitoring of herbal medicines in pharmacovigilance.

These guidelines aim to ensure the safe and effective use of herbal medicines and address the unique challenges associated with their monitoring. Here is a detailed overview of the WHO guidelines for the safety monitoring of natural medicines:

Objectives of the Guidelines:

The WHO guidelines for safety monitoring of natural medicines in pharmacovigilance aim to establish a framework for systematic surveillance and evaluation of the safety profile of drugs derived from natural sources. Here are the detailed objectives of these guidelines:

1. Standardization of Safety Assessment

Objective: Ensure consistent and standardized approaches to assessing the safety of natural medicines across different regions and healthcare settings.

    a. **Rationale:** Standardization facilitates comparability of safety data, enhances the reliability of risk assessments, and supports evidence-based decision-making in healthcare practice.

2. Enhancement of Pharmacovigilance Systems

Objective: Strengthen pharmacovigilance systems to effectively monitor and respond to adverse events related to natural medicines.

    a. **Rationale:** Natural medicines often lack comprehensive safety data due to variability in composition and quality. Enhanced pharmacovigilance systems enable early detection, reporting, and management of adverse reactions to improve patient safety.

3. Promotion of Public Health and Safety

Objective: Protect public health by identifying and mitigating risks associated with the use of natural medicines.

    a. **Rationale:** Natural medicines are widely used globally, and adverse reactions can have significant public health implications. By monitoring safety comprehensively, these guidelines aim to minimize risks and enhance the safe use of natural medicines.

4. Integration with Traditional and Complementary Medicine Practices

Objective: Integrate pharmacovigilance practices with traditional and complementary medicine systems to address unique safety considerations.

    a. **Rationale:** Many natural medicines are integral to traditional and complementary medicine practices worldwide. Integrating pharmacovigilance ensures that safety monitoring aligns with cultural and traditional practices, enhancing acceptance and compliance.

5. Capacity Building and Education

Objective: Build capacity among healthcare providers, regulators, and stakeholders to implement effective pharmacovigilance of natural medicines.

    a. **Rationale:** Pharmacovigilance of natural medicines requires specialized knowledge and skills due to their diverse sources and compositions. Capacity building enhances surveillance capabilities, data interpretation, and regulatory compliance.

6. Facilitation of Global Collaboration

Objective: Foster collaboration among countries, organizations, and stakeholders to share safety data and best practices in pharmacovigilance.

    a. **Rationale:** Natural medicines are used globally, and safety concerns often transcend national borders. Collaborative efforts facilitate data sharing, harmonize regulatory approaches, and strengthen international responses to emerging safety issues.

7. Guidance for Research and Development

Objective: Provide guidance for research and development initiatives to generate robust safety data for natural medicines.

    a. **Rationale:** Research gaps exist in the safety profiles of many natural medicines. Guidelines encourage targeted research, clinical trials, and post-marketing studies to fill knowledge gaps and inform evidence-based practice.

8. Ethical Considerations and Patient Rights

Objective: Uphold ethical principles and protect patient rights in the monitoring and reporting of adverse events related to natural medicines.

  a. **Rationale:** Patient safety and informed consent are paramount in pharmacovigilance. Guidelines emphasize ethical conduct, transparency, and respect for patient autonomy to maintain trust and credibility in safety monitoring efforts.

Framework for Safety Monitoring:

1. Risk Assessment and Prioritization

  i. **Objective:** Identify and evaluate potential risks associated with natural medicines based on their composition, pharmacological properties, and historical use.

  ii. **Activities:**

   a. **Literature Review:** Conduct systematic reviews of scientific literature, traditional knowledge, and clinical trial data to assess the safety profiles and identify known risks of natural medicines.

   b. **Expert Consultation:** Engage multidisciplinary experts including pharmacologists, toxicologists, traditional medicine practitioners, and epidemiologists to assess risks and prioritize monitoring efforts.

   c. **Risk Ranking:** Prioritize natural medicines for safety monitoring based on the severity of potential adverse effects, patterns of use, and public health impact.

2. Surveillance and Monitoring Systems

  i. **Objective:** Establish and maintain robust systems for monitoring and reporting adverse events associated with natural medicines in real-world settings.

  ii. **Activities:**

a. **Adverse Event Reporting:** Implement mechanisms for healthcare professionals, consumers, and patients to report adverse reactions and events related to natural medicines.

b. **Database Management:** Maintain centralized pharmacovigilance databases or systems to collect, analyze, and monitor safety data continuously.

c. **Signal Detection:** Utilize statistical methods and data mining techniques to detect signals of potential safety concerns from reported adverse events.

d. **Post-Marketing Studies:** Conduct studies to monitor the long-term safety and effectiveness of natural medicines after they have been marketed.

3. Risk Communication and Public Health Response

i. **Objective:** Communicate safety information effectively to healthcare providers, regulators, and the public to mitigate risks associated with natural medicines.

ii. **Activities:**

a. **Safety Alerts and Advisories:** Issue timely safety alerts, advisories, and warnings based on emerging safety signals or significant adverse events.

b. **Educational Campaigns:** Develop and disseminate educational materials to raise awareness about potential risks, safe use practices, and adverse effects of natural medicines.

c. **Patient Counseling:** Provide clear and accessible information to patients regarding potential adverse effects, contraindications, and precautions associated with natural medicines.

d. **Regulatory Actions:** Implement regulatory measures such as labeling updates or restrictions in response to safety concerns identified through pharmacovigilance.

4. Collaboration and Capacity Building

  i. **Objective:** Foster collaboration among stakeholders and build capacity to enhance safety monitoring of natural medicines globally.

  ii. **Activities:**

    a. **International Cooperation:** Facilitate collaboration between countries, regulatory agencies, and research institutions to share safety data, best practices, and regulatory experiences.

    b. **Training and Workshops:** Conduct training programs, workshops, and seminars to strengthen pharmacovigilance capabilities among healthcare professionals, regulators, and researchers.

    c. **Technical Assistance:** Provide technical support and guidance to countries and organizations in establishing or improving pharmacovigilance systems specifically tailored for natural medicines.

    d. **Research Collaboration:** Foster partnerships for research initiatives aimed at addressing knowledge gaps in the safety and efficacy of natural medicines.

5. Evaluation and Continuous Improvement

  i. **Objective:** Evaluate the effectiveness of safety monitoring activities and implement continuous improvements to enhance patient safety and regulatory oversight.

  ii. **Activities:**

    a. **Outcome Assessment:** Assess the impact of safety monitoring interventions on reducing adverse events and improving patient outcomes associated with natural medicines.

    b. **Feedback Mechanisms:** Solicit feedback from stakeholders, including healthcare providers and patients, to identify areas for improvement in safety monitoring practices.

c. **Adaptation to Emerging Issues:** Adjust monitoring strategies and guidelines in response to new scientific evidence, technological advancements, and evolving patterns of natural medicine use.

d. **Regulatory Review:** Periodically review and update regulatory frameworks and guidelines based on lessons learned, emerging safety concerns, and advancements in pharmacovigilance practices.

Key Elements of Safety Monitoring:

1. Risk Assessment and Prioritization

i. **Objective:** Systematically identify and assess potential risks associated with natural medicines to prioritize safety monitoring efforts.

ii. **Activities:**

a. **Literature Review:** Conduct comprehensive reviews of available scientific literature, traditional knowledge, and clinical trial data to understand the safety profiles and identify known risks of natural medicines.

b. **Expert Consultation:** Engage multidisciplinary experts including pharmacologists, toxicologists, traditional medicine practitioners, and epidemiologists to evaluate risks and prioritize monitoring activities.

c. **Risk Ranking:** Prioritize natural medicines based on the severity of potential adverse effects, patterns of use, and public health impact for focused safety monitoring.

2. Surveillance Systems and Data Collection

i. **Objective:** Establish robust systems for the continuous surveillance and collection of safety data related to natural medicines.

ii. **Key Elements:**

a. **Adverse Event Reporting:** Implement mechanisms for healthcare professionals, consumers, and patients to report adverse reactions and events associated with natural medicines.

b. **Database Management:** Maintain centralized pharmacovigilance databases or systems to collect, collate, and analyze safety data from various sources.

c. **Signal Detection:** Utilize statistical methods, data mining techniques, and epidemiological approaches to detect signals of potential safety concerns from reported adverse events.

d. **Post-Marketing Studies:** Conduct studies to monitor the long-term safety and effectiveness of natural medicines in real-world settings following their market authorization.

3. Risk Communication and Public Health Response

i. **Objective:** Disseminate safety information effectively to healthcare providers, regulators, and the public to mitigate risks associated with natural medicines.

ii. **Key Elements:**

a. **Safety Alerts and Advisories:** Issue timely alerts, advisories, and warnings based on emerging safety signals or significant adverse events related to natural medicines.

b. **Educational Campaigns:** Develop and distribute educational materials to increase awareness about potential risks, safe use practices, and adverse effects of natural medicines among healthcare professionals and consumers.

c. **Patient Counseling:** Provide clear and accessible information to patients regarding potential adverse effects, contraindications, and precautions associated with the use of natural medicines.

> d. **Regulatory Actions:** Implement regulatory measures such as updates to product labeling, restrictions, or withdrawals in response to safety concerns identified through pharmacovigilance activities.

4. Collaboration and Capacity Building

i. **Objective:** Foster collaboration among stakeholders and build capacity to enhance safety monitoring of natural medicines globally.

ii. **Key Elements:**

> a. **International Cooperation:** Facilitate collaboration between countries, regulatory agencies, and research institutions to share safety data, best practices, and regulatory experiences related to natural medicines.
>
> b. **Training and Capacity Development:** Conduct training programs, workshops, and seminars to strengthen pharmacovigilance capabilities among healthcare professionals, regulators, and researchers involved in monitoring natural medicines.
>
> c. **Technical Assistance:** Provide technical support and guidance to countries and organizations in establishing or strengthening pharmacovigilance systems tailored for natural medicines.
>
> d. **Research Collaboration:** Foster partnerships for research initiatives aimed at addressing knowledge gaps in the safety and efficacy of natural medicines through epidemiological studies, clinical trials, and post-marketing surveillance.

5. Evaluation and Continuous Improvement

i. **Objective:** Evaluate the effectiveness of safety monitoring activities and implement ongoing improvements to enhance patient safety and regulatory oversight.

ii. **Key Elements:**

a. **Outcome Assessment:** Assess the impact of safety monitoring interventions on reducing adverse events and improving patient outcomes associated with natural medicines.

b. **Feedback Mechanisms:** Solicit feedback from stakeholders, including healthcare providers, patients, and regulators, to identify areas for enhancement in safety monitoring practices.

c. **Adaptation to Emerging Issues:** Adapt monitoring strategies, guidelines, and regulatory frameworks in response to new scientific evidence, technological advancements, and evolving patterns of natural medicine use.

d. **Regulatory Review:** Periodically review and update regulatory policies, guidelines, and labeling requirements based on lessons learned, emerging safety concerns, and advancements in pharmacovigilance practices.

Stakeholder Involvement:

In the WHO guidelines for safety monitoring of natural medicines, stakeholder involvement plays a crucial role in ensuring comprehensive and effective pharmacovigilance. Stakeholders encompass a wide range of individuals, organizations, and institutions involved in the development, regulation, distribution, prescribing, and use of natural medicines. Here's a detailed overview of stakeholder involvement in these guidelines:

1. Healthcare Professionals

i. **Role:** Healthcare professionals, including physicians, pharmacists, nurses, and traditional medicine practitioners, play a pivotal role in pharmacovigilance.

ii. **Involvement:**

a. **Reporting Adverse Events:** Healthcare professionals are responsible for identifying and reporting adverse events associated with natural medicines to pharmacovigilance systems.

b. **Clinical Assessment:** They provide clinical insights into the safety profiles of natural medicines based on patient outcomes and adverse event reports.

c. **Educational Outreach:** Healthcare professionals are involved in educational initiatives to increase awareness about safety concerns and best practices in the use of natural medicines.

2. Regulatory Authorities

i. **Role:** Regulatory agencies at national and international levels oversee the approval, marketing authorization, and post-marketing surveillance of natural medicines.

ii. **Involvement:**

a. **Regulatory Oversight:** They establish and enforce regulatory frameworks, guidelines, and standards for the safety monitoring of natural medicines.

b. **Signal Detection:** Regulatory authorities collaborate with pharmacovigilance centers to detect signals of potential safety issues and initiate appropriate regulatory actions.

c. **Risk Communication:** They communicate safety alerts, advisories, and regulatory decisions related to natural medicines to healthcare professionals, consumers, and the public.

3. Pharmacovigilance Centers and Systems

i. **Role:** Dedicated pharmacovigilance centers and systems are responsible for monitoring and evaluating the safety profiles of medicines, including natural medicines.

ii. **Involvement:**

a. **Data Collection and Analysis:** Pharmacovigilance centers collect, collate, and analyze safety data from various sources, including adverse event reports and epidemiological studies.

b. **Signal Detection and Assessment:** They use pharmacovigilance methodologies to detect and assess signals of potential safety concerns associated with natural medicines.

c. **Reporting to Regulatory Authorities:** Pharmacovigilance centers report safety data and findings to regulatory authorities to inform regulatory decisions and actions.

4. Patients and Consumers

i. **Role:** Patients and consumers of natural medicines provide valuable insights into safety concerns and adverse effects through direct experience.

ii. **Involvement:**

a. **Reporting Adverse Events:** Patients and consumers are encouraged to report adverse events and reactions associated with natural medicines to healthcare providers or pharmacovigilance systems.

b. **Feedback and Communication:** Their feedback helps in understanding real-world safety issues and improving risk communication strategies related to natural medicines.

5. Academic and Research Institutions

i. **Role:** Academic and research institutions contribute to the scientific understanding of natural medicines' safety profiles through research and studies.

ii. **Involvement:**

a. **Clinical Trials and Studies:** They conduct pre-marketing and post-marketing studies to evaluate the safety, efficacy, and long-term effects of natural medicines.

b. **Evidence Generation:** Academic institutions generate scientific evidence through pharmacological and toxicological studies, epidemiological research, and systematic reviews that inform safety monitoring practices.

   c. **Capacity Building:** They provide training and education to healthcare professionals, researchers, and regulators to strengthen pharmacovigilance capabilities related to natural medicines.

6. Industry and Manufacturers

i. **Role:** Manufacturers and industry stakeholders are responsible for ensuring the quality, safety, and efficacy of natural medicines throughout their lifecycle.

ii. **Involvement:**

   a. **Quality Control:** They implement quality control measures to ensure the consistency and purity of natural medicines.

   b. **Post-Marketing Surveillance:** Manufacturers monitor and report adverse events associated with their products to regulatory authorities and pharmacovigilance systems.

   c. **Collaboration with Regulators:** They collaborate with regulatory authorities to comply with safety monitoring requirements and implement risk mitigation strategies.

Research and Development:

Research and development (R&D) in the context of WHO guidelines for safety monitoring of natural medicines within pharmacovigilance involves systematic efforts to advance scientific knowledge, enhance safety monitoring capabilities, and improve regulatory practices related to natural medicines. Here's an outline of R&D activities as per these guidelines:

1. Evidence Generation and Epidemiological Studies

i. **Objective:** Generate scientific evidence on the safety profiles, efficacy, and potential risks associated with natural medicines.

ii. **Activities:**

a. **Clinical Trials:** Conduct rigorous clinical trials to evaluate the safety and effectiveness of natural medicines in controlled settings before and after marketing authorization.

b. **Longitudinal Studies:** Undertake long-term observational studies to assess the real-world safety and efficacy of natural medicines in diverse patient populations.

c. **Meta-Analyses and Systematic Reviews:** Synthesize existing evidence through meta-analyses and systematic reviews to identify trends, gaps, and emerging safety concerns related to natural medicines.

2. Pharmacological and Toxicological Research

i. **Objective:** Investigate the pharmacokinetics, pharmacodynamics, and toxicological profiles of active compounds in natural medicines.

ii. **Activities:**

a. **Laboratory Studies:** Conduct in vitro studies to explore mechanisms of action, interactions with biological systems, and potential toxicities of natural medicine components.

b. **Animal Studies:** Utilize animal models to evaluate safety endpoints, including acute and chronic toxicity, organ toxicity, and reproductive toxicity associated with natural medicines.

c. **Safety Pharmacology:** Assess the effects of natural medicines on cardiovascular, respiratory, and central nervous system functions through specialized safety pharmacology studies.

3. Risk Assessment and Signal Detection

i. **Objective:** Identify, assess, and prioritize potential safety concerns and adverse events associated with natural medicines.

ii. **Activities:**

a. **Signal Detection Methods:** Develop and apply statistical algorithms, data mining techniques, and signal detection tools to analyze pharmacovigilance databases and identify signals of potential safety issues.

b. **Risk Evaluation:** Evaluate identified signals through expert review, risk-benefit assessments, and consideration of contextual factors such as patient demographics, concomitant medications, and disease states.

c. **Quantitative Risk Assessment:** Quantify risks associated with natural medicines based on epidemiological data, exposure levels, and adverse event frequencies to inform regulatory decisions.

4. Methodological Advancements

i. **Objective:** Improve methodological approaches and tools for safety monitoring and risk assessment of natural medicines.

ii. **Activities:**

a. **Pharmacovigilance Systems:** Develop and implement advanced pharmacovigilance systems capable of capturing, analyzing, and reporting safety data specific to natural medicines.

b. **Data Integration:** Integrate diverse sources of safety data, including electronic health records, patient registries, and social media platforms, to enhance surveillance capabilities.

c. **Outcome Measures:** Standardize outcome measures and endpoints in clinical trials and observational studies to facilitate comparative effectiveness research and meta-analyses.

5. Capacity Building and Training

i. **Objective:** Strengthen global capacity in pharmacovigilance and natural medicines research to enhance safety monitoring practices.

ii. **Activities:**

a. **Training Programs:** Develop and deliver training modules, workshops, and educational resources for healthcare professionals, researchers, regulators, and industry stakeholders on pharmacovigilance principles and best practices.

   b. **Technical Assistance:** Provide technical support and guidance to countries and institutions in establishing or strengthening pharmacovigilance infrastructure and capabilities specific to natural medicines.

   c. **Collaborative Networks:** Foster partnerships and collaborative networks among research institutions, regulatory agencies, and international organizations to share knowledge, resources, and expertise in natural medicines research and safety monitoring.

International Collaboration:

International collaboration plays a critical role in the WHO guidelines for safety monitoring of natural medicines within pharmacovigilance. It facilitates the exchange of knowledge, resources, and best practices among countries and organizations to enhance the safety monitoring of natural medicines globally. Here's an overview of international collaboration efforts as per these guidelines:

1. Data Sharing and Harmonization

   i. **Objective:** Facilitate the sharing of safety data and harmonization of pharmacovigilance practices across countries and regions.

   ii. **Activities:**

   a. **Data Exchange:** Establish mechanisms for the exchange of safety data related to natural medicines between national pharmacovigilance centers, regulatory authorities, and international organizations.

   b. **Harmonization of Standards:** Align pharmacovigilance standards, methodologies, and reporting requirements to ensure consistency and interoperability in safety monitoring practices.

c. **Joint Analysis:** Collaborate on joint data analysis initiatives to identify global trends, emerging safety signals, and patterns of adverse events associated with natural medicines.

2. Capacity Building and Training

i.   **Objective:** Build and strengthen pharmacovigilance capacity in natural medicines among healthcare professionals, regulators, and researchers worldwide.

ii. **Activities:**

a. **Training Workshops:** Organize international workshops, seminars, and training programs on pharmacovigilance principles, safety monitoring, and regulatory requirements specific to natural medicines.

b. **Technical Assistance:** Provide technical support and guidance to countries with limited resources to enhance their pharmacovigilance infrastructure and capabilities.

c. **Knowledge Sharing:** Share expertise, best practices, and lessons learned in pharmacovigilance through collaborative networks, webinars, and online platforms.

3. Research and Evidence Generation

i.   **Objective:** Foster collaborative research initiatives to generate scientific evidence on the safety, efficacy, and quality of natural medicines.

ii. **Activities:**

a. **Multinational Studies:** Collaborate on multinational clinical trials, epidemiological studies, and systematic reviews to evaluate the safety profiles and effectiveness of natural medicines across diverse populations.

b. **Data Pools:** Pool data from multiple countries and regions to conduct robust meta-analyses and comparative effectiveness research on natural medicines.

c. **Research Consortia:** Establish research consortia and partnerships to address knowledge gaps, prioritize research agendas, and leverage resources for conducting high-quality research in natural medicines.

4. Regulatory Harmonization and Alignment

i. **Objective:** Harmonize regulatory approaches and facilitate mutual recognition of safety assessments for natural medicines among regulatory authorities globally.

ii. **Activities:**

    a. **Regulatory Networks:** Participate in international regulatory networks and forums to discuss regulatory challenges, share regulatory experiences, and develop consensus on safety monitoring practices for natural medicines.

    b. **Mutual Recognition:** Promote mutual recognition agreements and collaborative frameworks that facilitate the acceptance of safety data, regulatory approvals, and post-marketing surveillance findings across jurisdictions.

    c. **Harmonized Guidelines:** Develop and endorse harmonized guidelines, standards, and best practices for the evaluation, approval, and safety monitoring of natural medicines to ensure global alignment and regulatory consistency.

5. Emergency Response and Crisis Management

i. **Objective:** Collaborate on emergency preparedness and response strategies for managing safety concerns and adverse events related to natural medicines.

ii. **Activities:**

    a. **Rapid Information Sharing:** Establish protocols for rapid information sharing and communication during public health emergencies or significant safety events involving natural medicines.

    b. **Joint Risk Assessments:** Conduct joint risk assessments and coordinated response efforts to mitigate risks, issue safety alerts, and implement regulatory actions as needed.

    c. **Capacity Support:** Provide technical assistance and capacity support to countries affected by safety incidents involving natural medicines to strengthen their response capabilities and ensure timely interventions.

Implementation and Evaluation:

Implementation and evaluation are crucial components of the WHO guidelines for safety monitoring of natural medicines within pharmacovigilance. They involve putting into practice the recommended strategies and continuously assessing their effectiveness to ensure the safe use of natural medicines. Here's a detailed overview:

1. Implementation Strategies

    a. **Guideline Adoption:** Encourage countries to adopt and adapt the WHO guidelines for safety monitoring of natural medicines into their national pharmacovigilance frameworks.

    b. **Capacity Building:** Provide technical assistance and training to healthcare professionals, regulators, and researchers on implementing pharmacovigilance practices specific to natural medicines.

    c. **Regulatory Integration:** Integrate safety monitoring requirements for natural medicines into national regulatory frameworks and guidelines.

    d. **Establishment of Pharmacovigilance Systems:** Develop and strengthen pharmacovigilance systems capable of collecting, analyzing, and reporting safety data related to natural medicines.

2. Key Elements of Implementation

a. **Data Collection:** Implement mechanisms for the systematic collection of safety data, including adverse event reports and epidemiological studies, for natural medicines.

b. **Signal Detection:** Utilize pharmacovigilance methodologies to detect signals of potential safety issues associated with natural medicines and initiate appropriate regulatory actions.

c. **Risk Communication:** Develop strategies for communicating safety information to healthcare providers, patients, regulators, and the public regarding the safe use of natural medicines.

d. **Collaboration:** Foster collaboration among stakeholders, including international organizations, regulatory authorities, healthcare professionals, and industry stakeholders, to enhance safety monitoring efforts.

3. Evaluation and Continuous Improvement

a. **Outcome Assessment:** Evaluate the effectiveness of implemented safety monitoring strategies and interventions in reducing adverse events and improving patient outcomes related to natural medicines.

b. **Feedback Mechanisms:** Solicit feedback from stakeholders, including healthcare providers, patients, and regulatory authorities, to identify strengths, weaknesses, and areas for improvement in pharmacovigilance practices.

c. **Adaptation to Emerging Issues:** Adjust safety monitoring strategies and guidelines based on new scientific evidence, technological advancements, and emerging safety concerns related to natural medicines.

d. **Regulatory Review:** Periodically review and update regulatory policies, guidelines, and labeling requirements to ensure they reflect current knowledge and best practices in pharmacovigilance for natural medicines.

AYUSH GUIDELINES FOR SAFETY MONITORING OF NATURAL MEDICINE

AYUSH (Ayurveda, Yoga & Naturopathy, Unani, Siddha, and Homoeopathy) is a governmental body in India responsible for the development and propagation of traditional systems of medicine. The Ministry of AYUSH has established guidelines for the safety monitoring of natural medicines, aiming to ensure their safe and effective use. These guidelines focus on pharmacovigilance activities specific to traditional medicines, addressing the unique challenges associated with these products. Below is a detailed overview of the AYUSH guidelines for safety monitoring of natural medicine:

1. Objectives of the AYUSH Guidelines:

a. **Ensure Patient Safety:** Protect consumers from potential adverse effects of AYUSH medicines.

b. **Promote Safe Use:** Encourage the rational use of AYUSH medicines through proper monitoring and reporting systems.

c. **Support Regulation:** Assist regulatory authorities in making informed decisions regarding the approval and monitoring of AYUSH medicines.

d. **Enhance Knowledge:** Improve the understanding of the safety profiles of AYUSH medicines.

2. Framework for Safety Monitoring:

The AYUSH guidelines emphasize a structured approach to safety monitoring, which includes the following components:

A. Regulatory Framework

a. **National Policy:** Development of a national policy and regulatory framework for AYUSH medicines, integrating pharmacovigilance activities.

b. **Legislation:** Establishment of laws and regulations to support the safety monitoring of AYUSH medicines.

c. **Registration and Licensing:** Systems for the registration and licensing of AYUSH medicines to ensure quality control and safety.

B. Pharmacovigilance Systems

a. **Adverse Event Reporting:** Establishment of systems for the reporting of adverse events related to AYUSH medicines, including spontaneous reporting systems where healthcare professionals and consumers can report adverse effects.

b. **Active Surveillance:** Implementation of active surveillance methods such as cohort event monitoring and targeted spontaneous reporting to proactively gather safety data.

c. **Data Collection and Analysis:** Development of standardized methods for the collection and analysis of safety data related to AYUSH medicines.

3. Key Elements of Safety Monitoring:

A. Identification of AYUSH Medicines

a. **Standardization:** Ensuring that AYUSH medicines are standardized and accurately identified by their botanical name, part of the plant used, and the method of preparation.

b. **Quality Control:** Implementation of quality control measures to ensure consistency in the composition and potency of AYUSH medicines.

B. Adverse Event Reporting and Management

a. **Reporting Forms:** Development of specific reporting forms for adverse events related to AYUSH medicines, capturing detailed information about the product, dosage, duration of use, and the adverse event.

b. **Database:** Maintenance of a centralized database for adverse event reports to facilitate data analysis and signal detection.

c. **Signal Detection:** Use of statistical methods to identify signals of potential safety concerns from the adverse event data.

4. Stakeholder Involvement:

A. Healthcare Professionals

  a. **Training and Education:** Providing training for healthcare professionals on the safe use of AYUSH medicines and the importance of reporting adverse events.

  b. **Reporting Encouragement:** Encouraging healthcare professionals to report adverse events and share information about the safety of AYUSH medicines with their patients.

B. Consumers

  a. **Public Awareness:** Conducting public awareness campaigns to educate consumers about the potential risks of AYUSH medicines and the importance of reporting adverse events.

  b. **Reporting Systems:** Providing accessible and user-friendly reporting systems for consumers to report adverse events.

5. Research and Development:

  a. **Clinical Studies:** Promotion of clinical studies and research to gather evidence on the safety and efficacy of AYUSH medicines.

  b. **Pharmacovigilance Research:** Support for research on pharmacovigilance methods specifically tailored to AYUSH medicines.

6. International Collaboration:

  a. **Data Sharing:** Facilitation of the sharing of safety data and experiences between countries to improve the global understanding of AYUSH medicine safety.

  b. **Harmonization:** Work towards harmonizing pharmacovigilance practices and regulatory standards for AYUSH medicines across different countries.

7. Implementation and Evaluation:

  a. **National Centers:** Establishment of national pharmacovigilance centers dedicated to monitoring the safety of AYUSH medicines.

b. **Continuous Improvement:** Regular evaluation and updating of the pharmacovigilance system to incorporate new knowledge and improve its effectiveness.

c. **Feedback Mechanism:** Creation of mechanisms for feedback from stakeholders to continuously improve the safety monitoring process.

SPONTANEOUS REPORTING SCHEMES FOR BIODRUG ADVERSE REACTIONS

Spontaneous reporting schemes are a cornerstone of pharmacovigilance, especially for drugs of natural origin (biodrugs). These schemes rely on healthcare professionals, patients, and consumers to report adverse drug reactions (ADRs) on a voluntary basis. Below is a detailed overview of spontaneous reporting schemes for biodrug adverse reactions in the context of pharmacovigilance of drugs of natural origin.

1. Definition and Importance

Spontaneous reporting schemes involve the unsolicited submission of information about suspected adverse reactions to drugs, including those of natural origin. These reports are crucial for:

a. **Early Detection:** Identifying new, rare, or serious ADRs that may not have been observed in clinical trials.

b. **Signal Generation:** Providing data to generate safety signals that warrant further investigation.

c. **Risk Assessment:** Contributing to the assessment of the risk-benefit profile of biodrugs.

d. **Regulatory Actions:** Informing regulatory decisions, such as label changes, restrictions, or withdrawals.

2. Components of a Spontaneous Reporting Scheme

A. Reporting Sources

a. **Healthcare Professionals:** Physicians, pharmacists, nurses, and other healthcare providers are primary reporters due to their clinical expertise.

b. **Patients and Consumers:** Direct reports from patients and consumers provide firsthand accounts of ADRs and can highlight issues not captured by healthcare providers.

B. Reporting Systems

a. **National Reporting Systems:** Managed by national regulatory authorities, such as the FDA's MedWatch in the USA or the MHRA's Yellow Card Scheme in the UK.

b. **Regional and Institutional Systems:** Hospitals, clinics, and regional health authorities may have their own reporting systems that feed into the national database.

c. **Online Platforms and Apps:** Increasingly, web-based platforms and mobile applications are used to facilitate easier and faster reporting.

3. Information Collected

A comprehensive spontaneous report typically includes:

a. **Patient Information:** Age, sex, medical history, and concomitant medications.

b. **Drug Information:** Name of the biodrug, dose, route of administration, and duration of use.

c. **Adverse Reaction Details:** Description of the ADR, onset time, severity, outcome, and any interventions required.

d. **Reporter Information:** Contact details and professional background of the reporter.

4. Challenges in Spontaneous Reporting for Biodrugs

A. Underreporting

a. **Lack of Awareness:** Healthcare professionals and consumers may not be aware of the importance of reporting ADRs.

b. **Perceived Safety:** Biodrugs are often perceived as safer than synthetic drugs, leading to underreporting of ADRs.

c. **Time Constraints:** The process of reporting can be time-consuming and may deter busy healthcare professionals.

B. Data Quality

a. **Incomplete Reports:** Missing or incomplete information can limit the usefulness of reports.

b. **Causality Assessment:** Determining the causal relationship between the biodrug and the ADR can be challenging due to the complex nature of natural products.

C. Variability in Biodrugs

a. **Batch-to-Batch Variability:** Differences in the composition of biodrugs between batches can complicate the identification of ADRs.

b. **Complexity of Composition:** Biodrugs often contain multiple active compounds, making it difficult to attribute ADRs to specific components.

5. Improving Spontaneous Reporting for Biodrugs

A. Education and Awareness

a. **Training Programs:** Regular training for healthcare professionals on the importance of pharmacovigilance and the process of reporting ADRs.

b. **Public Campaigns:** Awareness campaigns to educate patients and consumers about the significance of reporting ADRs.

B. Facilitating Reporting

a. **Simplified Reporting Forms:** User-friendly forms that are easy to complete.

b. **Multiple Reporting Channels:** Offering various reporting methods, including online, mobile apps, and paper forms.

C. Feedback and Communication

a. **Acknowledgement:** Providing feedback to reporters to acknowledge their contribution and encourage future reporting.

b. **Information Dissemination:** Sharing information about reported ADRs and subsequent actions taken to keep stakeholders informed.

6. Examples of Spontaneous Reporting Systems

A. FDA MedWatch

a. **Scope:** Accepts reports from healthcare professionals, patients, and consumers about ADRs and other safety issues related to drugs, including biodrugs.

b. **Submission Methods:** Reports can be submitted online, via mail, or by fax.

B. Yellow Card Scheme (UK)

a. **Scope:** Managed by the Medicines and Healthcare products Regulatory Agency (MHRA), it collects reports of ADRs related to all medicines, including herbal and traditional medicines.

b. **Submission Methods:** Online reporting, mobile app, or by phone.

7. Case Studies in Spontaneous Reporting

A. St. John's Wort

a. **Issue:** Reports of interactions with other medications, leading to reduced efficacy of drugs like oral contraceptives and anticoagulants.

b. **Outcome:** Increased awareness and updated product labeling to warn about potential interactions.

B. Kava

a. **Issue:** Reports of hepatotoxicity leading to serious liver damage.

b. **Outcome:** Regulatory actions including warnings, restrictions, and in some cases, bans on kava-containing products.

BIO DRUG-DRUG INTERACTIONS WITH SUITABLE EXAMPLES

Bio drug-drug interactions (DDIs) are critical considerations in pharmacovigilance for drugs of natural origin. These interactions can lead to altered pharmacokinetics and pharmacodynamics, potentially causing reduced efficacy or increased toxicity. Below is a detailed overview of bio drug-drug interactions, with suitable examples.

Introduction to Bio Drug-Drug Interactions:

Bio drug-drug interactions occur when a drug of natural origin (biodrug) affects the action or metabolism of another drug. These interactions can be:

a. **Pharmacokinetic Interactions:** Affect the absorption, distribution, metabolism, or excretion (ADME) of the other drug.

b. **Pharmacodynamic Interactions:** Alter the pharmacological effects of the other drug, leading to additive, synergistic, or antagonistic effects.

Mechanisms of Bio Drug-Drug Interactions:

Bio drug-drug interactions (DDIs) occur when the pharmacokinetics or pharmacodynamics of a biodrug are altered by another drug. These interactions can affect the efficacy and safety of drugs derived from natural sources. Understanding the mechanisms of these interactions is crucial for pharmacovigilance and optimizing patient care. Below are detailed mechanisms of bio drug-drug interactions:

1. Pharmacokinetic Interactions

A. Absorption Interactions:

a. **Mechanism:** Drugs can alter the absorption of biodrugs by affecting gastrointestinal (GI) pH, gastric emptying time, or GI motility.

b. **Example:** Proton pump inhibitors (PPIs) reduce gastric acid secretion, potentially decreasing the absorption of weakly basic biodrugs like alkaloids.

B. Distribution Interactions:

a. **Mechanism:** Drugs can compete for protein binding sites or alter tissue distribution of biodrugs.

b. **Example:** Nonsteroidal anti-inflammatory drugs (NSAIDs) displacing biodrugs like warfarin from plasma proteins, leading to increased free drug concentrations and risk of bleeding.

C. Metabolism Interactions:

a. **Mechanism:** Drugs can induce or inhibit drug-metabolizing enzymes (e.g., cytochrome P450 enzymes) responsible for biodrug metabolism.

b. **Example:** St. John's Wort induces CYP3A4, accelerating the metabolism of certain chemotherapy agents like irinotecan, reducing their efficacy.

D. Excretion Interactions:

a. **Mechanism:** Drugs can affect renal or hepatic excretion of biodrugs.

b. **Example:** Diuretics increasing renal clearance of biodrugs like lithium, potentially reducing therapeutic levels and efficacy.

2. Pharmacodynamic Interactions

A. Receptor Interactions:

a. **Mechanism:** Drugs can compete for or modulate the same receptor sites, altering biodrug effects.

b. **Example:** Beta-blockers antagonizing the effects of sympathomimetic biodrugs used for respiratory conditions.

B. Additive or Synergistic Effects:

a. **Mechanism:** Drugs can amplify or reduce the effects of biodrugs through additive or synergistic interactions.

b. **Example:** Concurrent use of sedatives or opioids with CNS-depressant biodrugs like valerian root potentiating sedation and respiratory depression.

C. Physiological Interactions:

a. **Mechanism:** Drugs can alter physiological processes, affecting biodrug metabolism or activity.

b. **Example:** NSAIDs reducing renal blood flow and GFR, impacting the excretion of biodrugs like methotrexate and increasing the risk of toxicity.

3. Combined Mechanisms

A. Multiple Pathway Interactions:

a. **Mechanism:** Drugs can affect biodrugs through multiple pathways simultaneously, compounding their effects.

b. **Example:** HIV protease inhibitors inhibiting both CYP3A4 and P-glycoprotein, altering the metabolism and excretion of biodrugs like digoxin.

Examples of Bio Drug-Drug Interactions:

Bio drug-drug interactions (DDIs) involving drugs derived from natural sources can significantly impact their pharmacokinetics and pharmacodynamics. These interactions are crucial to monitor in pharmacovigilance to ensure patient safety and optimize therapeutic outcomes. Here are detailed examples of bio drug-drug interactions:

1. St. John's Wort (Hypericum perforatum) and Antidepressants

Mechanism:

a. St. John's Wort induces the activity of cytochrome P450 enzymes, particularly CYP3A4 and CYP2C9, in the liver. This induction accelerates the metabolism of various drugs, reducing their plasma concentrations and efficacy.

Example:

a. **Antidepressants (e.g., SSRIs):** St. John's Wort reduces the effectiveness of selective serotonin reuptake inhibitors (SSRIs) such as sertraline and fluoxetine. This interaction can lead to worsening of depression symptoms due to decreased serum levels of SSRIs.

Outcome and Action:

a. **Outcome:** Patients may experience treatment failure or inadequate symptom control for depression.

b. **Action:** Healthcare providers are advised to avoid concurrent use of St. John's Wort with SSRIs and consider alternative antidepressant therapies to manage depression effectively.

2. Ginkgo biloba and Anticoagulants

Mechanism:

a. Ginkgo biloba contains bioactive compounds that inhibit platelet aggregation and may interfere with the anticoagulant effects of medications like warfarin.

Example:

a. **Anticoagulants (e.g., Warfarin):** Concurrent use of Ginkgo biloba with warfarin can increase the risk of bleeding due to additive anticoagulant effects or altered platelet function.

Outcome and Action:

a. **Outcome:** Patients may experience prolonged bleeding times or increased risk of hemorrhage.

b. **Action:** Close monitoring of international normalized ratio (INR) levels is recommended, with adjustments in warfarin dosage based on clinical assessment to minimize bleeding risks.

3. Garlic (Allium sativum) and Antihypertensives

Mechanism:

a. Garlic supplements have hypotensive effects and may potentiate the actions of prescribed antihypertensive medications.

Example:

a. **Antihypertensives (e.g., ACE Inhibitors):** Garlic can enhance the blood pressure-lowering effects of medications like captopril or enalapril, leading to excessive hypotension.

Outcome and Action:

a. **Outcome:** Patients may experience symptoms such as dizziness, lightheadedness, or fainting due to lowered blood pressure.

b. **Action:** Healthcare providers should monitor blood pressure closely and adjust antihypertensive dosages as necessary to prevent symptomatic hypotension.

4. Milk Thistle (Silybum marianum) and Chemotherapy Drugs

Mechanism:

a. Milk thistle contains flavonolignans that may inhibit drug-metabolizing enzymes and affect the metabolism of chemotherapy agents.

Example:

a. **Chemotherapy Drugs (e.g., Irinotecan):** Concurrent use of milk thistle with irinotecan, a chemotherapy drug metabolized by UDP-glucuronosyltransferase enzymes, can alter its metabolism and efficacy.

Outcome and Action:

a. **Outcome:** Reduced plasma concentrations of irinotecan may lead to suboptimal therapeutic responses or treatment failure in cancer patients.

b. **Action:** Monitoring of chemotherapy drug levels and clinical responses is essential. Consideration of alternative therapies or adjustments in chemotherapy dosages may be necessary to maintain therapeutic efficacy.

5. Green Tea (Camellia sinensis) and Cardiovascular Medications

Mechanism:

a. Green tea contains catechins and caffeine, which can interact with cardiovascular medications through various mechanisms including enzyme inhibition and altered drug metabolism.

Example:

a. **Cardiovascular Medications (e.g., Beta-blockers):** Green tea catechins can inhibit the metabolism of beta-blockers like metoprolol or propranolol, potentially increasing their plasma concentrations and adverse effects.

Outcome and Action:

a. **Outcome:** Patients may experience enhanced beta-blockade effects such as bradycardia or hypotension.

b. **Action:** Healthcare providers should educate patients on the potential interactions between green tea and cardiovascular medications. Monitoring of heart rate and blood pressure is recommended, with adjustments in medication dosages as needed to avoid adverse cardiovascular effects.

Monitoring and Management of Bio Drug-Drug Interactions:

Monitoring and managing bio drug-drug interactions (DDIs) involving drugs derived from natural sources are critical for ensuring patient safety and optimizing therapeutic outcomes. Here's a detailed overview of strategies for monitoring and managing these interactions:

1. Pharmacovigilance and Surveillance Systems

A. Adverse Event Reporting:

    a. Establish robust systems for healthcare providers and patients to report suspected bio drug-drug interactions to pharmacovigilance centers.

    b. Encourage timely reporting of adverse events associated with concurrent use of biodrugs and conventional medications.

B. Database Management:

    a. Maintain comprehensive databases to collect, monitor, and analyze data on reported bio drug-drug interactions.

    b. Utilize data analytics to identify trends, patterns, and potential risks associated with specific biodrugs and their interactions.

C. Signal Detection:

    a. Implement signal detection methodologies to identify new or previously unrecognized bio drug-drug interactions.

    b. Monitor literature, clinical trial data, and real-world evidence to stay updated on emerging interactions.

2. Healthcare Provider Education and Training

A. Awareness Programs:

    a. Conduct educational programs and workshops for healthcare providers on the pharmacokinetics, pharmacodynamics, and potential interactions of biodrugs.

b. Emphasize the importance of vigilance in assessing patient profiles for concurrent medication use and potential interactions.

B. Decision Support Tools:

a. Integrate decision support tools into electronic health records (EHRs) to alert healthcare providers about potential bio drug-drug interactions during prescribing.

b. Provide access to up-to-date databases and reference materials on biodrug interactions for clinical decision-making.

C. Interdisciplinary Collaboration:

a. Foster collaboration between pharmacists, physicians, nurses, and other healthcare professionals to ensure comprehensive assessment and management of bio drug-drug interactions.

b. Encourage open communication and consultation among healthcare team members to optimize patient care.

3. Patient Monitoring and Counseling

A. Patient Assessment:

a. Conduct thorough medication reconciliation and assessment of patient medication histories, including the use of biodrugs and conventional medications.

b. Identify and document potential bio drug-drug interactions based on individual patient profiles.

B. Patient Counseling:

a. Educate patients about the risks and potential consequences of bio drug-drug interactions.

b. Provide clear instructions on medication adherence, timing of doses, and potential dietary considerations to minimize interactions.

C. Monitoring Parameters:

a. Establish monitoring parameters specific to biodrugs and their potential interactions with conventional medications.

b. Monitor clinical responses, laboratory values (e.g., INR for anticoagulants), and adverse effects related to interactions.

4. Regulatory and Policy Measures

A. Labeling Requirements:

a. Enforce stringent labeling requirements for biodrugs to include information on potential drug interactions.

b. Ensure clear and comprehensive patient information leaflets and package inserts that highlight bio drug-drug interactions.

B. Post-Marketing Surveillance:

a. Conduct ongoing post-marketing surveillance to monitor the real-world safety and effectiveness of biodrugs in the context of drug-drug interactions.

b. Update safety communications and regulatory guidelines based on new data and emerging interactions.

C. Pharmacogenomic Testing:

a. Consider pharmacogenomic testing to identify genetic variants that may predispose patients to bio drug-drug interactions.

b. Tailor treatment plans based on individual genetic profiles to optimize therapeutic outcomes and minimize risks.

5. Case Management and Documentation

A. Case Studies and Analysis:

a. Document and analyze case studies of reported bio drug-drug interactions to understand underlying mechanisms and clinical implications.

b. Share findings through scientific publications, conferences, and educational forums to enhance awareness and knowledge among healthcare providers.

B. Risk Assessment and Mitigation Strategies:

a. Develop risk assessment tools and mitigation strategies for managing specific bio drug-drug interactions identified through pharmacovigilance.

b. Implement preventive measures and treatment protocols to minimize adverse outcomes associated with interactions.

BIO DRUG-FOOD INTERACTIONS WITH SUITABLE EXAMPLES

Bio drug-food interactions occur when foods affect the absorption, metabolism, or action of drugs derived from natural sources (biodrugs). These interactions can significantly impact the efficacy and safety of biodrugs, making it essential to monitor and manage them effectively in pharmacovigilance. Below is a detailed overview of bio drug-food interactions, with suitable examples.

Introduction to Bio Drug-Food Interactions:

Bio drug-food interactions happen when the presence of food alters the pharmacokinetics (absorption, distribution, metabolism, and excretion) or pharmacodynamics (effects and mechanisms) of biodrugs. These interactions can result in:

a. **Altered Absorption:** Food can enhance or inhibit the absorption of biodrugs.

b. **Modified Metabolism:** Food components can induce or inhibit the enzymes that metabolize biodrugs.

c. **Changed Excretion:** Food can affect the renal or biliary excretion of biodrugs.

d. **Altered Effect:** Food can modify the pharmacological action of biodrugs.

Mechanisms of Bio Drug-Food Interactions:

Bio drug-food interactions are significant in pharmacovigilance due to their potential to alter the efficacy and safety of drugs derived from natural sources (biodrugs). Understanding these mechanisms is crucial for predicting, monitoring, and managing such interactions. Below are detailed mechanisms by which food can interact with biodrugs.

1. Absorption

A. Gastrointestinal pH:

a. **Mechanism:** Food can alter the pH of the gastrointestinal (GI) tract, impacting the solubility and absorption of biodrugs.

b. **Example:** Acidic foods like citrus fruits can increase the stomach's acidity, enhancing the absorption of weakly acidic drugs but reducing the absorption of weakly basic drugs.

B. Complex Formation:

a. **Mechanism:** Certain foods can form insoluble complexes with biodrugs, reducing their absorption.

b. **Example:** Calcium in dairy products can bind to tetracyclines and quinolones, forming insoluble complexes that reduce the absorption of these antibiotics.

C. Gastric Emptying:

a. **Mechanism:** Food can delay gastric emptying, affecting the rate at which biodrugs are absorbed.

b. **Example:** High-fat meals slow gastric emptying, delaying the absorption of rapidly absorbed drugs like certain antiretrovirals.

D. Alteration of GI Transit Time:

a. **Mechanism:** Foods high in fiber can accelerate or slow down GI transit time, affecting drug absorption.

b. **Example:** High-fiber foods can speed up GI transit, reducing the absorption window for some drugs, such as digoxin.

2. Distribution

A. Protein Binding:

a. **Mechanism:** Foods can influence the binding of biodrugs to plasma proteins, altering the free drug concentration.

b. **Example:** High-fat meals can increase free fatty acids in the blood, displacing drugs like warfarin from albumin and increasing the risk of bleeding.

B. Tissue Distribution:

a. **Mechanism:** Foods can affect the distribution of drugs into tissues by altering cell membrane permeability.

b. **Example:** Certain fatty foods may enhance the distribution of lipophilic drugs into adipose tissues.

3. Metabolism

A. Enzyme Induction:

a. **Mechanism:** Some food components can induce the activity of drug-metabolizing enzymes, increasing the metabolism of biodrugs.

b. **Example:** Cruciferous vegetables (like broccoli) can induce CYP1A2, accelerating the metabolism of drugs like theophylline, reducing its efficacy.

B. Enzyme Inhibition:

a. **Mechanism:** Foods can inhibit the activity of drug-metabolizing enzymes, decreasing the metabolism of biodrugs.

b. **Example:** Grapefruit juice contains furanocoumarins that inhibit CYP3A4 enzymes, leading to increased plasma levels of drugs like statins, potentially causing toxicity.

C. First-Pass Metabolism:

a. **Mechanism:** Foods can affect the extent of first-pass metabolism in the liver, impacting drug bioavailability.

b. **Example:** High-fat meals can increase the first-pass metabolism of some drugs, reducing their bioavailability.

4. Excretion

A. Renal Excretion:

a. **Mechanism:** Foods can influence renal blood flow, glomerular filtration rate (GFR), and urinary pH, affecting the excretion of biodrugs.

b. **Example:** High-protein diets can increase renal blood flow and GFR, enhancing the excretion of drugs like lithium.

B. Biliary Excretion:

a. **Mechanism:** Foods can alter bile flow, impacting the excretion of drugs via the bile.

b. **Example:** High-fat meals can increase bile production, which may enhance the excretion of certain lipophilic drugs.

5. Pharmacodynamic Interactions

A. Synergistic Effects:

a. **Mechanism:** Foods can enhance the pharmacological effects of biodrugs.

b. **Example:** Consuming alcohol with sedative herbs like valerian can potentiate the sedative effects, leading to increased drowsiness or sedation.

B. Antagonistic Effects:

a. **Mechanism:** Foods can counteract the effects of biodrugs.

b. **Example:** Foods high in vitamin K, such as green leafy vegetables, can antagonize the effects of anticoagulants like warfarin, reducing its efficacy and increasing the risk of clotting.

6. Case Studies Illustrating Bio Drug-Food Interactions

A. Grapefruit Juice and Statins:

a. **Mechanism:** Inhibition of CYP3A4 by grapefruit juice increases statin levels.

b. **Outcome:** Increased risk of statin-induced myopathy and rhabdomyolysis.

B. Milk and Tetracyclines:

a. **Mechanism:** Calcium in milk binds to tetracyclines, forming insoluble complexes.

b. **Outcome:** Reduced antibiotic absorption and efficacy.

C. High-Fiber Foods and Digoxin:

a. **Mechanism:** Fiber binds to digoxin, reducing its absorption.

b. **Outcome:** Decreased effectiveness of digoxin in managing heart failure.

Examples of Bio Drug-Food Interactions:

Bio drug-food interactions can significantly impact the pharmacokinetics and pharmacodynamics of drugs derived from natural sources (biodrugs). These interactions are crucial in pharmacovigilance for ensuring drug safety and efficacy. Below are detailed examples of bio drug-food interactions.

1. Grapefruit Juice

Mechanism:

    a. Grapefruit juice contains furanocoumarins, which inhibit the cytochrome P450 3A4 (CYP3A4) enzyme in the intestine. This inhibition can lead to increased bioavailability and plasma levels of drugs metabolized by CYP3A4.

Examples:

    a. Statins (e.g., Atorvastatin, Simvastatin): Increased risk of muscle toxicity, including myopathy and rhabdomyolysis, due to higher plasma concentrations.

    b. Calcium Channel Blockers (e.g., Felodipine, Nifedipine): Enhanced blood pressure-lowering effects, potentially leading to hypotension.

    c. Immunosuppressants (e.g., Cyclosporine): Elevated drug levels, increasing the risk of nephrotoxicity and other adverse effects.

2. Milk and Dairy Products

Mechanism:

    a. Calcium in dairy products can bind to certain biodrugs, forming insoluble complexes that reduce drug absorption.

Examples:

    a. Tetracyclines (e.g., Doxycycline): Reduced antibiotic absorption, leading to decreased therapeutic effectiveness.

    b. Quinolones (e.g., Ciprofloxacin): Lower absorption and efficacy, potentially leading to treatment failure.

3. High-Fat Meals

Mechanism:

a. High-fat meals can enhance the solubility and absorption of lipophilic biodrugs, potentially leading to higher plasma levels and increased effects or side effects.

Examples:

a. **Cannabinoids (e.g., THC):** Increased absorption and enhanced psychoactive effects, potentially leading to overdose or heightened side effects.

b. **Itraconazole:** Enhanced absorption, increasing the risk of adverse effects such as hepatotoxicity.

4. Green Leafy Vegetables

Mechanism:

a. Green leafy vegetables are high in vitamin K, which can counteract the effects of anticoagulants by promoting blood clotting.

Example:

a. **Warfarin:** Reduced anticoagulant effect, increasing the risk of thrombosis and treatment failure. Patients on warfarin are often advised to maintain a consistent intake of vitamin K to avoid fluctuations in drug effectiveness.

5. Fiber-Rich Foods

Mechanism:

a. High-fiber foods can bind to certain drugs in the gastrointestinal tract, reducing their absorption.

Example:

a. **Digoxin:** Decreased absorption and efficacy in managing heart failure and arrhythmias due to binding of digoxin to dietary fiber.

6. Alcohol

Mechanism:

a. Alcohol can induce or inhibit various cytochrome P450 enzymes and has central nervous system depressant effects that can interact with other sedative biodrugs.

Examples:

a. Valerian Root: Enhanced sedative effects, leading to increased drowsiness and risk of respiratory depression.

b. Kava: Potentiation of kava's sedative effects, increasing the risk of severe sedation and potential liver toxicity.

7. Caffeine

Mechanism:

a. Caffeine can inhibit or induce various enzymes and can have stimulant effects that interact with other stimulants or sedatives.

Examples:

a. Ephedra (Ma Huang): Increased stimulant effects, potentially leading to hypertension, palpitations, and anxiety.

b. Ginseng: Potential for additive stimulant effects, causing increased heart rate and blood pressure.

8. Cruciferous Vegetables

Mechanism:

a. Cruciferous vegetables (e.g., broccoli, Brussels sprouts) contain compounds that can induce cytochrome P450 1A2 (CYP1A2), potentially increasing the metabolism of certain drugs.

Example:

a. Theophylline: Enhanced metabolism of theophylline, leading to reduced plasma levels and decreased efficacy in treating respiratory conditions like asthma and COPD.

9. Pomegranate Juice

Mechanism:

a. Pomegranate juice contains compounds that can inhibit cytochrome P450 2C9 (CYP2C9), affecting the metabolism of drugs that are CYP2C9 substrates.

Example:

a. **Warfarin:** Increased levels of warfarin, leading to a higher risk of bleeding due to reduced metabolism of the drug.

Monitoring and Management of Bio Drug-Food Interactions:

Monitoring and managing bio drug-food interactions are essential aspects of pharmacovigilance for ensuring the safety and efficacy of drugs derived from natural sources (biodrugs). This involves a comprehensive approach that includes patient education, healthcare professional training, regulatory measures, and robust reporting systems. Below are detailed strategies for monitoring and managing bio drug-food interactions.

1. Patient Education

A. Awareness:

a. Educate patients about the potential interactions between their medications and certain foods.

b. Provide clear instructions on what foods to avoid or consume in moderation while taking specific biodrugs.

B. Dietary Guidelines:

a. Develop and distribute dietary guidelines specific to the biodrugs being prescribed.

b. Use visual aids, brochures, and digital resources to enhance patient understanding.

C. Consistent Dietary Habits:

a. Encourage patients to maintain consistent dietary habits to minimize fluctuations in drug absorption and effectiveness.

b. Monitor patient adherence to dietary guidelines during follow-up visits.

D. Medication Labels and Leaflets:

a. Ensure that medication labels and patient information leaflets include warnings about potential food interactions.

b. Highlight key food interactions in bold or with symbols for easy identification.

2. Healthcare Professional Training

A. Knowledge and Awareness:

a. Train healthcare professionals to recognize and manage potential food interactions with biodrugs.

b. Include bio drug-food interactions as part of continuing education programs for pharmacists, doctors, and nurses.

B. Communication Skills:

a. Enhance communication skills to facilitate open dialogue between healthcare providers and patients about dietary habits and medication use.

b. Encourage healthcare providers to ask patients about their diet during consultations and medication reviews.

C. Decision Support Systems:

a. Implement decision support systems in electronic health records to alert healthcare providers about potential food interactions when prescribing biodrugs.

3. Regulatory Measures

A. Labeling Requirements:

a. Enforce stringent labeling requirements for biodrugs to include information about potential food interactions.

b. Ensure that labels are clear, accurate, and easy to understand.

B. Guidelines and Recommendations:

a. Develop and disseminate guidelines for managing bio drug-food interactions.

b. Collaborate with regulatory agencies to update guidelines regularly based on new evidence and research findings.

C. Post-Marketing Surveillance:

    a. Conduct post-marketing surveillance to monitor and evaluate the real-world impact of bio drug-food interactions.

    b. Use data from adverse event reporting systems to identify emerging food interaction issues.

4. Reporting Systems

A. Adverse Event Reporting:

    a. Implement robust systems for reporting and analyzing adverse drug-food interactions.

    b. Encourage healthcare professionals and patients to report any suspected interactions to pharmacovigilance centers.

B. Database Management:

    a. Maintain comprehensive databases to track and evaluate interaction data.

    b. Use data analytics to identify trends and patterns in bio drug-food interactions.

C. Feedback Mechanisms:

    a. Establish feedback mechanisms to inform healthcare providers and patients about reported interactions and preventive measures.

    b. Regularly update safety communications based on new data and research findings.

5. Monitoring Systems

A. Therapeutic Drug Monitoring (TDM):

    a. Use TDM to measure drug levels in patients' blood, particularly for biodrugs with narrow therapeutic windows.

    b. Adjust dosages based on TDM results and observed interactions with food.

B. Pharmacogenomic Testing:

    a. Implement pharmacogenomic testing to identify patients who may be more susceptible to drug-food interactions due to genetic variations.

b. Tailor drug therapy and dietary recommendations based on individual genetic profiles.

C. Clinical Trials:

a. Design clinical trials to specifically investigate the effects of food on the pharmacokinetics and pharmacodynamics of biodrugs.

b. Include diverse populations and dietary habits in clinical trial designs to capture a broad range of interactions.

6. Case Studies in Monitoring and Management

A. Grapefruit Juice and Statins:

a. **Issue:** Increased reports of muscle toxicity in patients taking statins with grapefruit juice.

b. **Action:** Updated labeling to warn against the consumption of grapefruit juice with certain statins and continued monitoring of adverse events.

B. Milk and Antibiotics:

a. **Issue:** Reports of reduced efficacy of tetracycline and quinolone antibiotics when taken with dairy products.

b. **Action:** Recommendations to avoid dairy products when taking these antibiotics and educate patients on proper administration.

C. Warfarin and Vitamin K-Rich Foods:

a. **Issue:** Fluctuations in INR levels and risk of clotting or bleeding due to inconsistent intake of vitamin K-rich foods.

b. **Action:** Educate patients on maintaining a consistent intake of vitamin K and monitor INR levels closely.

Multiple Choice Questions

1. What is the primary goal of pharmacovigilance?

    A) To develop new drugs

    B) To detect and prevent adverse effects of drugs

C) To market herbal products

D) To regulate drug prices

2. Which of the following is a challenge in pharmacovigilance of natural products?

A) Standardized dosages

B) Synthetic drug composition

C) Complexity of composition

D) Uniform cultivation conditions

3. What is the role of the FDA in the context of natural products in the United States?

A) Developing new herbal medicines

B) Regulating dietary supplements

C) Promoting natural product use

D) Conducting clinical trials

4. What method involves comparing patients with adverse effects to those without to identify potential risk factors?

A) Active surveillance

B) Spontaneous reporting

C) Case-control studies

D) Cohort studies

5. What is a key objective of the WHO guidelines for the safety monitoring of natural medicines?

A) Standardization of drug manufacturing

B) Enhancement of pharmacovigilance systems

C) Development of new herbal drugs

D) Marketing of natural products

6. Which food component can inhibit the enzyme CYP3A4, leading to increased plasma levels of certain drugs?

A) Calcium

B) Vitamin K

C) Grapefruit juice

D) Fiber

7. What is the impact of St. John's Wort on SSRIs like sertraline and fluoxetine?

A) Enhanced efficacy

B) Reduced metabolism

C) Increased adverse effects

D) Reduced efficacy

8. What is the effect of calcium in dairy products on antibiotics like tetracyclines?

A) Increased absorption

B) Reduced absorption

C) Enhanced therapeutic effect

D) Increased side effects

9. Which natural product can interact with anticoagulants like warfarin by inhibiting platelet aggregation?

A) Garlic

B) Ginkgo biloba

C) Green tea

D) Milk thistle

10. What is the mechanism of action of high-fat meals on the absorption of lipophilic drugs?

A) Reduced solubility

B) Enhanced absorption

C) Increased excretion

D) Reduced metabolism

11. Which reporting system in the UK collects reports of adverse reactions related to all medicines, including herbal and traditional medicines?

A) MedWatch

B) Yellow Card Scheme

C) AYUSH

D) EMA

12. Which herb is known for its interaction with chemotherapy drugs by potentially altering their metabolism and efficacy?

A) Garlic

B) Green tea

C) St. John's Wort

D) Saw Palmetto

13. Which natural product is associated with hepatotoxicity, leading to regulatory actions in several countries?

A) Kava

B) Ginkgo biloba

C) Milk thistle

D) Garlic

14. What is the primary role of pharmacovigilance centers in the context of natural products?

A) Marketing herbal medicines

B) Conducting clinical trials

C) Monitoring and evaluating safety profiles

D) Developing new drugs

15. What is the main challenge associated with the underreporting of adverse effects of natural products?

A) Lack of regulatory standards

B) Perception of inherent safety

C) Complexity of composition

D) Variability of products

16. Which component in green leafy vegetables can counteract the effects of anticoagulants like warfarin?

    A) Fiber

    B) Calcium

    C) Vitamin K

    D) Iron

17. What is the role of public education in the context of pharmacovigilance of natural products?

    A) Developing new herbal medicines

    B) Raising awareness about potential risks

    C) Conducting clinical trials

    D) Regulating drug prices

18. Which natural product is used for benign prostatic hyperplasia (BPH) and can potentially alter the metabolism of BPH medications?

    A) Saw Palmetto

    B) Garlic

    C) St. John's Wort

    D) Ginkgo biloba

19. What is the mechanism of interaction between high-fiber foods and drugs like digoxin?

    A) Enhanced absorption

    B) Reduced excretion

    C) Increased bioavailability

    D) Reduced absorption

20. What is the impact of milk thistle on the metabolism of chemotherapy agents like irinotecan?

    A) Enhanced metabolism

    B) Reduced metabolism

    C) Increased efficacy

D) Reduced toxicity

Short Answer Type Questions (Subjective)

1. Define pharmacovigilance and explain its significance in the context of drugs of natural origin.
2. What are the primary challenges in monitoring the safety of natural products?
3. Describe the role of the US FDA in regulating natural products.
4. How does the composition variability of natural products affect pharmacovigilance?
5. What is the purpose of spontaneous reporting systems in pharmacovigilance?
6. How can healthcare professionals contribute to the pharmacovigilance of natural products?
7. What are some common adverse effects associated with St. John's Wort?
8. Explain the term "underreporting" in the context of pharmacovigilance of natural products.
9. What measures can be taken to improve consumer awareness about the risks of natural products?
10. Describe the interaction between grapefruit juice and statins.
11. How does the WHO facilitate safety monitoring of herbal medicines?
12. What are the key components of the AYUSH guidelines for the safety monitoring of natural medicines?
13. Explain the mechanism by which Ginkgo biloba interacts with anticoagulants.
14. Why is it important to standardize the composition of natural products in pharmacovigilance?
15. What is the role of active surveillance in pharmacovigilance of natural products?

16. How can international collaboration enhance the safety monitoring of natural medicines?

17. What are the benefits of including case-control studies in pharmacovigilance?

18. Describe the impact of high-fiber foods on the absorption of digoxin.

19. What is the significance of signal detection in pharmacovigilance?

20. How do high-fat meals influence the pharmacokinetics of lipophilic drugs like cannabinoids?

Long Answer Type Questions (Subjective)

1. Discuss the regulatory framework for the pharmacovigilance of natural products in different regions, focusing on the roles of the US FDA, EMA, and WHO.

2. Explain the various methods used in pharmacovigilance to monitor and assess the safety of natural products. Highlight the strengths and limitations of each method.

3. Describe the challenges and solutions in the pharmacovigilance of natural products, focusing on complexity, variability, and lack of standardization.

4. Discuss the importance of healthcare professional education and training in improving the pharmacovigilance of natural products.

5. Analyze the role of consumer awareness and public education in minimizing the risks associated with the use of natural products.

6. Describe the mechanisms of bio drug-drug interactions and provide examples of significant interactions involving natural products.

7. Explain the process of signal detection in pharmacovigilance and its importance in identifying new safety concerns related to natural products.

8. Discuss the case studies of St. John's Wort, Ginkgo biloba, and Kava, highlighting the pharmacovigilance actions taken and their outcomes.

9. Examine the role of international collaboration in harmonizing pharmacovigilance practices for natural products. Provide examples of successful collaborative efforts.

10. Describe the strategies for monitoring and managing bio drug-food interactions, including patient education, healthcare professional training, and regulatory measures.

Answer Key

1. B) To detect and prevent adverse effects of drugs

2. C) Complexity of composition

3. B) Regulating dietary supplements

4. C) Case-control studies

5. B) Enhancement of pharmacovigilance systems

6. C) Grapefruit juice

7. D) Reduced efficacy

8. B) Reduced absorption

9. B) Ginkgo biloba

10. B) Enhanced absorption

11. B) Yellow Card Scheme

12. B) Green tea

13. A) Kava

14. C) Monitoring and evaluating safety profiles

15. B) Perception of inherent safety

16. C) Vitamin K

17. B) Raising awareness about potential risks

18. A) Saw Palmetto

19. D) Reduced absorption

20. B) Reduced metabolism